Anomalistic Psychology

AIM HIGHER WITH *PALGRAVE INSIGHTS IN PSYCHOLOGY*

Also available in this series:

978-0-230-24986-8

978-0-230-27222-4

978-0-230-30150-4

978-0-230-24988-2

978-0-230-24941-7

978-0-230-25265-3

978-0-230-29537-7

978-0-230-24944-8

978-0-230-24987-5

978-0-230-24942-4

978-0-230-29640-4

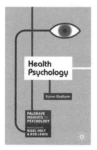

978-0-230-24945-5

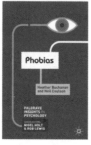

978-0-230-29536-0

978-0-230-30273-0

To find out more visit **www.palgrave.com/insights**

Anomalistic Psychology

Nicola J. Holt,
Christine Simmonds-Moore,
David Luke and
Christopher C. French

**PALGRAVE
INSIGHTS** IN
PSYCHOLOGY

SERIES EDITORS:
**NIGEL HOLT
& ROB LEWIS**

palgrave
macmillan

First published 2012 by
PALGRAVE MACMILLAN

Palgrave Macmillan in the UK is an imprint of Macmillan Publishers Limited, registered in England, company number 785998, of Houndmills, Basingstoke, Hampshire RG21 6XS.

Palgrave Macmillan in the US is a division of St Martin's Press LLC, 175 Fifth Avenue, New York, NY 10010.

Palgrave Macmillan is the global academic imprint of the above companies and has companies and representatives throughout the world.

Palgrave® and Macmillan® are registered trademarks in the United States, the United Kingdom, Europe and other countries.

ISBN 978–0–230–30150–4

This book is printed on paper suitable for recycling and made from fully managed and sustained forest sources. Logging, pulping and manufacturing processes are expected to conform to the environmental regulations of the country of origin.

A catalogue record for this book is available from the British Library.

A catalog record for this book is available from the Library of Congress.

10   9   8   7   6   5   4   3   2   1
21   20   19   18   17   16   15   14   13   12

Printed in China

For my family, my parents Jean and John, my sister Georgina and my husband Lee, who made the writing of this book possible.

–Nicola J. Holt

To Steve Moore for everything, Sienna and Leif for putting up with my attachment to the computer and the Simmonds family for letting me be me.

–Christine Simmonds-Moore

For Anna and for my dad and in memory of my mum.

–David Luke

For my mum and in memory of my dad – with thanks for everything.

–Christopher C. French

Contents

Note from series editors

Anomalistic psychology is an understandably popular component of our subject. This area, perhaps more than any other, can astonish and amuse readers as well as inform and develop their understanding of psychology.

Nicola Holt and her team have developed a book that does all these things. The examples used in the text are certainly interesting and informative, but most importantly they are not superfluous and redundant. Instead they are used to carefully illustrate well-made and illuminating aspects of anomalistic psychology. Many of you considering reading this book will already know that this topic is not about ghost hunting and magic; rather, it is about how people arrive at their beliefs and what they regard as constituting evidence. It is, perhaps, best described as the study of extraordinary experiences or behaviours.

- *You may be reading this book in preparation for university.* Interest in anomalistic psychology continues to grow and as such it is likely to feature as part of an undergraduate course in psychology. The principles discussed here, not least those of careful experimenting and research, are described in such a way as to avoid confusion and facilitate the transfer of knowledge to related topics within psychology. Some existing books can be heavy and dry, but Nicola and the other contributors have provided an excellent, welcoming introduction to the topic.
- *This book may be part of your university course.* If this is the case, you are probably studying psychology or a related subject. The members of the author team are all well aware of the demands of an undergraduate course where anomalistic psychology plays a part,

so you can be confident that the coverage is both relevant and appropriately rigorous.

- *You may be reading this book as part of a pre-university course, such as A-level psychology.* If anomalistic psychology is an option that you are covering, the series of which this text is part has this in mind. The authors and editors have taken care to include coverage required by your A-level specification as well as additional material that will stretch and challenge your understanding of the topic. We hope this volume will encourage your appetite for further study. Directions about where information relevant to your A-level specification appears can be found in the Reading Guide.

Of course, the nature of this particular topic lends itself not only to those looking for a book to complement a course but also to a wider readership. Those interested in the paranormal and in extraordinary beliefs and experiences will find it fascinating and accessible. If you fall into this group, it may even whet your appetite for psychology and we look forward to welcoming you to the subject. We are delighted to include this book in the series.

NIGEL HOLT AND ROB LEWIS
Series Editors

Chapter 1

Introduction and overview

Historical records abound with accounts of visions, miraculous healings, encounters with spirits, and extraordinary human powers. Socrates claimed to hear voices (Smith, 2008), Herodotus (c. 440 BC) describes how the messages from the god Apollo, delivered by the Oracle at Delphi, were central to ancient Greek culture, and Genesis tells of the prophetic dreams of Jacob. Similar experiences persist in oral traditions across the world, from shamanistic trances (in which shamans appear to communicate with spirit guides) to gazing into polished stone in the hope of obtaining images of the future (Frazer, 1957). Extraordinary experiences, such as sightings of deceased relatives, **telepathy** (mind-to-mind communication) between friends or relatives, and the apparent ability to 'leave' and float above one's own body are commonly reported today, across all cultures. As psychologists, what are we to make of such experiences, and what, if anything, do they tell us about the nature of consciousness? For example, do they suggest that our personality survives death, and that our minds are more interconnected than conventional models of mind construe, or do they simply illustrate our remarkable powers of imagination?

What is anomalistic psychology?

Anomalistic psychology is the application of psychological methods to the study of anomalous experiences and associated beliefs. An anomaly is something that is rare or that deviates from the norm. An anomalous experience, then, is an "uncommon experience (e.g. **synaesthesia** [where the stimulation of one sense, such as colour vision, automatically stimulates another sense, such as sound]) or one that, although it may be experienced by a substantial amount of the population (e.g. experiences interpreted as telepathic), is believed to deviate from ordinary experience or from the usually accepted explanations of reality" (Cardeña, Lynn & Krippner, 2000, p. 4). Anomalous experiences include, but are not limited to, hallucinations, a perceptual experience that occurs despite the absence of an appropriate external stimulus (Bentall, 1990); **mystical experiences**, which may involve a sense of connection with a divine being and leave "a strong impression of having encountered a reality different from . . . the reality of everyday experience" (Wulff, 2000, p. 397); out-of-body experiences, where one's consciousness is experienced as separate from one's physical body (Alvarado, 2000); alien abduction experiences (French, Santomauro, Hamilton, Fox & Thalbourne, 2008); and subjective paranormal experiences, such as prophetic dreams (Targ, Schlitz & Irwin, 2000). Associated beliefs are multidimensional and include belief in the paranormal (e.g. **extrasensory perception** [ESP] or ghosts), magical, superstitious or 'new age' beliefs (such as in astrology, angels, the luckiness of black cats or past lives), and other extraordinary beliefs, such as in the Loch Ness monster, fairies or the Bermuda Triangle (Irwin, 1993). It is worth nothing that there are different types of anomalous beliefs. People who hold one type of belief (e.g. in an afterlife) do not necessarily hold others (e.g. in extraordinary life forms) (Lawrence, 1995).

Anomalous experiences and beliefs are distinct from our ordinary state of awareness or contravene conventional assumptions about reality. For example, we expect our self to be experienced as bounded by our own physical body and our thoughts exclusively to be our own. Anomalous experiences offer an apparent 'alternative reality' of sorts. They may involve changes in the dimensions of consciousness that make up our state of ordinary wakefulness, such as cognition, emotion, perception, and attention (Reed, 1988), or they may violate existential assumptions that seem self-evident and that we take for granted. The philosopher Broad (1953) defined four types of such assumptions, which he called 'basic limiting principles' – principles of causation (that an event cannot begin to have effects before it has happened), of mind on matter (i.e. that the mind cannot directly influence objects), of the mind's dependence on the brain, and of information acquisition (i.e. it is only possible to perceive a material object through the five ordinary senses). These four principles would be contravened by reports, when taken at face value, of **precognition** (acquiring information from the future), psychic healing, communication with spirits or out-of-body experiences, and telepathy (acquiring information directly from the mind of another) respectively.

Despite the unusual nature of anomalous experiences, they are relatively common. For example, in surveys of the general population, approximately 10% report having had at least one, non-drug-induced, vivid hallucinatory experience (Bentall & Slade, 1985), 35% a mystical experience (Greeley, 1975), 10% an out-of-body experience (Alvarado, 2000), 33–50% a telepathic experience (Targ, Schlitz & Irwin, 2000) and 7% a psychokinetic experience (mind-matter interaction) (Palmer, 1979). Likewise, polls by professional companies suggest that belief in the paranormal is common in Western culture, as well as cross-culturally (Haraldsson, 1985). A telephone poll by Ipsos MORI (2007) of 1005 randomly selected British adults found high levels of belief in life after death (47%), telepathy (41%), guardian angels (38%), ghosts (38%), reincarnation (23%), premonitions (58%), **precognitive dreams** (35%), and communication with the dead (32%). 'Anomalistic' beliefs and experiences then are highly prevalent. This alone makes them worthy fodder for psychological research. As psychologists, we can seek to better understand why and how they occur and what function they serve.

⊙ An example of an anomalous experience

Anomalistic psychology enables the application of different models to explain these fascinating and widespread experiences, requiring the juggling of a mixture of different (and sometimes competing) approaches and sub-disciplines of psychology. Before we consider some of these approaches, let us reflect on a first-hand report of an anomalous experience. The scenario described below was originally included in an article by Eleanor Sidgwick in 1891 (pp. 31–33) and concerns an apparition seen by a lady called Agnes Paquet following the death of her brother, Edmund.

Statement of Accident
On October 24th, 1889, Edmund Dunn, brother of Mrs Agnes Paquet, was serving as fireman on the tug *Wolf*, a small steamer engaged in towing vessels in Chicago Harbour. At about

3 o'clock a.m., the tug fastened to a vessel, inside the piers, to tow her up the river. While adjusting the tow-line Mr Dunn fell or was thrown overboard by the tow-line, and drowned. The body, though sought for, was not found until about three weeks after the accident, when it came to the surface near the place where Mr Dunn disappeared.

Mrs Paquet's statement goes as follows:

I arose about the usual hour on the morning of the accident, probably about six o'clock. I had slept well throughout the night, had no dreams or sudden awakenings. I awoke feeling gloomy and depressed, which feeling I could not shake off. After breakfast my husband went to his work, and, at the proper time, the children were gotten ready and sent to school, leaving me alone in the house. Soon after this I decided to steep and drink some tea, hoping it would relieve me of the gloomy feelings aforementioned. I went into the pantry, took down the tea canister, and as I turned around my brother Edmund – or his exact image – stood before me and only a few feet away. The apparition stood with his back toward me, or, rather, partially so, and was in the act of falling forward – away from me – seemingly impelled by two ropes or a loop of rope drawing against his legs. The vision lasted but a moment, disappearing over a low railing or bulwark, but was very distinct. I dropped the tea, clasped my hands to my face, and exclaimed, "My God! Ed is drowned".

At about half-past ten a.m. my husband received a telegram from Chicago, announcing the drowning of my brother. When he arrived home he said to me, "Ed is sick in hospital at Chicago; I have just received a telegram" to which I replied, "Ed is drowned; I saw him go overboard". I then gave him a minute description of what I had seen. I stated that my brother, as I saw him, was bareheaded, had on a heavy, blue sailor's shirt, no coat, and that he went over the rail or bulwark. I noticed that his pants' legs were rolled up enough to show the white lining inside. I also described the appearance of the boat at the point where my brother went overboard.

I am not nervous, and neither before nor since have I had any experience in the least degree similar to that above related.

My brother was not subject to fainting or vertigo.

Agnes Paquet

How would you explain this report? Eleanor Sidgwick considered factors such as false reporting, poor memory, incorrect observations, being unaware of ordinary modes of communication, and chance coincidence. The field of anomalistic psychology likewise attempts to explain anomalous experiences and paranormal beliefs in terms of known psychological and physical factors. These include cognitive biases, the inaccurate reconstruction of events, vivid imagination, coincidence, and deception, as well as considering underlying neurological causes, developmental antecedents, clinical implications, and social and cultural factors. For example, research on eye witness testimony shows how unreliable our memory is, being prone to misinformation effects and the creation of new or false memories (Loftus & Hoffman, 1989). Phenomena such as inattentional blindness, where salient stimuli in the perceptual field, such as a 'dancing' gorilla, are not perceived (Simons & Chabris, 1999), illustrate how our conscious awareness is selective and constructed, reflecting our biases and expectations. In addition, work from a **social constructionist** perspective reminds us how reports of experiences are narratives that are themselves shaped in the telling, through the selection of particular words to perform specific social actions (Wooffitt & Holt, 2011). Research since Sidgwick's has examined whether people who report paranormal experiences and beliefs are poorer at judging how probable an event is (Blackmore & Troscianko, 1985), are more prone to false memories (French, 2003), or to seeing meaning in randomness (**apophenia**) (Gianotti, Mohr, Pizzagalli, Lehmann & Brugger, 2001), and, on a positive note, are more imaginative or creative (Holt, 2007).

Returning to Agnes Paquet, might she have had anxious thoughts and images about relatives frequently (she says "I am not nervous"), might she have had prior reason for concern about her brother, might she have elaborated details of the event since its occurrence to make it more extraordinary, or might she have misreported the timing of hearing about her brother's death and seeing his apparition? Further, we might consider what factors might have predisposed her to having a hallucination: was she sleep-deprived or stressed, or did she have a fantasy-prone personality (she says that she has never had an experience like this before)? Hallucinations occur more frequently under conditions of bereavement, stress or trauma, as well as both sleep deprivation and sensory deprivation (Bentall, 1990; West, 1962). We might also question whether Agnes Paquet had a genuine paranormal experience, triggered by the extreme circumstance of her brother's death.

Thinking scientifically

What do the terms 'anomalistic psychology' and 'parapsychology' make you think of? You probably have your own beliefs and opinions about anomalous phenomena. However, be warned – the study of anomalous experiences can spur strong opinions and feelings; for example, either pro- or anti-belief in the paranormal. This isn't new. Over 100 years ago, one of the fathers of modern psychology, William James, is said to have warned of this topic: "A great many people think they are thinking when they are merely rearranging their prejudices." A challenge for you, then, when digesting the material in this book, and exploring it further, is to examine your own beliefs and to try to set any biases or preconceptions to one side – to maintain a sceptical attitude. This means having a questioning and probing perspective, the word 'sceptic' being derived from the Greek *skepsis*, meaning inquiry or doubt – in this context, neither being unquestioningly gullible nor rigidly debunking experiences, arguments, and evidence.

Anomalistic psychology is a good testing ground for a critical and sceptical attitude. Throughout this book we will include boxes, like this one, entitled 'Thinking scientifically', where we will highlight particular dilemmas that require a dispassionate stance.

The role of parapsychology

While anomalistic psychology examines anomalous experiences and beliefs without assuming that anything paranormal is involved, parapsychology questions this assumption. It was carefully vetted reports such as the case presented by Sidgwick (1891) that led some researchers (including Eleanor Sidgwick herself) to question whether or not a paranormal explanation might better explain some anomalous experiences. If Agnes Paquet's report is taken at face value, it appears that she gained knowledge of her brother's death, and the method of it, before being told of it by normal means. Her report is quite compelling with the inclusion of details, such as "a loop of rope drawing against his legs", that may have been accurate. However, despite attempts to obtain reliable accounts, first-person reports are unverifiable, due to the private nature of subjective experience. This led parapsychologists to develop an experimental approach.

Parapsychology is "the scientific study of paranormal or ostensibly paranormal phenomena, that is, **psi**" (Thalbourne, 2003, p. 84). 'Psi' is an umbrella term that includes a range of parapsychological phenomena, including ESP and **psychokinesis** (PK) ('mind over matter'). Irwin (1999, p. 6) defines an extrasensory experience as "one in which it appears that the experient's mind has acquired information directly, that is, seemingly without either the mediation of the recognized human senses or the processes of logical inference". For example, in the case of Agnes Paquet, might she have gained information precognitively, accessing the future event when she was told of her brother's death, might she have gleaned information telepathically from her husband, or might she have picked up information directly from the event of her brother's accident through **clairvoyance**? Parapsychologists focus on these phenomena (ESP and PK), although some also study experiences that pertain to the 'survival hypothesis' (the survival of the personality after death), such as apparitions, mediumship, and near-death experiences. Parapsychological research is contentious because of the ontological implications that its findings have (that is, implications for the nature of existence rather than just for our experience of it). This raises critical questions about the nature of consciousness, such as can mental intention directly affect the physical world and the thoughts, experiences, and behaviours of others? It also raises more general questions about the validity of its research protocols and the conclusions that can be drawn from empirical data, and more fundamentally about how science works and what science is.

◉ And then there's transpersonal psychology

Another related field that studies anomalous experiences is transpersonal psychology, which forms a subsection of the British Psychological Society (BPS). Transpersonal denotes experiences in which the sense of self extends beyond the personal (everyday ego-focused sense of self) to encompass an awareness of wider aspects of humankind, life, psyche or cosmos (Walsh & Vaughan, 1993). Transpersonal psychology focuses on the meaning of anomalous experiences and thus tends to take a qualitative and phenomenological approach. It is concerned with the transformative nature of anomalous experiences. For example, a transpersonal psychologist might be interested in the meaning that Agnes Paquet's experience held for her personally, what the experience was like, and how it subsequently affected her life and worldview. Presumably, having had such a profound experience might have changed her outlook on life (perhaps leading to a more spiritual worldview) and may have had implications for her well-being (positive or negative). Transpersonal psychologists have been instrumental in developing new criteria for the *Diagnostic and Statistical Manual for Mental Disorders (DSM-IV)* that seek to distinguish between anomalous experiences that occur in the context of psychopathology and those that are associated with spirituality and a sense of meaningfulness (Lukoff, Lu & Turner, 1992). They have also developed counselling methods for people who are struggling to deal with anomalous experiences, without assuming that these experiences are delusory (Grof & Grof, 1989).

◉ Different approaches, different origins

These approaches, of anomalistic, para-, and transpersonal psychology, have different historical antecedents and reflect different ways of thinking about anomalous experiences. Anomalistic psychology has its roots in psychiatry and the medical model, such as the work on hallucinations and delusions by Pierre Janet (1859–1947) (Alvarado, 2005), as well as the psychology of superstition (Lehmann, 1893, cited by Zusne & Jones, 1989, p. 11). Parapsychology traces its routes to the formation of the Society for Psychical Research (SPR) in 1882 by a collective of Cambridge scholars. Their remit was to investigate "that large body of debatable phenomena designated by such terms as mesmeric, psychical and 'spiritualistic' . . . in the same spirit of exact and unimpassioned enquiry which has enabled Science to solve so many problems" (Weaver, 2009). Yet, the society was formed with the view to take such phenomena seriously against an increasingly dismissive academic climate. Transpersonal psychology grew out of humanistic psychology, such as the work of Abraham Maslow (1971) on personal growth and **peak experiences** (which are healthy and are characterised by a diminished awareness of self, amplified awareness of the external world, and intense positive emotion). However, taken more broadly, these three approaches form part of one field, and both parapsychology and transpersonal psychology may be seen as sub-disciplines of anomalistic psychology. The authors of this book have backgrounds in all three approaches, and this is reflected in the content. The stances of both anomalistic psychology and parapsychology in particular are taken and questioned but, ultimately, they operate in synthesis, both asking important questions.

In and out of fashion

The study of anomalous experiences has waxed and waned in psychology. Along with topics such as consciousness and methods such as **intro-spection**, interest in anomalous experiences was rife in the early days of psychology and has risen in popularity again. At the turn of the 19th century the study of anomalous experiences was mainstream, marked by William James's famous text *The Varieties of Religious Experience*, and early research by the SPR on topics such as apparitions and mediumistic trances were presented in papers at the Second International Congress of Experimental Psychology, held in London in 1892 (Watt, 2005a). Although work in these areas continued in the unfashionable shadows, consciousness and conscious experience waned as topics of psychological enquiry after the rise of behaviourism, and the narrow focus of cognitive science, and this continued until the early 1990s. Although humanistic and transpersonal psychology began to study expansive states of consciousness in the 1960s, this topic was rejected by mainstream psychology. It is an interesting fact that 50% of all books ever published on consciousness have been published since the 1980s (Radin, 1997), and this interest in inner experience has led to a reinvigoration in the study of different types of experience, including those considered to be anomalous. Accordingly, cognitive and neuropsychological methods, as well as qualitative and social approaches, have been integrated into the search to understand anomalous experiences. As such, the current era could be considered the golden age for research in this field, with many resources to draw on and many questions that remain unanswered.

The value of studying anomalous experiences

Whether or not anomalous experiences are veridical (e.g. Agnes's case suggesting that ESP occurs), they are an important area for psychological scrutiny for a number of reasons. Anomalistic psychology extends our understanding of the nature of conscious experience and potentially expands the notion of what is 'normal'. It illustrates just how peculiar our minds are and how fragile our construction of consensual experience is. Anomalistic psychology explores profound questions, such as can our minds survive without our bodies, and, to what extent are all of our experiences imaginary constructions, akin to hallucinations? Anomalous experiences can have a profound impact on people's lives. For example, a spontaneous mystical or near-death experience can be life-changing, providing a sense of increased meaningfulness and inter-connection. However, sometimes anomalous experiences are associated with fear and anxiety, such as in the case described below. Psychologists can accrue and communicate useful knowledge about such experiences, which has implications for how people deal with and interpret them.

Alternative explanations of an anomalous experience

> EB is a 22-year-old Caucasian woman requesting evaluation for a two-year history of 'spells of paralysis'. These began after an auto accident that was not associated with head trauma, but did result in a broken ankle. She described the accident as intensely terrifying. During recovery, she began having episodes of emerging from sleep to a state of being fully awake but unable to move, accompanied by a sense of fear and breathlessness. Sometimes, she would have visual imagery or strange sensations, such as feeling a distinct foreign pres-ence in the room, seeing shadows, or hearing footsteps. Typically, episodes would occur from a nocturnal awakening, and could hap-pen at any time of night. . . . She admitted reluctance to discuss these events with a physician for fear of being labelled mentally ill.
>
> (McCarty & Chesson, 2009, p. 83)

Rather than accepting a paranormal explanation for this experience (such as visitations by spirits or aliens), or worrying about one's sanity, it may be a relief to learn of an alternative interpretation in this case – that of **sleep paralysis** (French & Santomauro, 2007). This temporary state, where one is unable to move or speak, occurs between sleeping and waking. It may be accompanied by **hypnopompic** hallucinations – the interjection of dream-like imagery into one's perception of the environment – and is thought to be due to the dysregulation of dreaming sleep. Sleep paralysis is rel-atively common. For example, Spanos et al. (1995) found that 21% of their sample of undergraduate students had had at least one isolated experience of sleep paralysis. To be offered a psychological explanation for such experiences may allay fears – in this case, fears that have become so severe that EB is afraid to go to sleep. Meanwhile, as psychologists, we can also acknowledge and investigate the potentially healthy role of paranormal explanations, it having been argued that they can provide a sense of meaning and control (Boden & Berenbaum, 2004).

👁 Belief in the paranormal

Extreme experiences aside, paranormal beliefs can indirectly affect decision-making and behaviour in everyday life. A high level of belief in the paranormal might be associated with the reading of tarot cards or regular visits to a proclaimed psychic, to the purchase of books and films on supernatural topics, and to the attribution of paranormal explanations for events that others might put down to coincidence. Psychologists are particularly interested in the latter, that is, in the reasoning processes that govern the attribution of events to a paranormal source. Research in this area has implications for how belief in the paranormal is construed. For example, it has been argued to be incompatible with scientific understanding and indicative of poor reasoning (Irwin, 1993). The American organisation National Science Foundation (2000) has voiced concern that high levels of belief in the paranormal are suggestive of a lack of scientific literacy and critical thinking, and a blurring of fact and fiction that renders citizens' judgement suspect. This is a bold claim. Do such beliefs undermine one's ability to function as rational, intelligent beings? Or is such a position stigmatising, and do such beliefs merely form part of a different worldview, one that has advantages such as creativity (Thalbourne, 2005), or is it promoting social cohesion through a supernatural sense of connection (Hood, 2009)? Might such beliefs correctly reflect an underlying **ontology**, which can be backed up by empirical evidence, such as a belief in ESP (Radin, 1997)? As well as being associated with cognitive deficits in some quarters, anomalous experiences and beliefs have also been linked with dysfunction and deviance. For example, certain paranormal beliefs form part of the symptomatology of schizophrenia (*DSM-IV*, American Psychiatric Association, 1994). Thus, important questions that anomalistic psychology can help to address are whether this is justified and whether anomalous experiences and belief in the paranormal are associated with mental health, and, if so, in what way. It seems unlikely that the large proportion of people who believe in the paranormal in our culture are all at risk of schizophrenia. Anomalistic psychology raises and seeks to answer many questions about paranormal beliefs and experiences. Research can help us to learn more about their correlates, types, prevalence, predictors, antecedents, and consequences.

⊙ Overview

This book is divided into three sections, which will address different topics: explanations for anomalous experiences and beliefs; theoretical and methodological issues in the study of paranormal experiences; and research into specific anomalous experiences (apparitions, near-death and out-of-body experiences, and psychic mediumship). These sections, and the chapters within, follow the structure of the A-level syllabus, but we have aimed the content at undergraduate and postgraduate readers too.

In Section 1 we will discuss explanations for anomalous experiences and beliefs, including superstition. In Chapter 2 we will focus on cognitive explanations, including cognitive biases (such as a misunderstanding of the likelihood of events occurring, which has implications for whether an event is put down to coincidence or is given a paranormal explanation). In Chapter 3 we will explore the predictive value of individual difference factors, such as intelligence, extraversion, and fantasy-proneness. Given the prevalence of anomalous experiences and beliefs in the general population, can we predict who is most likely to report them based on which we all vary? In Chapter 4 of this section we will consider why people tend to be superstitious and believe in luck, and what function this serves. Do superstitious behaviours (such as wearing a lucky jumper to take an examination) provide a sense of control, for instance? Here, we focus on psychological models. Other non-psychological factors, such as social and environmental issues, may be important explanatory factors too, and these have been covered in more detail in other texts. For instance, Irwin (2009) evaluates the evidence for the **social marginality hypothesis** – the idea that belief in the paranormal is more prevalent among a demographic that has low levels of autonomy and is marginalised. Further work has considered the role of physical factors, such as naturally occurring electromagnetic fields and infrasound, as triggers of hallucinations and paranormal experiences (Irwin & Watt, 2007). We focus on variables associated with three other reasons that Irwin (2009) proposes for why people hold anomalous beliefs: the **cognitive deficits hypothesis** (that people lack the critical and intellectual ability to dismiss potential anomalous events as being due to chance); the **worldview hypothesis** (that particular attitudes and behaviours, such as being religious or having a subjective outlook that prioritises personal experience above objective facts, lead to anomalous beliefs); and the **psychodynamic functions hypothesis** (that people hold anomalous beliefs because they serve a useful function, such as reducing anxiety by making the world seem more ordered and predictable).

In Section 2 we will focus on the scientific status of research in parapsychology and the examination of the claim that some anomalous experiences are veridical. The status of parapsychology as a science will be evaluated. Is parapsychology a pseudoscience (more akin to astrology than psychology), a protoscience (in its early stages), or can it be taken seriously as 'a science'? Indeed, what is science? In Chapter 6 we will examine some of the methodological approaches that parapsychologists have used in order to test experimentally whether psi occurs. We will discuss the problems that need to be circumvented when designing experiments and difficulties that arise when assessing the outcomes of numerous experiments. Such problems have implications for psychology and science more widely.

In Section 3 we will focus on specific anomalous experiences and examine them through different sub-disciplines of psychology, including biological, individual differences, cognitive, social, and parapsychological approaches. We will consider the related near-death and out-of-body experiences, apparitions, and mediumistic experiences. These illustrate what our minds are capable of in extremis, such as appearing to leave the body when approaching death, or seeing a recently departed loved one when grieving. Subjective reports of such phenomena offer unique challenges to psychologists who attempt to explain and understand them; for example, agreement through intersubjective validation of the 'core' **phenomenology** of such experiences and how we can best study spontaneous and infrequent experiences – they cannot be created 'on demand' in an experiment.

It is hoped that this book will provide a preliminary introduction to the field of anomalistic psychology and will inspire you to explore the topic further, following the suggestions for further reading that you will find at the end of each chapter.

Further reading

Cardeña, E., Lynn, S. & Krippner, S. (2000) *Varieties of anomalous experience: Examining the scientific evidence.* Washington, DC: American Psychological Association.

Online resources

- The Anomalistic Psychology Research Unit at Goldsmiths University: www.gold.ac.uk/apru/
- The Parapsychological Association: www.parapsych.org
- The Society for Psychical Research: www.spr.ac.uk
- The Transpersonal Psychology subsection of the BPS: www.bps.org.uk/tps

Explanations for Anomalous Experiences and Belief in the Paranormal

Chapter 2

Cognitive explanations

The previous introductory chapter presents us with population percentages for a number of different paranormal beliefs. One recent Gallup survey shows that 73% of North Americans believe in at least one type of paranormal phenomenon (Moore, 2005). Clearly, then, paranormal beliefs are not uncommon, but they do challenge current scientific thinking, so psychologists have looked to explain why these beliefs exist and how they are formed. Attempting to categorise paranormal beliefs, Schmeidler (1985) proposed four reasons for the formation of paranormal beliefs:

1 personal experience;
2 influence of friends, religion, media or culture;
3 careful analysis of the scholarly literature for and against such phenomena;
4 merely to serve a psychological need.

When people were actually asked why they believe in paranormal phenomena, they most often responded that it was because they had had a paranormal experience themselves, with other people's experiences being the next most common reason, followed by media influences (Clarke, 1995). These findings satisfy the first two points above, but rarely does anyone report that the scientific evidence has convinced them to have a paranormal belief. Indeed, recent experimental research shows that reported belief in extrasensory perception (ESP) may go against scientific opinion if participants are told that the belief is popular among the public (Ridolfo, Baxter & Lucas, 2010), though this study needs replicating. The notion of belief as a psychological need is obviously never cited as a reason by believers and will be addressed in the next chapter.

Supporting the main reason reported for believing in the paranormal, an individual's beliefs in certain phenomena tend to correlate quite well with having had a corresponding experience (Clarke, 1995), such that people who report having had a telepathic experience are also likely to believe in telepathy. So clearly people's beliefs are related to their experiences, but are these experiences genuine or do they merely stem from an ambiguous experience that is in some way misinterpreted as paranormal? This hypothesis, that people are somehow making an error in processing an ordinary event, has been labelled the cognitive deficits hypothesis by Irwin (2009) and will be the focus of this chapter, particularly in relation to probability judgements and coincidences. Leaving aside the possibility that people's paranormal experiences may actually be genuine in some cases, the other main proposals for why people believe in the paranormal are the worldview hypothesis, the social marginality hypothesis, and the psychodynamic functions hypothesis (Irwin, 2009), which were outlined in the introduction.

◉ The cognitive deficits hypothesis

Researchers sceptical of paranormal claims and parapsychological research findings have tended to focus on the notion of faulty cognitive processes at work in the appraisal of anomalous experiences. Although such researchers rarely term it as such, Irwin (2009, p. 77) calls this the cognitive deficits hypothesis and points out that the underlying connotation is that paranormal believers are "illogical, irrational, credulous, uncritical and foolish". However, very little research, for instance, considers the possibility that paranormal believers may have potentially positive psychological characteristics, such as heightened empathy (Irwin, 2003) or creativity, the latter of which is discussed in the next chapter.

Reviewing a number of ways in which paranormal belief may be due to faulty cognition, French and Wilson (2007) have associated such beliefs with biases and deficits in perception, memory, critical thinking, **syllogistic reasoning**, probabilistic reasoning, conceptualising randomness, and evaluating meaningfulness, and with a greater susceptibility to suggestion and an increase in **subliminal** sensitivity. Given that it is not possible to cover all these areas in detail here, the remainder of this chapter will consider a few of these possible faulty cognitions – focusing mainly on perception, memory, probabilistic reasoning, and coincidences. We will then evaluate the cognitive deficits hypothesis at the end.

Coincidences: How good (bad) are we at gauging probabilities?

As humans we are wonderfully predisposed to notice patterns and observe coincidences, and it is such awareness that makes us good natural scientists. By observing the position of the sun in the sky as it coincided with the seasons, our ancestors could determine the length of the year and the solstices, enabling them to time the planting of crops necessary for survival as an agrarian community. Sometimes coincidences occur that require us to make a judgement between chance and some other explanation for the cause: in fact, for social scientists, all quantitative research outcomes in psychology are based upon probability, so we have to make these decisions all the time; fortunately, in psychology we have statistics to guide us. In the everyday world we are literally "swimming in an ocean of coincidences" (Diaconis & Mosteller, 1989, p. 860), but we have no life raft of certainty with which to navigate the probabilities.

How do such decisions about coincidences get resolved in everyday life? Imagine you are thinking of somebody and the phone rings and it is that very person calling you. How do you determine the probability that this person would call you just as you were thinking about them? This is not as easy as it seems, is it? There are a number of factors that have to be considered. You would have to consider how often you think about this person generally, and the more often you think about them then the more likely it is that they will call at the same time. You would also have to consider how often the person calls you. Are these enough factors? What about all the times you think about this person and they don't call, as well as all the times they call and you weren't thinking about them? Mistakenly overlooking such non-coincidences and only considering the obviously 'available' coincidences has been called **judgement by availability** (Tversky & Kahneman, 1974). Now we are beginning to properly weigh up the odds, but there is more. What about **hidden causes** (Diaconis & Mosteller, 1989), such as shared factors that made you both think about each other? Perhaps this is the day of the year on which you both shared a particular event, or perhaps you both saw a news story about a particular place you both went to together. You can see now that these kinds of factors are hard to quantify or even to identify, thus they are hidden. Yet, they could lead to what looks like an improbable event.

When surveyed, a large number of people suggest that they have had the experience of somebody unexpectedly calling them as they were thinking about them, such that they considered it to be an instance of telepathy. In one survey, 51% of randomly selected Londoners said that they had experienced telephone telepathy (Sheldrake, 2000), and in a similar survey in California, 71% reported experiencing the same phenomenon (Brown & Sheldrake, 2001). Given the common occurrence of this experience, Sheldrake asserts that telephone telepathy is a genuine phenomenon and he has conducted several controlled experimental studies which support this notion (Sheldrake & Smart, 2003a, 2003b). Some independent research has also supported Sheldrake's findings (Lobach & Bierman, 2004) although some has had mixed results (Schmidt, Erath, Ivanova & Walach, 2009). So, the jury is still out until further research is conducted. Experiments aside, some psychologists (e.g. Holt & Lewis, 2009) have proposed that those reporting telephone telepathy experiences in surveys may be misjudging the improbability of the events, perhaps by failing to consider the times when thinking about people did not result in a phone call or omitting to factor in those times when someone called but they were not thinking about them.

The birthday problem

Here's another example. Assume you are in a psychology class and two people turn out to have the same birthday. How many people would there have to be in the classroom for it to be more likely than not that two people would share the same birthday (excluding 29 February)? Clearly there needs to be a minimum of two people, and with 366 people it would be certain that someone would share the same date, but at what number of people does the coincidence have a greater than even chance of occurring? The surprisingly low answer is just 23, which is much lower than we might expect, and this is probably because we generally fail to consider the multiple combinations of different people pairing with each other but instead think in terms of just one person (usually us) pairing with everyone else in the room (Esgate & Groome, 2001). This is related to what Marks and Kammann (1980, p. 166) call the **principle of equivalent**

oddmatches, whereby a *particular* 'oddmatch', such as you and me sharing the same birthday, is not seen to be equivalent to *any* other oddmatch, such as anybody else in the room sharing the same birthday, and so the coincidental event is given special probabilistic status when, actually, it is much more likely than it is perceived. Furthermore, Falk (1989) demonstrated that people found coincidences that happened to themselves to be far more surprising than those that happened to other people, and this in turn introduces an egocentric bias that makes personal coincidences seem subjectively less likely (Watt, 2005b).

Predicting that those having psychic experiences and beliefs, such as telephone telepathy, may be making poor judgements of probability, Blackmore and Troscianko (1985) incorporated the birthday problem and similar puzzles into a measure of probabilistic reasoning in two studies. The first study found no difference between believers and disbelievers in ESP in their accuracy of probability estimation, but the second one did, with believers making worse judgements of probability, as predicted. This latter finding was replicated (Brugger, Regard & Landis, 1991), but further studies failed to find a difference in probability estimates between ESP believers and non-believers, even with a large scale survey of more than 6000 respondents (Blackmore, 1997). Furthermore, when the measure was extended to paranormal believers rather than just believers in ESP, several studies were unable to replicate the effect (e.g. Mathews & Blackmore, 1995; Roberts & Seager, 1999; Stuart-Hamilton, Nayak & Priest, 2006). So, at best the probability judgement hypothesis only applies to some ESP believers some of the time, and so is definitely not a robust effect and, perhaps, is not even a genuine effect.

"Million to one chances crop up nine times out of ten"

Despite the lack of a robust relationship between paranormal beliefs and poor probabilistic reasoning, researchers sceptical of paranormal claims continue to draw upon such misjudgements in the explanation of various psychic-like experiences, such as precognitive dreams (e.g. Blackmore, 1990; Esgate & Groome, 2001; Hines, 2003; Mueller & Roberts, 2001; Wiseman, 2011; Zusne & Jones, 1989). Take the following example of a precognitive dream taken from the personal journal of the novelist Charles Dickens (cited in Ullman, Krippner & Vaughan, 2002, p. 6):

> On Thursday night of last week ... I dreamed that I saw a lady in a red shawl with her back towards me .... On her turning round

I found that I didn't know her, and she said, 'I am Miss Napier'. All
the time I was dressing next morning, I thought – what a prepos-
terous thing to have so very distinct a dream about nothing! and why
Miss Napier? for I never heard of any Miss Napier. That same Friday
night . . . came into my retiring-room Miss Boyle and her brother,
and the lady in the red shawl whom they present as 'Miss Napier'!

A cross-cultural comparison of a Gallup-style randomised survey found
that 60% of US citizens and 44% of British residents reported having had
a paranormal experience (Haraldsson & Houtkooper, 1991). According to
one case collection analysis, of all the precognition cases, 60% of them
occurred in dreams (Van de Castle, 1977). In another random survey in
the US, of the 53% of participants reporting ESP experiences, 70% of
them had had an experience occur in a dream and 85% of these had had
more than one such experience (Palmer, 1979). Boiling down Palmer's
figures, 31% of a random survey reported having multiple dream ESP
experiences. How is it then that so many people report having had a
precognitive dream: are these genuine or can poor probabilistic reasoning
account for them?

A common occurrence is for people to publicly report having had
dream precognitions of tragic events, such as the famous sinking of the
Titanic in 1912 with the loss of more than 1500 lives (Stevenson, 1960),
or the destruction of the French colony of St Pierre on the island of
Martinique, when the neighbouring volcano exploded in 1902 killing all
but two of the 30,000 inhabitants (Dunne, 1927). Using the example of
aeroplane crash disasters, Esgate and Groome (2001) suggest that these
accidents are regularly reported on the news and that disaster dreams
are also fairly common, so the likelihood of the two events coinciding by
chance has a high degree of probability. But is it possible to put some
figures on it? Having studied my dreams and written them down every
day for 18 months, I can safely say that I never dreamed of aeroplanes
during that whole time, let alone of crashing aeroplanes, so for me at least,
dreaming of aeronautical disasters is not that common, though perhaps
that's because I never watch the news. So how common are such disaster dreams and how common are the events, it's hard to say, but some
researchers have tried to quantify them.

On 21 October 1966, the Welsh mining village of Aberfan experienced
an awful disaster when a massive coal-tip slid down a mountainside partially destroying Pantglas Junior School, killing 144 people, of whom

128 were schoolchildren. Local residents had previously expressed public concern that the coal-tip might collapse. However, the event occurred suddenly and was so tragic that it was unprecedented in the long history of Welsh mining. A week later Barker (1967) launched an appeal in the London *Evening Standard* that was syndicated in the national press, requesting people who had foreknowledge of the event to write in. Barker received 60 letters relating to the event, 36 of which (60%) were from people who had had a supposed premonition in a dream. Although the survey mostly attracted responses from London and the surrounding area, a moving letter was received from the minister in Aberfan regarding the dream of a ten-year-old girl the night before the disaster. The letter was countersigned by the girl's parents and told how on the morning of the disaster the girl had tried to tell her uninterested mother about her dream. Her mother had not wanted to hear the dream but the girl insisted and said, "I dreamt I went to school and there was no school there. Something black had come down all over it!" (Barker, 1967, p. 173). The week previously the girl had expressed how she was not afraid to die and that she would be with her school friends, Peter and June, when she did. Having perished in the disaster, the girl was buried between her two friends in the communal grave. A number of similar dreams, though less dramatic, came from people who were not connected to the event.

Trying to interpret such accounts by ordinary means, critics of paranormal claims have often considered such dreams in terms of the **law of truly large numbers** (Diaconis & Mosteller, 1989). For instance, let's assume that such coincidences have odds of 1 in 10,000 and that typically people remember just one dream a night. With a population of roughly 60 million in the UK we would expect 3.6% of them to have such a dream each year, which would be about 2 million impressive cases in the UK annually (French & Wilson, 2007). If we extend the odds for truly uncanny dreams to 1 in 1,000,000 – a figure which the mathematician Littlewood (1953) required for an event to be 'surprising' – then this figure drops to about 20,000 impressive cases per year, but echoes the author Terry Pratchett's comical line from the book *Mort* that "million to one chances crop up nine times out of ten". It's a funny comment but if you think about it, oddly, it starts to make sense. Returning to the Aberfan case, Wiseman (2011) considers the odds in a slightly different way. The average person has 60 years of adult dreaming, 365 days of the year, which equates to 21,900 nights of dreams. Assuming that events like the Aberfan disaster only occur once in each generation, and the average person only dreams of such a disaster once in a lifetime, then the odds of such a dream are roughly 22,000 to one, but when we consider that there were about 45 million Britons in 1966, then this equates to roughly 2000 people dreaming the event. According to Wiseman (2011) the law of truly large numbers accounts for Barker's perhaps impressive collection of dreams of the Aberfan disaster.

This all seems rather compelling, but unfortunately this type of reasoning is open to endless criticism. Wiseman's calculation assumes that the coincidence of the dream with the event can occur any time throughout one's life, but clearly dreaming of the disaster *after* the event doesn't really count as precognition, so it rather depends on the average age of people when they have such dreams, not how long they live. The average age of those submitting dreams to Barker was 43 years. Discounting the first three years, say, when children do not generally report dreams, then the average number of dreaming years is 40, not 60 as Wiseman would have it. More importantly than this, though, we must consider the time span before the event in which people had a corresponding dream. In Barker's study, 26% had their dream the night before the event, 56% had it within two days of the event, 82% had it within two weeks of the event, and everyone had it within two months of the event. The average time span was actually about ten days.

So we see that it isn't strictly correct to use a lifetime of dreams, or even half a lifetime of dreams, as the calculation upon which to base the probability of dreaming of a disaster. On average we have just ten nights on which to base it. Expanding the calculation, however, Wiseman (2011) points out that, actually, we each dream an average of four times a night for a period of about 20 minutes, so the number of factors is more complex than first considered. In an effort to demonstrate how probable dreaming the future is, Hines (2003) estimates that we normally have at least 250 dream themes a night. Unfortunately, dream researchers estimate that we lose around 95% of our dreams due to poor recall (Hobson & McCarley, 1977) and even in studies where participants are expected to remember their dreams, mean recall is about 2.8 dreams per week. There is about a 40% chance of recalling anything of the previous night's dream on any particular day (Schredl, 2009). So we see that the average person would probably recall just four dreams in the average period of ten days in which people apparently have premonitory dreams of natural disasters. Let's generously assume that about nine million people actually read Barker's 1966 newspaper request (the readership of *The Sun* in 2008 was about 7.7 million), then for 36 people out of nine million to have one of their four dreams in a ten-day period match that of the Aberfan disaster, the likelihood of these dreams occurring is about one in a million. Truly then, Terry Pratchett was right, million to one chances happen nine times out of ten, or at least million to one chances are almost always guaranteed to occur, which is the point he was trying to make.

The danger is, of course, that the speculation can roll on and on. What about all the people who may have read the paper but didn't actually read Barker's request, or who may have had such a dream but didn't write in, because they were too busy or couldn't be bothered or thought they may be ridiculed, or who didn't believe in precognition anyway? Alternatively, we can use Wiseman's figure of expecting 2000 people to dream the event and calculate that, with an average of four dreams per person per ten-day average precognition period, the likelihood of any one person having dreamed such an event is one in 8000, which somehow doesn't seem surprising enough. When we look at other research, what we find is that 60% of people taking part in a daily dream diary study over a two-week period actually report having precognitive dreams, and averaged across all participants these dreams occur about 2% of the time, such that 1 in every 50 dreams is apparently precognitive (Schredl, 2009). Other diary studies report precognitive dreams occurring as frequently as one in every ten (Bender, 1966; de Pablos, 1998, 2002). Can the law of truly large numbers account for these figures?

It is a curious point to note that each of the writers proposing probability estimates to demonstrate how common premonitory coincidences really are all generate wildly different figures to support their case (e.g. Blackmore, 1990; Charpak & Broch, 2004; Esgate & Groome, 2001; Hines, 2003; Mueller & Roberts, 2001; Wiseman, 2011; Zusne & Jones, 1989). Clearly such speculation is endless and is bound to go round and round in circles, because no amount of *estimating* of the probabilities of such and such an event occurring can actually tell you how likely it *genuinely* is. That is, no amount of speculating and estimating can tell us whether the dreams were genuinely precognitive or just a matter of misjudging the probabilities. Obviously, on some occasions people are bound to make poor probability judgements in these matters, though the relationship between poor probability judgements and belief in the paranormal is slim at best, so how do we actually determine if dreams are genuinely precognitive or not? The sensible scientific approach, of course, would be to conduct rigorously controlled experimental studies in which the probabilities for success are clearly predetermined, rather than making wild and untestable estimations about how likely real world coincidences actually are. As Shermer (1997, p. 48) states in his research of paranormal beliefs, "what we need are controlled experiments, not anecdotes".

⊙ Controlling probabilities for predicting the future

While cases of supposedly paranormal experiences are interesting, and may even lead to a greater understanding concerning a particular phenomenon, Stokes (1985, p. 399) notes that "there is a consensus in the parapsychological community that the evidence from spontaneous cases is insufficient to prove the existence of psi and that experimental evidence is required in order to rule out the existence of sensory cues, confabulation, coincidence, inference, delusion, and memory distortion".

Thinking scientifically → **Is dreaming the future just wishful thinking?**

Attempting to actually test people for their ability to have psychic dreams, Ullman and Krippner established a programme of research at the Maimonides Medical Centre in Brooklyn in 1962. The relationship between **rapid eye movement** (REM) sleep and vivid dreams had only recently been discovered at that time and the Maimonides dream laboratory protocol utilised **electroencephalograph** (EEG) monitors to identify the REM sleep stage of their participants. As the dreamer slept a 'sender' in a distant room would concentrate on psychically transmitting a randomly chosen and secret image to the dreamer in the soundproof room. Having fallen asleep with the intention of dreaming the target, the dreamers were woken during REM and would describe their dreams in as much detail as possible, which was recorded. In the morning, the dreamer would typically judge 12 art prints, one of which was a duplicate of the target, and they would rank the prints in relation to how closely they resembled their dreams of the previous night. Several independent judges would later rank the corresponding dream transcripts and images, and the rank scores were reduced to 50:50 hits (ranked in the top 6) or misses (ranked in the bottom 6) (Van de Castle, 1977).

The Maimonides programme ran for 16 years and produced more than 50 research articles, condensed into a book (Ullman, Krippner & Vaughan, 2002). The entire 15 studies have been independently reviewed by several researchers and found to be successful (Radin, 1997; Sherwood & Roe, 2003; Van de Castle, 1977). Compared to the chance hit rate of 50%, the actual overall combined hit rate was 63%, which, with more than 300 trials, was highly statistically significant with odds against chance of about 75 million to one (Radin, 1997). So the entire 16-year research programme would have to be repeated 75,000,000 times to get results this good by chance alone! Despite some valid criticisms of the earliest studies concerning **sensory leakage**, which were soon rectified, no plausible counter-explanations exist for the results (Roe, 2010; Sherwood & Roe, 2003). However, independent **replication** of the Maimonides research was not forthcoming during the lab's existence.

Despite the lack of direct replications, only a few of which have been attempted due to a lack among later researchers of the resources that were available to the Maimonides team, there have, however, been a number of simplified conceptual replications. These later studies have been conducted without sleep labs or EEG monitoring by having dreamers sleep at home. These studies also adopted clairvoyance designs, without a sender, and precognition designs, where the target is selected only when judging is complete. Reviewing the 21 studies published between 1977 and 2002, the combined results of more than 400 trials gave chance scoring overall much like the Maimonides studies (Sherwood & Roe, 2003). Overall, it can be said at this time that the experimental dream ESP research appears to demonstrate the weak but consistent ability of individuals to demonstrate psi during dreaming, and that there are currently no good counter-explanations for this effect.

⊙ Perception and memory biases

Besides the possibility of believers having poor probabilistic reasoning as part of the cognitive deficits hypothesis, it is also proposed that other aspects of faulty cognition such as memory and perception may play a role. Many of the studies taking this approach are based on research into eyewitness testimony, and apply the methodology of this area to paranormal beliefs. Believers are considered to maintain their convictions because they have witnessed events that they interpreted as being paranormal but which were in fact due to faulty perception and memory processes. Paranormal believers are therefore hypothesised to have worse memory and perceptual skills than non-believers and some studies support this hypothesis. For instance, in one study (Wiseman & Morris, 1995), participants were shown a conjuring trick in which a metal key bends by apparently paranormal means. Those believing in the paranormal were more likely than non-believers to announce that the demonstration was genuinely paranormal, as might be expected, but they also had poorer recall of the details of the demonstration, such as not recalling that the key went out of sight at one point. However, in a similar key-bending study (Wiseman & Greening, 2005), paranormal believers were found to be no more susceptible than non-believers to a misleading suggestion that the key was still bending after the trick, even though around 40% of participants hearing this suggestion reported witnessing the continued bending of the key. It's hard not to think of this study as being a bit like the scene from the film *The Matrix* where the small bald boy bends the spoon merely by concentrating and says to Neo, "it is not the spoon that bends, it is only yourself".

The Matrix aside, not only do these trick metal-bending studies report mixed findings concerning paranormal believers but they also mix cognitive processes, and French and Wilson (2007) rightly note that it is unclear whether such experiments aim to demonstrate memory bias or perceptual bias. Taking a purer approach to the issue Wilson and French (2006) utilised a test of false memories. Participants were given a questionnaire asking them a number of leading questions concerning the details of prominent tragedies that have appeared in the news in recent years, such as the 9/11 destruction of the World Trade Centre twin towers. After a number of questions concerning genuine television footage, participants are asked leading questions concerning the contents of non-existent television footage, such as the CCTV footage of the Bali bombing or, in a later study, Princess Diana's death (Dagnall, Parker & Munley, 2008). Up to 81% of the participants reported seeing the non-existent television footage, which the researchers interpreted as a susceptibility to false memory. Of note for the cognitive deficits hypothesis, both studies found that paranormal believers were more likely to mistakenly report having seen the non-existent television footage.

As compelling as this finding is, given that it has been independently replicated, the researchers appear to have overlooked the possibility that their findings merely demonstrate a *response bias* rather than a propensity for believers to have false memories. Response bias is the term given to the tendency for participants to systematically respond to a questionnaire in a way which does not answer the question accurately. The nature of this systematic misreporting may be due to either an *acquiescence bias* – where respondents return positive responses regardless of the question, as often occurs with children – or may take the form of a *response set*, whereby respondents become set in the direction of their responses when confronted with lists of positively worded questions, such that they just answer in the affirmative once they have answered a few questions in the same way. Frequently, and it is considered good research practice (Schott & Bellin, 2001), research questionnaires are developed with a random order of both positively and negatively worded questions to avoid response bias, but in the case of the studies under discussion both the measure of false memory susceptibility and the measure of paranormal belief were entirely positively worded. It is possible that the relationship between these two measures does not indicate a genuine tendency of paranormal believers to be susceptible to false memories, but merely reflects a tendency of those responding positively on one measure to also respond positively on the other.

Evaluating the cognitive deficits hypothesis

Weighing up the evidence for the cognitive deficits hypothesis in their recent reviews, Irwin (2009) and French and Wilson (2007) conclude that there is little evidence for the suggestion that believers in the paranormal are inferior to non-believers in their critical thinking and general intelligence (see the following chapter for an analysis of this). Furthermore, there is mixed, or at best limited, support for the proposition that poor probabilistic reasoning is related to paranormal belief, as has been demonstrated. But some support is available for the idea that, while believers may not have worse probabilistic reasoning, they may have a greater tendency to find meaning in random patterns (French & Wilson, 2007), a factor which is related to creativity and is discussed in the next chapter. Apparently there are also a number of studies which demonstrate that believers require less evidence before they jump to a conclusion, although, ironically, French and Wilson (2007) only provide one referenced example to support this claim (Brugger & Graves, 1997).

Irwin (2009) also concludes that there is no good evidence for the relationship between memory bias and paranormal belief, except for some new research suggesting that believers are more susceptible to generating false memories (Dagnall, Parker & Munley, 2008; Wilson & French, 2006). However, the false memory relationship research may actually be due to response biases of various types, because all the questions in these two studies were positively worded. Nevertheless, there is some interesting evidence emerging for a relationship between a tendency towards having anomalous experiences and non-conscious processing, such as a sensitivity to pick up subliminal information, that is, information that is received through the senses below the threshold of conscious awareness (French & Wilson, 2007). Research also indicates that paranormal believers are more suggestible than non-believers and that this may be linked to the capacity for dissociation (Irwin, 2009), which is something like the tendency to go into an altered state of consciousness and detach from reality while awake, and has been linked to childhood trauma (again, this is discussed in more detail in subsequent chapters, in relation to out-of-body experiences and mediumship).

In summary, while some of the proposed factors have no relationship to paranormal belief, some other cognitive processes do, at least to a modest degree. However, many of the relationships are based on very few studies and often with mixed findings, and much further research is needed in this developing field. So, while French and Wilson (2007, p. 17) profess that "many of the other postulated cognitive biases do seem to be reliably related to paranormal belief and experience", Irwin (2009, p. 90) contests that "the cognitive deficits hypothesis appears to be rather more successful as a polemical device for sceptical commentators than as an empirically grounded theory of paranormal belief". That is, Irwin believes that the cognitive deficits hypothesis is used as an argument for explaining paranormal belief far more than is warranted by the available evidence.

One of the pitfalls of this research is that the underlying connotation of the cognitive deficits approach, that paranormal believers are "illogical, irrational, credulous, uncritical and foolish" (Irwin, 2009), is in danger of leading proponents of the hypothesis to take an arrogant and derogatory perspective towards believers, because, by implication, the non-believing researcher is therefore logical, rational, incredulous, critical, and, *importantly*, clever. In recent years a movement rejecting supernatural and mystical beliefs in favour of scientific ones has emerged, somewhat self-righteously labelling its adherents 'brights'. However, confessed brights such as Dennett (2007, p. 21) have suggested that "those who are not brights are not necessarily dim". Nevertheless, while some researchers sceptical of the paranormal profess not to consider themselves superior to those who aren't opposed to such beliefs, they have tended to consider paranormal believers as being psychologically infantile, archaic, and technologically regressive (Alcock, 1981; Hood, 2009), delusional, pathological (Vyse, 1997; Zusne & Jones, 1989), mal-adaptive (Vyse, 1997), and, perhaps ironically, religiously dogmatic and closed-minded with regards to scientific evidence (Alcock, 1981; Hines, 2003).

Another problem is that just as it doesn't matter how many people report paranormal experiences it is still not evidence for its genuine exis-tence (Blackmore, 1990), so too can no amount of demonstrating that paranormal believers have worse cognitive abilities than non-believers disprove the existence of the paranormal. Furthermore, much of the cog-nitive deficits research is merely correlational, and therefore no **causal link** can be assumed. Even the few **true experiments** into paranor-mal belief that there are can, at best, only demonstrate that paranormal believers have a tendency to believe in paranormal phenomena for all the wrong reasons; they can never actually demonstrate that paranor-mal phenomena cannot occur. To do this, experimental research test-ing paranormal claims is required (see the chapter on methodological issues).

On the positive side, research into the relationship between cognitive factors and paranormal belief is helping to illuminate ways in which peo-ple may be susceptible to irrational and credulous thinking, and may help prevent people from being duped by financially motivated fads and gurus. Such research can also assist in the continuing quest to determine how, when, and why people believe in paranormal phenomena, and lead us towards a greater understanding of the psychology of the paranormal, be that in terms of parapsychology or anomalistic, cognitive, social or transpersonal psychology, all of which have much to offer.

👁 Further reading

French, C., & Wilson, K. (2007) Cognitive factors underlying paranormal beliefs and experiences. In S. Della Sala (ed.), *Tall tales about the mind and brain: Separating fact from fiction* (pp. 3–22). Oxford: Oxford University Press.

Irwin, H. (2009) *The psychology of paranormal belief: A researcher's handbook.* Hatfield: University of Hertfordshire Press.

Chapter 3

Personality and individual difference explanations

In the previous chapter we focused on cognitive explanations for the reporting of anomalous experiences and beliefs. However, might it be that some people are more likely to engage in certain cognitive processes that perhaps underpin anomalous experiences and beliefs, such as seeing meaning in randomness or being sensitive to subliminal cues? In this chapter we ask whether certain 'types' of people are predisposed to having anomalous experiences and holding unusual beliefs. We will explore a number of attributes of persons (personality traits, abilities, and cognitive styles) that might predict 'anomaly-proneness' (how likely someone is to have anomalous experiences and beliefs). Is there an 'anomaly-prone' profile and, if so, what is it? For example, do people report experiences such as seeing a ghost because they are prone to imaginative flights of fancy? Are people who visit tarot readers more anxious and afraid of the future, seeking to make the unknown seem predictable and safe? Do believers in the paranormal prefer an 'intuitive' to a 'rational' way of thinking about life events? Or are those who have had mystical experiences or lucid dreams open to experience, seeking unusual experiences through an intrepid desire for novelty, or entertaining unusual beliefs due to curiosity and open-mindedness? In this chapter we will also examine some potential underlying biological mechanisms that have been put forward to explain why some people might be anomaly-prone, such as fluctuations of electrical activity in the **temporal lobes** or increased communication between the two hemispheres of the brain. Finally, we will consider some models of the relationship between personality and anomaly-proneness. For instance, does childhood trauma lead to withdrawal into an imaginative inner world and the construction of a worldview in which anomalous phenomena are possible?

Some of the individual difference factors that we will discuss overlap with constructs that were introduced in the previous chapter. For example, some variables, such as critical thinking, can be seen as a 'cognitive style', a preference for a particular form of information processing. Or certain traits might be associated by their very nature with particular cognitive processes; for example, people who score highly on the personality trait of schizotypy (non-clinical expressions of traits that are analogous to symptoms of schizophrenia) are more likely to see meaning in randomness (Farias, Claridge & Lalljee, 2005).

We will begin by examining a number of personality traits that have been investigated in relation to 'the anomalous'. Personality traits can be defined as behaviours that are relatively consistent across situations in a person. These include extraversion (sociable and outgoing traits), neuroticism (moody and anxious traits), and openness-to-experience (curious and exploratory traits) (Costa & McCrae, 1992). Given the prevalence of anomalous beliefs and experiences in the general population, it seems likely that they relate to these core traits (Goulding & Parker, 2001). By examining this we might also glean insights into the functions that anomalous experiences and beliefs serve, such as reducing fear of the unknown (which might be linked to neuroticism) or stimulating imaginations (which might be related to openness-to-experience) (Auton, Pope & Seeger, 2003; Gallagher, Kumar & Pekala, 1994).

◉ Extraversion and sensation seeking

Extraversion is a complex variable relating to one's sociability, excitement and sensation seeking, impulsivity, and level of outgoingness (among other components, such as positive affect) (Friedman & Schustack, 2006).

Extraverts "like excitement and stimulation and tend to be cheerful in disposition. They are upbeat, energetic, and optimistic" (Costa & McCrae, 1992, p. 15).

Why might extraversion be related to anomaly-proneness? Eysenck (1967) proposed that extraverts have a low level of cortical arousal (electrical activity in the cerebral cortex of the brain) and thus are driven to maintain an optimal level of arousal by seeking sensory stimulation. This may impact upon anomaly-proneness in two ways. First, Eysenck (1967) reasoned, low levels of cortical arousal, which are associated with quiet relaxed states, might be conducive for anomalous experiences, allowing weak stimuli (which ESP information might be, or an unusual idea) to enter awareness, akin to moments of inspiration. This is supported by the finding that extraverts perform better on ESP tasks (Honorton, Ferrari & Bem, 1992). Second, extraversion might be related to anomalous experiences through the quest for excitement and stimulation, perhaps being more likely to encounter experiences and situations that might trigger them, such as meditation or the taking of psychedelic drugs (Maltby & Day, 2001) or through the excitement that unconventional and mysterious ideas might hold (Kumar, Pekala & Cummings, 1993).

Extraversion appears to be related to the reporting of anomalous experiences more robustly than the holding of paranormal beliefs (e.g. MacDonald, 2000). For example, extraversion has been found to predict out-of-body, mystical, precognitive, and hallucinatory experiences and lucid dreams (the awareness of being asleep while dreaming) (Francis & Thomas, 1996; Gallagher et al., 1994; MacDonald, 2000; Maltby & Day, 2001; Rattet & Bursik, 2001).

A number of studies have examined whether this might be due to sensation seeking, the degree to which individuals crave excitement (Zuckerman, Kolin, Price & Zoob, 1964). Significant **correlation**s have been found between sensation seeking and anomaly-proneness (e.g. Gallagher et al., 1994). However, sensation seeking can be expressed in different ways, such as susceptibility to boredom (finding repetition aversive), disinhibition (engaging in uninhibited social activities), adventure and thrill seeking (such as participating in dangerous high-speed sports), and seeking novel or unconventional experiences. Kumar et al. (1993) found that belief in the paranormal was associated with seeking novel and thrilling experiences only. This supports the hypothesis that extraverts have anomalous experiences because they seek out such experiences, or those that trigger them.

Gallagher et al. (1994) explored this further. They found that anomalous experiences were associated with *internal* sensation seeking (daydreaming and fantasy) to a greater extent than external sensation seeking (thrill seeking and the taking of drugs). The taking of drugs alone could not explain the link between sensation seeking and anomaly-proneness. This led them to conclude that anomalous beliefs and experiences are related to specific aspects of extraversion and sensation seeking – those which involve enjoying unconventional and novel internal thoughts and daydreams.

Based on this body of evidence, Irwin (2009) describes anomaly-prone individuals as sociable (rather than introverted and socially withdrawn) but as preferring to reflect on their own subjective worlds than the needs of other people.

◉ Openness-to-experience and fantasy-proneness

Openness-to-experience is a broad factor characterised by interest in a wide range of experiences. "Open individuals are curious about both inner and outer worlds, and their lives are experientially richer. They are willing to entertain novel ideas and unconventional values, and they experience both positive and negative emotions more keenly than do closed individuals" (Costa & McCrae, 1992, p. 15). Openness is assessed across six aspects of being: values, feelings, ideas, aesthetics, fantasy, and actions.

Openness-to-experience appears to be a robust predictor of anomaly-proneness (e.g. Eudell & Campbell, 2007). Indeed, such is the relationship between openness-to-experience and anomaly-proneness that one of the developers of the five-factor model of personality, McCrae (1994), suggested that the openness factor be extended to include a further subfactor indicative of a "fluid and permeable structure of consciousness" (1994, p. 251), characterised by anomaly-proneness.

Despite some overlap with the construct of sensation seeking, Smith, Johnson and Hathaway (2009) found that openness-to-experience independently predicted anomaly-proneness, and was a better, more powerful, predictor. In particular, one sub-factor, openness to fantasy, appears to be important (Smith et al., 2009; Zingrone, Alvarado & Dalton, 1998–1999). People with high fantasy scores have a vivid imagination, daydreaming "not simply as an escape but as a way of creating for themselves an interesting inner world. They elaborate and develop their fantasies and believe that imagination contributes to a rich and creative life" (Costa & McCrae, 1992, p. 17). This supports the finding in the previous section that seeking out novel inner experiences predicted anomaly-proneness.

Fantasy-proneness has been studied as a trait in its own right, characterising people who have a very rich inner life to the extent that daydreams can seem 'real', so that they might even confuse imagined and real life events (Wilson & Barber, 1983). Fantasy-proneness is related to the reporting of anomalous experiences and belief in the paranormal (e.g. Irwin, 1993). A related trait is imaginative **absorption**, where people become fully involved or 'absorbed' in their own thoughts and/or activities, such as watching a film (Tellegen & Atkinson, 1974). People scoring highly on absorption are "open to self-altering experiences" and are more likely to have anomalous experiences (e.g. Hunt, Dougan, Grant & House, 2002).

However, as is usual with individual differences research, work in this area has been largely **correlational** and cannot inform us about *why* people who are open to fantasy are more likely to report having anomalous experiences and beliefs. One suggestion is that fantasy-prone people confuse reality and imagination due to the vividness of internal experiences. Williams (1997) suggested that "many paranormal experiences like hallucinations can be considered to be failures of adequate reality-testing" (p. 30). An alternative explanation is that fantasy-prone people might be more likely to see meaning in random or coincidental events (Brugger & Taylor, 2003). Thus, fantasy-prone people might be more likely to engage in the cognitive biases discussed in the previous chapter. Or, they might simply attend to things that others do not, having a richer and more diverse array of experiences from which to construct meaning. Rather than embellishing events and misconstruing ambiguous experiences as being anomalous, or being suggestible and easily deluded, open people may simply be more tolerant of unusual ideas or enjoy speculating about the possibility of anomalous phenomena. They may encounter more 'triggers' for anomalous experiences, such as being moved by nature or art (Laski, 1961). They might shift into altered states of consciousness more easily than other people.

It has also been proposed that people fantasise as a means to avoid negative stimuli and to cope with uncontrollable life events, enabling them to separate their sense of self from events in the real world and thus protect themselves (Irwin, 1990). In a later section we explore developmental models which consider paranormal beliefs and experiences in relation to childhood trauma, which, it is suggested, precipitates a retreat into fantasy (Irwin, 2009).

In the next section we will consider the relationship between anomaly-proneness and personality traits that have implications for mental health: neuroticism, schizotypy, and locus of control. Much of the research on individual differences and anomaly-proneness has focused on dysfunction, deviance, and deficiency (Irwin, 1993). However, there has been a growing impetus in recent years to increase understanding of situational and psychological factors that differentiate between thriving and need for care among those who report being prone to anomalous experiences (Bak et al., 2003). This has been driven both by its implications for clinical intervention and diagnosis (Lukoff, 2007), and the possibility of extending understanding of normal variation in human experience and its relation to functioning in everyday life (Claridge, 1997). As such, the healthy role of anomalous experiences is an emerging topic (Simmonds-Moore, in press).

Neuroticism

'Neuroticism' measures a general tendency to experience negative moods and emotions, including anxiety, fear, sadness, hostility, embarrassment, anger, guilt, and disgust. It also assesses the degree to which emotions are disruptive. People who score highly on neuroticism are less able to control their impulses and cope poorly with stress. Further, neurotic individuals tend to feel self-conscious (Costa & McCrae, 1992). Conversely, individuals with low neuroticism scores are calm, relaxed, emotionally stable, and unflappable.

Why might neuroticism be associated with anomaly-proneness? Two models have been proposed. First, that paranormal beliefs act as a coping mechanism to help allay high levels of anxiety (giving an increased sense of control) (Wiseman & Watt, 2004). For example, fears about the future may be reduced by attempting to predict events through the use of tarot cards or by consulting a psychic. Secondly, it has been suggested that belief in the paranormal is a by-product of the 'over-emotionality' and irrationality inherent in neuroticism (Williams, Francis & Robbins, 2007).

Significant positive correlations have been found between neuroticism and superstition (e.g. Wiseman & Watt, 2004; Wolfradt, 1997) and global belief in the paranormal (e.g. Williams et al., 2007). However, other studies have not supported this (e.g. MacDonald, 2000). As such, the picture is unclear. It might be that only particular dimensions of paranormal belief, such as superstition, relate to neuroticism. Superstition may be more directly related to behaviours that reduce anxiety, such as taking a lucky charm to an exam.

Anomalous experiences also relate differentially to neuroticism. A number of studies have failed to find a relationship between neuroticism and both mystical experiences (e.g. Caird, 1987; Francis & Thomas, 1996) and paranormal experiences (Zingrone et al., 1998–1999). Spanos and Moretti (1988) found that of mystical, diabolic, and out-of-body experiences, only diabolic experiences were significantly related to neuroticism. They described diabolical experiences as "a sense of being acted upon by an evil presence, being given messages or being overtaken or possessed by Satan" (Spanos & Moretti, 1988, p. 106). People who score highly on the anxiety component of neuroticism are also more likely to experience **depersonalisation** experiences (e.g. observing oneself as a stranger) (Wolfradt & Meyer, 1998).

Research has distinguished between 'positive' anomalous experiences (characterised by unity and integration, e.g. mystical experiences) and 'pathological' experiences (characterised by dissociation and fragmentation, e.g. depersonalisation experiences) (Hunt et al., 2002; Kohls & Walach, 2007). Only experiences of the latter have been significantly predicted by neuroticism (as well as with narcissism, low self-esteem, anxiety, and an external locus of control), while mystical experiences, the **flow** state, lucid dreams, and out-of-body experiences have been significantly and positively associated with a sense of meaningfulness in life, optimism, well-being, and emotional stability (e.g. Ayers, Beaton & Hunt, 1999; Csikszentmihalyi, 1992; Kennedy, Kanthamani & Palmer, 1994; LaBerge & Gackenbach, 2000).

From this, we can conclude that, at best, neuroticism might only predict one's likelihood of having *certain types* of anomalous experiences and beliefs. Why this might be requires further exploration. For example, might anomalous experiences be *interpreted* as being frightening if one scores highly on neuroticism?

👁 Locus of control

Locus of control refers to the degree to which people attribute the outcomes of their behaviour to their own characteristics or actions (thus having an "internal locus of control") or to factors beyond their control, such as powerful others, institutions, chance or fate (an "external locus of control") (Rotter, 1990). Self-efficacy and well-being have been linked with having an internal locus of control, through an ensuing sense of mastery and competence (Frenkel, Kugelmass, Nathan & Ingraham, 1995).

Why might locus of control be related to anomaly-proneness? Certain paranormal beliefs – for example, communication with spirits – assume the interjection of paranormal agencies in one's daily life, and people might ascribe control to such external forces. Indeed, there is a body of work that supports a link between having an external locus of control and paranormal belief (e.g. Groth-Marnat & Pegden, 1998), although not all studies have found this effect (e.g. Watt, Watson & Wilson, 2007).

However, other research suggests that the picture is more complex than this and that locus of control is only related to certain types of belief. This makes sense when one considers that while some forms of belief concern external agents or forces (e.g. Spiritualism and belief in God), or a fatalistic perspective (e.g. superstitious beliefs, such as having seven years of bad luck if one breaks a mirror), others, such as a belief in psychokinesis or clairvoyance, do not. Indeed, the latter involve a sense of one's own agency and ability to affect the world through one's own psi.

Dag (1999) found that only traditional religious beliefs and a belief in witchcraft were associated with an external locus of control and Tobacyk, Nagot, and Miller (1988) found that only superstition was related to an external locus of control. Further supporting the idea that locus of control relates differently to different types of belief, Davies and Kirkby (1985) found two relationships in their data. They found that having an external locus of control predicted religious beliefs and that having an internal locus of control predicted belief in psi phenomena (and witchcraft, in contrast to Dag [1999]). Interestingly, McGarry and Newberry (1981) found that, among high believers in the paranormal, those with a high degree of involvement in the paranormal (for example, being a professional psychic) had an internal locus of control, suggesting that another factor needs to be considered, the degree of expertise and skill. Among professionals, the practice of paranormal abilities helped them to feel in control of their lives. Perhaps they felt empowered by their perceived abilities (Irwin, 2009).

Again, as with neuroticism, this reminds us that not all anomalous experiences and beliefs are the same and they appear to have different predictors. For example, an external locus of control might relate only to paranormal beliefs that invoke external agents.

Thinking scientifically

Many of the studies that we have reviewed in this chapter rely on correlational analyses. We must then bear in mind the maxim that 'correlation is not causation'. Just because, for example, neuroticism correlates with belief in the paranormal, we cannot infer that one causes the other.

Further, many of the correlations reported are small to medium (in the range of .2 to .4, on a scale from 0 to 1). This means that constructs only overlap to a small degree. For example, Williams et al. (2007) point out that the effect size in their study was small. Neuroticism and belief in the paranormal scores correlated with each other with a correlation coefficient of .27 ($r = .27$, $p < .001$). Another way of expressing this is to say that neuroticism only explained 7.29% of the variance in paranormal belief scores (this percentage is calculated by squaring the correlation coefficient of .27). This clearly suggests that other factors play an important role, and that in reality, although this effect was statistically significant, it doesn't predict paranormal belief very well.

For this reason research might better look at the predictive value of a range of variables and see how these predict anomaly-proneness together. For example, Swami, Chamorro-Premuzic, and Shafi (2010) used structural equation modelling to assess the relationship between various factors and belief in extraterrestrial life. Together personality traits (openness-to-experience and social conformity) explained 21% of the variance in belief scores and demographic factors explained a further 16% (education level, political orientation, and religiosity). Thus, together these factors explained about a third (37%) of the variance in belief in extraterrestrial life scores. This is an improvement on 7%, but still doesn't predict belief very well. Of course, such findings need to be related to a meaningful explanatory model too, describing how factors interact and why.

Schizotypy

Schizotypy (derived from the term "schizophrenic genotype") is a disposition toward developing schizophrenia (Claridge, 1997). However, several authors have argued that this disposition is distributed on a continuum in the general population, so that symptoms associated with schizophrenia (such as hallucinations and delusions) can exist in watered down forms, and people differ in the extent to which they manifest these (Bentall, 2003; Crow, 2008). As such, schizotypy is a personality trait (Claridge, 1997). The fully dimensional approach toward schizotypy considers that schizotypal traits are not indicative of psychopathology, and indeed may have some usefulness in their diluted forms. High scorers on schizotypy may be more likely to experience psychotic breakdown, but an analogy can be made with anxiety, which is useful for humans. We all need the fight-flight response if we find ourselves in situations where we are faced with danger. However, at higher levels anxiety may become maladaptive – for example, in the case of phobias. In addition, anxiety may interact with other factors to result in disease – e.g. a heart attack. Schizotypy may also be underpinned by useful traits, which may become less useful if they manifest at very high levels. This may only result in disease (schizophrenia) if other factors come into play. There is some evidence that those who score high on schizotypy can be well-adjusted. For example, the so-called 'happy' or 'benign' schizotype is psychologically healthy and exhibits adaptive traits such as creativity and a sense of meaning in life (e.g. Brod, 1997; Goulding, 2005).

Schizotypy is actually a multidimensional variable that is comprised of four factors: **positive schizotypy (magical thinking**, hallucinations, paranormal experiences, and altered perceptual experiences, such as one's face appearing to look different than usual), cognitive disorganisation (attentional difficulties and disorganised thoughts), negative schizotypy or introvertive anhedonia (a preference for solitude and a lack of enjoyment from socialising), and impulsive nonconformity (reckless behaviours) (Claridge & Beech, 1995). Positive schizotypy is most associated with anomalous phenomena (e.g. Simmonds, 2003; Simmonds & Roe, 2000). However, consideration of the three other factors of schizotypy is important for understanding anomalous experiences and their relationship to mental health. Cluster analysis, a statistical technique which groups individuals into types according to their responses on a particular set of variables, has recently been applied to schizotypy scores (e.g. Loughland & Williams, 1997). This has found three or four clusters which reflect: happy schizotypy (people who score high on positive schizotypy but low on all other factors of schizotypy); low schizotypy (people who score low on all schizotypy factors); high schizotypy (people who score high on all schizotypy factors); and negative/disorganised schizotypy (people who score high on negative schizotypy and cognitive disorganisation).

Both happy and high schizotypes are prone to anomalous experiences and beliefs. However, there are mental health differences between the two. Happy schizotypes exhibit better mental health than high schizotypes, and may be more creative (Goulding, 2005; Holt, Simmonds-Moore & Moore, 2008). This may be partially due to the absence of negative schizotypy in the happy schizotypal profile, with its flat affect and social withdrawal, which has previously been found to have a detrimental effect on mental health (Chapman, Chapman, Kwapil, Eckblad & Zinser, 1994). However, it mostly seems to derive from low scoring on cognitive disorganisation, which seems to be important in the way in which anomalous experiences are appraised. A lack of cognitive disorganisation may make it easier to form a logically consistent belief system with which to make sense of anomalous experiences, which makes for a more healthy self (Schofield & Claridge, 2007). These recent findings imply that anomaly-proneness is neutral in terms of mental health, and other factors are more important in terms of whether a high scorer on positive schizotypy will be mentally healthy (flat affect and cognitive disorganisation).

It is of note that positive schizotypy is very similar to other anomaly-prone personality traits – **transliminality** and **boundary thinness**. All three traits may be measuring the same thing (Hartmann, 1991; Thalbourne & Maltby, 2008). Boundary thinness has been described as a cognitive style characterised by a fluid and "open" "organization of the mind" (Levin, Gilmartin & Lamontanaro, 1998, p. 25) and is predictive of a wide range of anomalous experiences (Hartmann, Harrison & Zborowski, 2001). Thalbourne and Maltby (2008, p. 1618) define transliminality as "a hypersensitivity to psychological material originating in (a) the unconscious, and/or (b) the external environment" that is likewise a robust predictor of anomaly-proneness (Thalbourne & Houran, 2000). It has been suggested that positive schizotypy, transliminality, and boundary thinness are all underpinned by "neural interconnectedness" and have a hyperawareness of subtle or irrelevant cues. These cues (which might be subliminal) could be misinterpreted as having a paranormal source (or might be associated with genuine parapsychological experiences). Indeed, Crawley, French, and Yesson (2002) did find that transliminal individuals were better at detecting subliminal primes in an ostensible test of ESP, from which attributions of genuine psychic ability could be inferred.

The remaining individual difference constructs that we will consider in this chapter may be conceived as abilities: intelligence, critical thinking, and creativity. Rather than dysfunction, the research on intelligence and critical thinking addresses whether or not anomaly-proneness is associated with deficits – the cognitive deficits hypothesis. This proposes, for example, that people believe in the paranormal because they lack the intellectual ability to recognise that their reasoning or perception is flawed – due to the cognitive biases discussed in the previous chapter. In contrast, creativity is interesting because it is a valuable ability, due to the useful products and ideas that ensue, and is one of the few positive variables that has been related to anomaly-proneness (Holt, in press).

⦿ Intelligence and critical thinking

Intelligence has been defined in multiple ways, including the ability to think abstractly, the skills to solve problems in daily life, and a capacity to acquire knowledge (Maltby, Macaskill & Day, 2010). Despite the prevalence of the cognitive deficits hypothesis, intelligence is surprisingly understudied as a predictor of anomaly-proneness (Irwin, 1993; 2009). Further, the results are inconsistent. A small number of early studies reported an association between superstitiousness and low intelligence scores. However, Thalbourne and Nofi (1997) argued and found that superstition was a different construct from belief in the paranormal (which they defined as a belief in extra-sensory perception, psychokinesis, and life after death), and found that only superstition was associated with low intelligence. Further studies have likewise found that scores on intelligence tests do not predict belief in the paranormal (e.g. Wiseman &Watt, 2002). However, Smith, Foster, and Stovin (1998) did report that low intelligence predicted belief in the paranormal (in particular Spiritualism, psi, and precognition). These studies have used different measures of both intelligence and belief in the paranormal, which may account for the discrepancy. Nevertheless, overall, this body of work does not provide support for the cognitive deficits hypothesis – general cognitive ability has not proved to be a good predictor of anomaly-proneness.

Perhaps, then, more specific cognitive ability measures might provide evidence for the cognitive deficits hypothesis. We will briefly review here research on critical thinking, which measures reasoning in relation to real life problems (refer also to the previous chapter on understanding of probability). Tests of critical thinking measure people's ability to evaluate information logically. For example, the Watson Glaser Critical Thinking Appraisal Scale (1964) measures one's ability to evaluate the validity of inferences drawn from factual statements, recognise assumptions, evaluate whether arguments follow from facts, weigh up evidence, and decide if conclusions are valid. Alcock and Otis (1980) reported poorer performance on critical thinking among believers in the paranormal. However, this was not replicated in subsequent studies (e.g. Morgan & Morgan, 1998) although their study did report significant correlations between the sub-factor of evaluating inferences and both superstition and belief in Spiritualism.

Further studies have assessed critical thinking by asking participants to evaluate research papers. Alcock and Otis (1980) randomly assigned low and high believers in the paranormal to one of two conditions in which they were asked to critically evaluate a paper either on pain tolerance or on psychokinesis. No significant differences between low and high believers were found in their critical evaluation of both papers. Gray and Mill (1990) recorded the number of cues that people required, when evaluating three fictitious abstracts, to notice that all of the experiments described lacked control conditions. The ability to do this well was associated with lower paranormal belief, supporting the cognitive deficits hypothesis. However, Roe (1999) pointed out a flaw in this research. The study worked with both English and biology students, and the English students had both a higher belief in the paranormal and less training in how to design a well-controlled experiment. So, there was a **confound** between belief in the paranormal and knowledge of scientific principles.

Roe (1999) suggested that cognitive dissonance (tension that ensues from holding conflicting ideas at the same time) could play an important role when thinking critically – people might be more likely to evaluate research as being poor when it does not conform to their beliefs (thereby reducing cognitive dissonance). For example, '*skeptics*' might be more critical of a paper that supports the occurrence of psychokinesis than

'believers' in the paranormal, but also, 'believers' might be more critical of a paper that contests the occurrence of psychokinesis than '*skeptics*'.
Roe (1999) measured participants' belief in the paranormal and randomly
assigned them to one of two conditions where they were asked to critically
evaluate the quality of a paper that was either pro- or anti-psi. In fact,
these papers both had the exact same flaws. Belief in the paranormal was
not related to ratings of study quality. However, ratings for the anti-psi
study depended upon prior belief. People were more likely to rate the
study as being of high quality if they had a lower belief in the paranormal, supporting the cognitive dissonance hypothesis. This outcome
suggests that the application of critical thinking abilities interacts with
a priori beliefs and motivations. The cause of belief in the paranormal,
Roe concludes, is much more complex than a matter of critical thinking
ability.

In sum, there is not strong evidence to support the cognitive deficits
hypothesis from individual differences in intelligence and critical thinking ability, although there is some evidence to suggest that superstition
might be associated with lower intelligence. Irwin (2009) suggests, rather,
that perhaps belief in the paranormal is related more to a cognitive *style*
than a cognitive ability – that is, a preference for a particular way of thinking. In support of this, Genovese (2005) and Wolfradt, Oubaid, Straube,
Bischoff, and Mischo (1999) found that believers in the paranormal were
more likely to have an intuitive thinking style (e.g. relying on instincts and
hunches). Interestingly, Wolfradt et al. (1999) reported that high believers
in the paranormal scored highly on *both* rational and intuitive thinking,
suggesting that they can use either style as context demands.

👁 Creativity

A common definition of creativity is the "sequences of thoughts and
actions that lead to a novel, adaptive production" (Lubart, 2000–2001,
p. 295). This criterion of 'adaptive novelty' requires that a creative product demonstrates both: 1) the recombination of existing sub-components
in an unusual way (Mednick, 1962); and 2) a product that is useful
or valuable. The criterion of adaptivity distinguishes creative thinking
from merely original and/or psychopathological thinking (Martindale,
1999). Correspondingly, the creative process is typically (but not always,
see Weisberg, 2006) described as biphasic, characterised by a recursive

looping between two forms of cognition: goal-oriented, structured cognition that is evaluative and leads to a 'correct', and thus 'useful', solution versus loose, unstructured cognition, which is open-ended and original (Guildford, 1967). It is this "loose, associative" cognitive style that has been linked with anomalous experiences (Martindale, 1977–1978).

Empirically, creativity has been consistently related to belief in the paranormal and overall, research suggests that there is an association between creative personality (inquisitive attitudes and motivations), artistic involvement, and paranormal belief (e.g. Thalbourne, 2005).

The situation is less clear when it comes to anomalous experiences. As with other variables considered in this chapter (such as extraversion and belief in the paranormal), creativity is a componential construct. It has been measured in different ways (as a trait, the ability to make unusual cognitive associations, or a behaviour such as painting or writing). Research suggests that only certain types of creativity are associated with anomaly-proneness as a trait (i.e. transliminality, boundary thinness, and positive schizotypy), in particular, involvement in the arts (e.g. Nettle, 2006). In addition, artistic creativity has been associated with mystical experiences, lucid dreams, and paranormal experiences (e.g. Ayers et al., 1999; Holt, Delanoy & Roe, 2004).

Thus, it seems clear that there is an association between reporting having had an anomalous experience and artistic creativity. However, again, the nature of this predominantly correlational self-report work does not allow us to infer causality. From it we cannot assess whether or not anomalous experiences are directly involved in the creative process or are incidental to it. This distinction is important because it enables us to discern whether or not anomalous experiences are functional, contributing to creative production and transformation.

The evidence for a direct link is sparse, but several strands of research can be used to inform our opinion on this matter: EEG work on creative **problem solving** (Martindale, 1999), neurofeedback training to help artists to enter a 'flow' or **hypnagogic** state (Egner & Gruzelier, 2003), and research that has attempted to interpolate an altered state of consciousness into the creative process in an experimental setting, through the use of hypnosis (Council, Bromley, Zabelina & Waters, 2007), perceptual isolation (Norlander, Kjellgren & Archer, 2002–2003), or the administration of alcohol or psychoactive drugs (Norlander & Gustafson, 1998; Sessa, 2008). Overall, this collection of experimental research supports a link between relaxed states and original ideation. For example, Martindale's

(1999) electroencephalogram (EEG) research showed that participants who produced the most creative ideas shifted into a relaxed state of consciousness (with low cortical arousal), whereas less creative participants did not. Norlander's work on perceptual isolation, where participants rested in a flotation tank before taking part in creativity tests, comes closest to establishing a causal link between anomalous experiences and creativity. This work suggests that altered, not just relaxed, states facilitate original ideation (involving a loss of self-awareness, the self leaving the body, or losing sense of space and time).

Why might creativity and anomaly-proneness be associated? This may be explained by a general link between creative attitudes and open belief systems and the seeking of novel experiences, as creative people tend to score highly on openness-to-experience (Feist, 1999). Alternatively, Gianotti, Mohr, Pizzagalli, Lehmann, and Brugger (2001) suggest that loose cognitive associations underpin the relationship. For example, linking two remote ideas might lead to an original idea (leading to a scientific insight or a clever metaphor), and linking two remote incidents might lead to the ascription of paranormality (for example, thinking of an old friend, bumping into this old friend on holiday, and deciding that one had had a precognitive experience). Finally, Taft (1969) proposes an emotional link between anomaly-proneness and creativity, where both involve openness to strong affective experiences, such as the positive affect involved in creative breakthroughs and the joy of mystical experiences.

◉ Biological underpinnings of anomaly-proneness

In this section, we will explore two biological factors which might underpin anomaly-prone personalities. These are temporal lobe lability and hemispheric dominance.

Temporal lobe lability

Temporal lobe lability is a continuum of experiences from 'normal' people through to epileptics in the general population (Persinger & Makarec, 1987). This is underpinned by a continuum of electrical activity within the temporal lobe structures of the brain. These structures include the primary auditory cortex, the secondary auditory and visual cortex, the limbic cortex, and the amygdalae (Kolb & Whishaw, 1996). These structures are involved in stimulus recognition, the categorisation of stimuli, long-term memory, short-term memory, emotion, and movement control. At the sub-cortical level are the mesiobasal structures, the hippocampus and amygdalae (comprising part of the limbic system). The hippocampi have a role as a 'key' to finding sensory and memory representations in the brain. They are also associated with spatial memory and smell perception (Kolb & Whishaw, 1996). The amygdalae are involved in attaching emotional tone and meaning to experiences and constitute a vigilance system serving to "alert the body to the presence of important objects in the environment" (Roll & Persinger, 1998). Thus, fluctuations in the activity of the temporal lobes have important implications for our general functioning, in particular affecting memory and emotion.

It has often been noted that increased electrical activity or anomalies in the activity of temporal lobe structures of the brain are associated with subjective paranormal and anomalous experiences, such as apparitions, a sense of a ghostly presence and mystical experiences (Fenwick, 2001). This includes experiences in temporal lobe epilepsy, head injury (in particular to the right temporal lobe of the brain), and transcranial stimulation studies (where the temporal lobes are electrically stimulated through apparatus placed on a person's head) (Fenwick, 2001; Persinger, 1996a).

It has been proposed that electrical activity in the temporal lobes may function on a continuum such that there is a benign or sub-clinical variety of 'seizure' that occurs in normal people (Persinger & Makarec, 1993). These 'micro-seizures' go unnoticed by the person experiencing them, but may alter his or her state of consciousness. Some people might be more prone to such fluctuations and so prone to anomalous experiences and beliefs (Persinger & Makarec, 1987). Temporal lobe lability can also alter as a result of meditation, hypoglycemia (prolonged fasting), fatigue, hypoxia (lack of oxygen), alterations in vascular flow associated with drugs, and the biochemical effects caused by personal crises (Persinger, 1989; Persinger & Makarec, 1987).

Temporal lobe lability might lead to the making of a type one error, the misattribution of events as being paranormal. This may occur in a number of ways, through attributing meaning, through making remote associations, and/or through errors in source monitoring.

Persinger (1993) suggests that temporal lobe lability causes people to attach odd beliefs and experiences with emotional and sometimes cosmic significance due to an over-activity of the normal mode of attaching meaning. Greater activity or influence of the usual activity of the amygdalae on the neo-cortex would result in an enhanced tendency to finding meaning and significance (even in random events).

Brugger and Graves (1997) suggest that a hyper-activation of the medial temporal lobes (in particular *hippocampal* activity) results in a disinhibition of associative processing. This allows for: 1) greater access to the contents of memory, particularly semantics (the meaning of words); and 2) more associations being made between events which may or may not be causally related. These tendencies could be implicated in anomalous experiences as there would be more information available and a greater likelihood of attributing meaningfulness and causality where none is present (a cognitive characteristic pertaining to the type one error).

Individuals with increased lability of the temporal lobe structures may be more likely to perceive imagined events as real. Mavromatis (1987) has suggested that the cortex is usually responsible for reality monitoring, and that during states of consciousness such as the hypnagogic state the functioning of the limbic system becomes primary while the role of the cortex diminishes. It would seem that any experience (whether from external or internal sources) is laid down as memory via the hippocampus, the function of which is to consolidate 'memories'. Persinger (1996b) asserted that irrespective of the source, once consolidated as memory, the impression may be remembered as real. The hippocampus does not distinguish between imagery from a mundane perception, a wish, thought, fantasy or dream. Persinger (1996b) concluded that any process that affects temporal lobe lability could potentially modify memory, change the sense of self and alter perception of reality. This might account for anomalous experiences and memories; for example, reports of alien abductions.

Hemispheric dominance

Recently, much research has found evidence that there may be differences in hemispheric organisation and dominance among those who are anomaly-prone. Effectively, there is a reduction in the usual dominance of the left hemisphere and more influence of the right hemisphere in both information processing and conscious experiences such that the anomaly-prone brain has reduced asymmetry (Pizzagalli et al., 2000).

Among high scorers on positive schizotypy, the usual lateralisation patterns across the two hemispheres of the brain are altered such that the right hemisphere has a greater role (e.g. Grimshaw, Bryson,

Atchley & Humphrey, 2010) (most people exhibit a dominance of the left hemisphere). Research also suggests that a relative 'over-activation' in right hemispheric processes may underpin the propensity to have paranormal beliefs and experiences. In contrast, the brain activity in sceptics appears to be more 'globally' activated (Gianotti, Faber & Lehmann, 2002). Interestingly, asymmetries are not only localised in the brain and cognitive laterality but are also apparent in body-based asymmetries. For example, those who have strong beliefs in paranormal phenomena also have more fluctuating asymmetry of finger length (Schulter & Papousek, 2008).

These biases can be summarised as having more availability of information associated with the functioning of the right hemisphere (via reduced dominance in the left hemisphere and increased connectivity between the hemispheres) which impacts on the tendency to experience and believe in paranormal and anomalous phenomena. A reduction in the input of the left hemisphere may imply a reduction in rational and logical thought processes, which could result in a greater tendency to label a normal event 'paranormal'. However, paranormal belief is heterogeneous, and not all research finds that those exhibiting paranormal belief have "cognitive deficits" (Irwin, 2009). Having more input of the right hemisphere allows for greater influence of the processes associated with this hemisphere. The right hemisphere is characterised by a proclivity to make 'loose' cognitive associations which may underpin the propensity to see connections and patterns where none are really there, the type one error or *apophenia* (Brugger, 2001; Gianotti et al., 2001). Gianotti et al. (2001) have proposed a continuum of loose associative processing, which underlies the tendency to think creatively, experience paranormal cognition, and at higher levels, to have psychopathological delusions, disordered thought processes or 'apophenia' – the "specific experience of abnormal meaningfulness" (p. 596). There is also empirical support for the proposal that this thinking style is associated with being prone to new age beliefs and practices (Farias et al., 2005).

If there is less dominance of the left hemisphere and more connectivity between the two hemispheres, then right hemisphere processes may occasionally project into (left hemispheric) conscious awareness. For example, Persinger has proposed that some anomalous experiences may be explained by a relative discrepancy in the arousal levels across the two hemispheres of the brain (Persinger & Richards, 1991). This results in intrusions of right hemispheric processes, such as the homologue (i.e.

equivalent representation) of the sense of self, into the left hemisphere (Munro & Persinger, 1992), which may be experienced as a **sense of presence**, out-of-body experience, or feelings of detachment from the body. Interestingly, other methods of increasing the synchronisation between right and left hemispheres, such as meditation, have also been associated with anomalous experiences (Atwater, 2004).

In summary, a tendency toward processing the world with greater input from the right hemisphere (as opposed to the left hemisphere dominance) may biologically predispose people to be anomaly-prone due to tendencies to perceive more complex and meaningful patterns where none are present (or may predispose people to be sensitive to veridical patterns). Also, interjections from the right hemisphere may lead to anomalous perceptions of one's sense of self and body.

Conclusions

In this chapter we have examined a range of personality and individual measures in relation to anomalous experiences and beliefs (extraversion, sensation seeking, openness-to-experience, fantasy-proneness, neuroticism, locus of control, schizotypy, intelligence, critical thinking, and creativity). In many cases the relationship between these variables and anomaly-proneness was not straightforward (e.g. for neuroticism and locus of control). This could often be attributed to the multidimensional nature of the constructs involved, for example, neuroticism appears to relate to certain anomalous experiences (such as depersonalisation) but not others (such as mystical experiences). Nevertheless, from the pattern of results we can generate a few working hypotheses about the anomaly-prone profile or profiles.

The anomaly-prone person may seek out novel and unconventional thoughts and experiences. As such they may score more highly on components of extraversion that relate to seeking excitement and also score highly on openness-to-experience. In particular, the anomaly-prone person might be open to fantasy, having a vivid imagination, and entering absorbed states of consciousness. They may prefer an intuitive to a rational thinking style. They may be artistically creative. Perhaps there is a common correlate of these factors (such as hemispheric dominance). Or, perhaps such people share a worldview, for example, being open-minded and curious about the nature of the world in which we live. The anomaly-prone person is not necessarily neurotic and anxious or unintelligent and incapable of critical thinking, neither do they necessarily have an external locus of control, although certain sub-factors of paranormal belief (e.g. superstition) and specific types of anomalous experiences (e.g. depersonalisation) may relate differentially to these factors, the ascertainment of which requires further research. As such, there may be different types of anomaly-prone profile, which relate differentially to a range of factors (personality, cognition, and adjustment).

However, as noted in the 'thinking scientifically' box, work examining single factors is limited, because they have little predictive value and are too simplistic. Models that examine how different factors interact to lead to different types of anomaly-proneness would be beneficial. There is some work in this area.

A model of anomaly-proneness by Irwin (1993, 2009) considers the interaction of situational factors and several of the variables that we have considered thus far, in particular fantasy-proneness and the **need for control** and anxiety due to childhood trauma.

Irwin (1993) suggested that traumatic childhood experiences, *or* parental encouragement of fantasy, cause a higher level of fantasy-proneness, which, as noted above, is associated with anomalous experiences and beliefs. Lawrence, Edwards, Barraclough, Church, and Hetherington (1995) tested this model. They confirmed that paranormal experiences can emerge through two different developmental pathways: a direct pathway from traumatic experience and an indirect pathway from fantasy (which can result from trauma or from parental encouragement of fantasy). According to Lawrence et al. (1995) a lack of control over external events, due to childhood trauma, may cause a turning inwards toward make-believe realms which might "permanently open doors to heightened visualisation ability" (p. 214). In Irwin's model this occurs in conjunction with a 'need for control', the need to make sense of traumatic and seemingly uncontrollable elements in life. The formation of paranormal beliefs might help a person to cope with these events, building a sense of meaning and control that is essential for well-being, and acting as a buffer against anxiety. They may also help to make sense of anomalous experiences. Reciprocally, the maintenance of such beliefs makes it more likely that future experiences will be interpreted as being anomalous.

Irwin (2009) has recently proposed an integrated causal model pertaining to the development of 'scientifically unaccepted beliefs' (SUBs). Irwin distinguishes between 'parapsychological beliefs' and 'beliefs in black magic' as psychometrically different, but correlated forms of SUBs. Irwin argues that beliefs are formed by cognition, either: a) an intuitive-experiential explanation for an anomalous experience or (less typically); b) analytical and rational information processing of academic articles or spiritual and arcane texts. The types of beliefs are proposed to emerge as a result of the information processing style and socio-cultural factors. However, there are also differences in the motivational processes at play, in essence, a need for a sense of mastery over the events in one's life. Paranormal beliefs may arise in those who have an external locus of control and serve to gain control over the events of a threatening world. This is particularly likely among people who had early childhood experiences with 'diminished control'; for example as a result of abuse or trauma. Activation of existing beliefs occurs via contextual stress, which may lead to vulnerability, a sense of loss of personal control, and anxiety/ helplessness. As such, Irwin notes that belief activation functions as an *adaptive* response which attenuates anxiety, and also serves to reinforce the SUB.

The research on personality and individual differences as predictors of anomaly-proneness gives us some insights into the different functions of belief in the paranormal. One, as discussed above, is a need for control over ambiguous and uncontrollable events. Another is a need for stimulation from novel and unconventional ideas and experiences, remaining open to and tolerant of ambiguity. Both may relate to different types of anomaly-proneness.

Further reading

Irwin, H. (2009) *The psychology of paranormal belief: A researcher's handbook*. Hatfield: University of Hertfordshire Press.

Chapter 4

Explanations for superstitious beliefs and behaviour

At the beginning of the 20th century, when psychology was being formed as a science, superstition was primarily investigated by teachers and educational psychologists, who hoped to replace the belief in black cats with black capes and mortar boards, and improve education by eradicating irrationality (Irwin, 2009). Superstition was also investigated at that time by anthropologists, who study other cultures, because this type of thinking was considered to be typical of pre-literate societies. Magical thinking was seen as a response to uncertainty, and ritual was seen as a means of dealing with anxiety. By the 1940s the **behaviourists** had taken a different approach and considered rituals to be learned patterns that occur when random rewards accompany the odd behaviours that are performed when confronted by challenges that have uncertain solutions. More recently, sociologists have considered superstitious behaviour to be merely a means of simply doing something that might help in uncertain situations, whereas parapsychologists have considered that perhaps some people genuinely are luckier than others and that they may be using their subtle and unconscious psychic abilities to affect their fortuity. Finally, social psychologists have considered superstitious belief to be the misapplication of a skill orientation to tasks determined by chance, thereby giving rise to superstitions stemming from an **illusion of control**.

There has long been a contention within psychology as to how to define superstition. The definitions have changed over the years as the theories of why people are superstitious have developed. Generally, however, the notion of luck is involved. In this chapter we will consider these definitions and each of the five major theories outlined above, for why people are superstitious. We will then consider when people are most superstitious and how these superstitions are believed to function.

◉ What is superstition?

We all have a good idea of what it means to be superstitious but the term superstition itself has long proved difficult to define within psychology and is still a matter of debate. One famous quip holds that being superstitious is actually unlucky, and while this is doubtful it does demonstrate the importance of luck in superstition. Supporting this, large surveys that have documented superstitious beliefs show that most superstitions clearly involve the notion of luck. For example, in one survey, college girls were asked to recall as many superstitions as they could remember, producing nearly 1000 distinct superstitions, of which 58% were explicitly concerned with tempering luck (Gould, 1921). Most other superstitions related specifically to omens of birth, death, marriage, health, wealth, and the arrival of strangers, and were more indirectly related to luck. The two most common superstitions were that walking under ladders was unlucky and that a black cat crossing one's path was a lucky omen. Indeed, the French painter Henri de Toulouse-Lautrec must have been aware of this because he was quoted as saying that one should never walk under a black cat. Painters aside, luck clearly seems to be important to the concept of superstition.

Specific definitions of superstitions vary and Jahoda (1969) dedicated the first ten pages of his book to pinning this down and yet finally arrived, somewhat vaguely, at "the kind of belief and action a reasonable man in present-day Western society would regard as being 'superstitious' " (p. 10). More recently, Planer (1980, p. 6) defined it broadly as "a belief affording the relief of an anxiety by means of an irrational notion". It can be noted that in both these latter cases neither 'reasonable' nor 'irrational' serve to reach far beyond a circular definition. Later, Zusne and Jones (1989) concluded that a superstition is a specific belief or act that involves magical thinking and is culturally transmitted or learned through reinforcement, and is resorted to under conditions of uncertainty. Here the use of the term irrational has been supplanted with the term magical, itself undefined. More recently, Thalbourne (1997, p. 221) offered a less laden definition of superstition as "a belief that a given action can bring good luck or bad luck when there are no rational or generally accept-able grounds for such a belief", bringing superstition back within the realm of luck, as have others, such as Wiseman and Watt (2005), who stated that it is a person's attempt to control and enhance their luck, and Irwin (2009) who asserted that the core element of superstitions is a belief in luck.

It should be noted, however, that luck can mean things other than that which falls under the notion of superstition, because some people interpret luck to mean random chance. Conversely, some superstitions relate to beliefs that are more specific than just something generally lucky happening, such as itchy palms indicating that money will come. So superstition and the belief in luck are not completely the same, though they are very closely related.

Alternatively, Wiseman and Watt (2004) proposed that superstitions could be classified as being either just negative or positive. This is not a new idea, however, and this classification echoes that of Sir James Frazer's (1922) over-simplified distinction between sorcery (i.e. rituals) as posi-tive magic and taboos as negative magic. Frazer was one of the last great 'armchair' anthropologists, having never visited the people he studied but having developed his ideas at his desk based solely on other peo-ple's reports of those different cultures. Wiseman and Watt's positive/negative distinction, like Frazer's, appears not to relate to genuine super-stitious behaviours because the ritual behaviours they use as examples of positive superstitions – such as knocking on wood, crossing fingers, and carrying lucky charms – can be used just as easily to ward off bad luck as to invite good luck. Surveys of superstitious beliefs and stud-ies of folk superstitions indicate that, in reality, all superstitions seem to have the dual purpose of attracting favourable influences and warding off unfavourable ones.

Amid all the circular definitions and categorisations of superstition, Hill (1968) provides a good system of classification by identifying just three distinct types of superstition: omens, taboos, and rituals:

- Omens are signs that forewarn of an event, such as a penny found in the street predicting good luck.

- Taboos are acts that must be *avoided* to avert bad luck, such as walking under ladders.
- Rituals are the opposite of taboos: they are acts that should be *conducted* to either avoid bad luck *or* ensure good luck, such as crossing one's fingers for luck.

Why are people superstitious?

Many superstitions are no more than social customs, some of which may go back a long way, with origins which have often been forgotten. For such **socially transmitted** customs it is clear that they have been adopted from one's immediate culture, such as family, friends, and the media, but this does not explain how people originally came to generate and believe in these superstitions or why they are still maintained. Some superstitions are much more recent, such as the belief in lucky rabbit's feet, and undoubtedly some superstitions are entirely new (Irwin, 2009). How is it then that superstitions get started, and why is it that people are superstitious? The following sections will explore the five main approaches to understanding why people are superstitious.

The behaviourist approach

Some researchers in the past have tried to identify why people engage in superstitious behaviours. An early approach by one of the most famous behaviourists, B. F. Skinner (1948), was an attempt to understand magical thinking by studying the most superstitious animal he could think of, which, strangely enough, was a pigeon. Skinner aimed to show how superstitious behaviour could be learnt through **operant conditioning** by demonstrating the idiosyncratic rituals displayed by pigeons in response to automated feeders. Given food rewards at staggered time intervals, pigeons would spontaneously develop behaviour strategies in the interval. These behaviours, which Skinner called adventitious, had no effect upon the delivery of the reward, which was granted by the automated feeder regardless. This effect has since been demonstrated conceptually with children (Wagner & Morris, 1987), high school students (Bruner & Revulski, 1961), and university students

(Ono, 1987), using the same paradigm of a timed automated reward which, unknown to the participants, was independent of the participant's behaviour.

For example, in one experiment (Ono, 1987) student participants were placed in a booth with three levers and were asked to try to get as many points as possible on a numerical counter, but were not told that the levers were independent of the counter activity, which was actually controlled by a timer. Just 10% of the participants in Ono's study developed what the researchers called 'persistent superstitious behaviour' for a noticeable but short period of the experiment. However, since it is apparent that the students in these experiments were told to try to affect the outcome of the reward system, these responses may be due to the **demand characteristics** of the experiment and may merely indicate their desire to conform to the experimenter's wishes, as is known to happen in psychology experiments (Milgram, 1963; Rosenthal, 1966). So, such responses may not be a true reflection of the development of 'spontaneous' superstitious behaviours but may actually be artefacts of the experimental protocol. Similarly, in Wagner and Morris's study, prior to the experimental session the children engaged in training sessions in which typical experimental behaviour (lever pressing) was encouraged and rewarded, thereby priming the children for such behaviour. It's hard to see how such pre-trained behaviour could be considered spontaneous.

Furthermore, the development of these supposed superstitious behaviours are typically only very temporary explorations in biasing the reward system rather than prolonged behaviour patterns, like real superstitious behaviours. This is important when it is considered that the experimental scenarios lack **ecological validity**, and that, in the short term, the repetition of any behaviour that results in a reward at a regular short-term interval (e.g. a coin every ten seconds) is worthwhile repeating for the participant because the exploration of other behaviours is unnecessary and may actually endanger the delivery of the reward. There are very few, if any, superstitious situations like this in the real world, although Hood (2009) suggests that sports players who have a successful game may attempt to repeat their actions for that game, and come to wear 'lucky' socks, shirts, shorts, or other items. However, if operant conditioning were responsible for this repeated action then it would tend to occur for people who win repeatedly while wearing the same item of clothing; otherwise the lack of persistent reinforcement would be unlikely to induce a 'conditioned' superstitious response. Consequently, this effect would probably only occur with very successful sports players; certainly there are some sports stars that utilise lucky talismans, but these rituals are not restricted to top league competitors and occur with game players of all standards, and even in games with a persistent lack of success, such as bingo.

A further criticism of Skinner's superstitious pigeon model is that upon encountering an unknown reward or punishment provider in the natural environment, it also follows that the person would explore other behaviour patterns just as soon as 'the system' stops producing rewards or starts incurring punishments, or when they become bored or satisfied with rewards (e.g. no longer hungry). Nevertheless, in the short term the repeated 'superstitious' behaviour is desirable over and above other behaviours merely because it is successful. Indeed, when it is not known how a system operates, the 'superstitious' ritual is superior to 'logical' scientific methods of **falsification** and hypothesis testing because such behaviour would run the risk of ceasing the reward. As the saying goes, 'if it ain't broke don't fix it'. If the same task were approached as a problem solving situation the 'superstitious' participant would be said to be using a **heuristic approach** which, although it only approximates to the best solution, is successful anyway and so does not need altering. The alternative 'logical' solution would be an **algorithmic approach** to the task that tests all possible solutions systematically and so would involve many more unsuccessful attempts before arriving at the correct solution (Greene, 1987).

Summary

So, although this behaviourist theory offers a possible mechanism through which certain superstitions may initially be formed, the supporting evidence with humans is based on limited and artificial situations in which it is unlikely that such behaviours would be maintained or even arise naturally. Furthermore, these behaviours might also be explained through experimental demand characteristics or in terms of heuristic problem solving. Additionally, it's clear that the behaviourist explanation fails to account for the bulk of superstitious beliefs as these are frequently socially transmitted. It is equally unclear how a belief in luck, which is not rewarded in any obvious way, may be explained in terms of conditioned responses.

Superstition and magical thinking

It's a somewhat obvious observation that competitive activities are rife with lucky behaviours. To support this there have been numerous studies showing that gamblers are often superstitious, and observational research has also identified specific superstitious behaviours designed to alter one's luck – such as rituals and the use of lucky mascots and gaming pieces – among crap shooters, pre-exam students, and bingo, golf, and baseball players. Several researchers, such as Gmelch (2001), view this superstitious behaviour as a belief in magic – magic in the occult sense not the illusory, stage magic sense. Albas and Albas (1989) also suggest that students engage, perhaps unwittingly, in acts of attempted magic when they utilise superstitious pre-exam behaviour to positively affect their test outcome, defining magic as "an action directed toward the achievement of a particular outcome with no logical relationships between the action and the outcome" (p. 604). Van Ginkel (1990) also identified the systematic use of superstitious behaviour to avoid unlucky outcomes as a magical ritual, but suggested that it also serves to reduce anxiety and uncertainty, as originally proposed by Malinowski (1948).

Bronislaw Malinowski is considered the father of cultural anthropology as he was the first anthropologist to actually spend time living among the people he studied, unlike those before him, such as Frazer. He suggested that magic is used as something that helps man "to master accident and ensnare luck" (Malinowski, 1948, p. 104), and considered systematic superstitious behaviour, often used for luck, as reactive patterns used to reduce anxiety fostered by activities that create a high degree of stress. Observational research on pre-literate societies indicated that those in higher-risk occupations, such as deep-sea fishing, engaged in more superstitious behaviour and magical rituals than those engaged in lower-risk occupations, such as freshwater fishing. Malinowski theorised that the rituals served to reduce anxiety, although it was not clearly proposed exactly how this works. Presumably, anxiety is reduced because one believes that the act will reduce the likelihood of the feared event occurring, and consequently in certain situations the reduced anxiety might also lead to increased confidence and enhanced performance, perhaps fulfilling the desired effect. However, despite assertions by researchers even today that ritual reduces the stress of uncertainty (e.g. Hood, 2009), there is still no conclusive evidence that it does, although there is plenty of indirect support for this notion.

Thinking scientifically → **The relationship between anxiety and superstition under different degrees of stress**

Malinowski's theory of ritual and superstition as anxiety-reducing functions has been supported by some direct empirical research. Shrimali and Broota (1987) demonstrated the relationship between stress, anxiety, and superstition by comparing self-reports of anxiety and superstition both before and after a surgical operation. Participants in the high-stress condition of major surgery reported greater superstition and anxiety than the minor surgery group. Additionally, for those in the major surgery group, reports of anxiety and superstition declined after the operation.

Evaluation: Although these findings clearly identify a relationship between stress, anxiety, and superstition, attention is drawn to the limitations of inferences about causality made from the results of **quasi-experimental** methodology; because participants were not randomly assigned to the different experimental groups so the differences between them may have been due to other causes. For instance, it is possible that those people going for major surgery had more anxious personalities.

All students are probably aware of the increase in superstitiousness that occurs around exam time. Offering further support for the stress-superstition relationship, Keinan (2002) found that students were more likely to exhibit knocking-on-wood behaviour in response to provoking questions on an exam day (high-stress condition) compared to a normal study day (low-stress condition). This effect was more pronounced among those reporting a greater need for control, though again no causal relationship can be assumed with quasi-experimental research. Keinan (1994) also found that, during the Gulf War, superstitious and magical beliefs were more prevalent among people living in areas prone to missile attacks compared with those who did not live in such places. This notion is supported by research apparently indicating a steep increase in magical thinking, superstition, and the use of lucky mascots by soldiers during the period of the First World War (Chambers, 2004). In evaluation, there is good evidence for the relationship between increased levels of stress, and therefore increased anxiety, and increased superstitious behaviour and belief – for highly stressful situations at least. However, surveys looking at the relationship between anxiety and superstitiousness *generally* tend to find weak relationships, if any at all. There is also a need to be cautious in assigning any causality to these relationships based on the type of experiments conducted.

Thinking scientifically → **Superstitious behaviour as the need to do something that might help**

Not all research unequivocally supports Malinowski's anxiety reduction theory. Gallagher and Lewis (2001) found that, although the percentage of sociology students who agree that luck is a factor in examinations rises from 33% to 58% from the start of term to the pre-exam lesson, there is no equivalent rise in the number of students reporting plans to practice superstitious activity for the examination. Furthermore, Gallagher and Lewis also note that although many students (68%) report plans to practice lucky rituals in the exam, approximately half of these (47%) actually report no belief that luck is a factor in the exam. The authors explain these findings with the notion of **instrumental activism**, which proposes that the high value placed on rational thinking in the West requires that people persevere to overcome obstacles however they can. This has been interpreted to mean that belief in instrumental activism – the sense that one should do something – overrides non-rational beliefs. Consequently, Gallagher and Lewis have proposed that instrumental activists exhibit a half-belief in luck, such that they do not believe in it but still practice the superstitious behaviours because these actions 'do something' rather than just 'say something', and action is the necessary function of the modern world.

Evaluation: Although Gallagher and Lewis's (2001) proposition offers an explanation of why people sometimes utilise socially transmitted superstitions, it does not indicate how these superstitions arise or even why people are superstitious in non-stressful situations. Furthermore, more support for their explanation is needed; their survey only counts reports of 'planned' superstitious action and does not actually measure superstitious behaviour. It may be that people do not actually do what they say they will do.

Summary

Several theorists and researchers have indicated that the irrational and ritualistic behaviour component of magical thinking and superstitious belief serves to reduce anxiety about feared possible outcomes and uncertainties. This relationship has been found in research investigating high-stress situations such as war, surgical operations, and exams. However, the research does not necessarily indicate that stress and anxiety cause increased superstition and, furthermore, this relationship between anxiety and superstition is not apparent in non-stressful situations. An alternative theory for the rise of superstitious behaviour in stressful situations is the Westerner's need to act, which is termed instrumental activism, but luck beliefs are clearly not restricted to the West. Instrumental activism has some limited experimental support but more research is needed.

👁 The need for control and the illusion of control

Following on from Malinowski's (1948) concept of stress-related superstition as an anxiety-reduction device, Friedland (1992) demonstrated how people with a greater need for control over events, such as those in higher-stress conditions, had a stronger tendency to make attributions to luck. This relationship between reliance on luck and the need to control events to reduce stress has often been described in terms of an illusion of control (Friedland, 1992). The illusion of control theory, proposed by Langer (1975), suggests that individuals may assume that they can utilise skill in situations determined only by chance and inappropriately perceive the situation to be controllable.

According to Zusne and Jones (1989), this illusion of control occurs particularly when the elements of control are unrelated to the task outcome. To illuminate this point, Zusne and Jones (1989) cite research by Ayeroff and Abelson (1976) which revealed that participants in telepathy experiments reported higher expected outcomes when they were given some degree of control over the experimental methodology compared with those who were not. The results indicated that the degree of control had no noticeable effect upon the outcome of the telepathy test and Zusne and Jones interpreted this as an instance of the illusion of control. However, it should be noted that this is not a particularly good example, because the experiment overall revealed no evidence of telepathic ability, so it cannot be ascertained if giving participants a degree of control could actually be related to the task outcome. In short, Zusne and Jones have failed to allow the possibility that the participants may actually be right, which would seem presumptuous in light of the unsettled scientific debate concerning the genuine existence of a very subtle type of telepathy.

Langer (1975) demonstrated how an illusion of control was more likely when factors from skill situations, such as competition, choice, familiarity, and involvement, were introduced into chance situations; for example, being allowed to roll one's own die or shuffle a pack of cards. Further to this, Langer and Roth (1975) also demonstrated how, with coin-flip guessing tasks, an initial success can lead to a greater expectation of subsequent success. They interpreted this in terms of illusion of control. However, research has shown how gamblers spontaneously distinguish between luck and chance (Keren & Wagenaar, 1985), and make the distinction that chance is uncontrollable, so there is no illusion of control with chance, but there is the perception of control of one's own luck.

Yet, Smith (1998) has stated that the belief in luck may itself be a manifestation of the illusion of control because the illusion of control over luck is seemingly possible, but there is seemingly no illusion of control over chance. This also relates to the finding that luck is sometimes considered to be controllable but that chance almost never is. It follows then, as noted by Wiseman and Watt (2005), that superstitious behaviour designed to improve the outcome of an event may be perceived as an act of luck over which one may believe that one has control. However, it should be noted that it is the researchers' responsibility to actually establish whether this control is illusory or not by establishing whether or not psi influences are possible.

Nevertheless, virtually all of the studies investigating the illusion of control (e.g. for a review see Thompson, Armstrong & Thomas, 1998) have utilised methods of investigation where psi is entirely possible, yet nearly all of these studies have made the assumption that psychic abilities are not possible and have failed even to test for such an effect. Such an assumption runs counter to the findings of experimental research into parapsychology generally, which tend to be positive about psi when considered as a whole, and the beliefs of approximately half the general public who consistently believe in the existence of these abilities.

Furthermore, Langer's illusion of control theory, though possibly flawed, only applies to those who perceive luck to be controllable, although luck is clearly not seen to be universally controllable or uncontrollable, it depends on the individual's beliefs. However, for some, the perception of control may still persist, although how illusory this control actually is remains debatable and depends on one's orientation towards the mere possibility of psychic abilities, rather than on the actual reality of them.

Summary

The concept of the illusion of control as an explanation for recourse to luck attributions has been useful for testing out ideas but does not consider the possibility that chance factors can be affected by non-ordinary human influences, such as telepathy. Yet, the findings of parapsychological research, though controversial, present a question mark to this assumption, bringing any illusion of control research into question if a parapsychological explanation is possible, and, indeed, this includes much if not all of the literature on this subject. Furthermore, the use of the illusion of control as an explanation for the maintenance of luck beliefs only logically applies when luck is considered to be controllable, and clearly this is not always the case. All these factors call into question Friedland's (1992) use of the illusion of control as an explanation for luck beliefs, and may even call into question the notion of illusory control itself when it is considered that many people maintain beliefs about the existence of psychic abilities, and the notion of illusion in this case is contingent upon the possible existence of psi, which is heatedly debated and ultimately boils down to the opinions of those on either side of the debate.

◉ Luck as a parapsychological factor

As a final consideration of why people may believe in luck, some researchers have chosen to consider at face value some peoples' belief that they can alter or even control their luck through rituals and superstitious behaviour. This line of research does not explain the types of behaviour engaged in but may account for the belief. The approach proposes that those who believe they have control over luck are either suffering from an illusion of control or they may be genuinely more lucky than other people – that is, they are able, somehow, to bend chance events in their favour. If some people can demonstrate this ability to alter chance events this then invites a consideration of the possible parapsychological nature of luck.

Could it be that people believe in luck because events really do consistently work against them (or in their favour) much more often than could be expected by chance, because that person is subtly affecting or predicting the world around them through non-ordinary means? It has been suggested by some parapsychologists that if psychic capabilities of clairvoyance, telepathy, precognition, and psychokinesis – collectively termed 'psi' – do exist then those people who are effective with them, either knowingly or not, may appear to be lucky. This hypothesis has been proposed in terms of Stanford's (1990) 'psi mediated instrumental response' (PMIR) model of psi that supposes that psi abilities exist in everybody but that they are very subtle, work both automatically and unconsciously in line with our desires, and have functioned in an evolutionarily adaptive manner to serve the survival needs of the organism. That is, that we may not be aware of our own psi but it can work quietly in our favour, although Stanford added that it only works in our favour if we have positive self-regard; otherwise, if we do not regard ourselves positively, we may unconsciously sabotage our own luck – hence bad luck.

If the existence of this automatic and unconscious psi were the case, people who are proficient with psi might unwittingly predict changes in their environment and possibly cause favourable changes through non-normal means so that they place themselves in a position in which event outcomes are seemingly lucky. If this was the case, it could be said that "psi may look like luck" (Broughton, 1992). Subsequently, some parapsychologists acknowledge that luck may be both a belief and a possible ability, and also accept as a working hypothesis the possibility of the existence of psi.

Consequently, a number of parapsychological studies have been conducted to investigate luckiness in relation to the production of psi under strict laboratory-controlled conditions. Of the twenty experimental studies investigating luck and psi that have been published between 1960 and 2008, nearly all of these studies reported a positive relationship between participants' perceived personal luckiness and psi score in the laboratory tests. However this primarily positive relationship was not significant in the majority of studies, but was significant in some (Luke, 2007). For instance, a series of four experiments looking at the participants' perceived luckiness and their ability to detect when somebody was staring at them from a remote location, both out of view and out of earshot, found that, overall, luckiness was significantly correlated with their scores on this **remote staring detection** task (Wiseman & Smith, 1994; Wiseman, Smith, Freedman, Wasserman & Hunt, 1995).

One of the reasons proposed for why the relationship between lucki-ness and psi is not consistent is due to the lack of an explicit definition of what people believe luck to be when they say that they are lucky. Devel-oping a questionnaire of beliefs about luck drawn from interviews with people who considered themselves to be lucky or unlucky, Luke (2007) used statistical techniques to determine that luck beliefs can best be thought of as falling into four basic categories, which are labelled Luck, Chance, Providence, and Fortune:

- Luck – 'luck' is primarily controllable, but also internal, stable, and non-random.
- Chance – 'luck' is random, unpredictable, unstable, and inert.
- Providence – 'luck' is managed by external higher beings or forces, such as God or fate.
- Fortune – 'luck' is used as a metaphor for life success rather than for literal events.

Thinking scientifically → **The relationship between luckiness, luck beliefs, and unconscious psi**

Wishing to test Stanford's PMIR model, which stipulates that psi is unconscious and automatic, Luke, Delanoy, and Sherwood (2008) asked participants to quickly identify from a set of four colour-ful random patterns which pattern they most preferred artistically. Unbeknown to the participants, after they made their choice on each of ten trials the computer would then also randomly select one of the four art images as the 'target'. If participants selected the same tar-get that the computer would later select then this was considered a 'hit'. At the end of the ten trials if the participant had a hit rate higher than chance (mean chance expectation is 25% correct) then they would be directed towards a pleasant task, such as rating erotic images of their preferred gender, whereas if they scored lower than chance they would be directed towards an unpleasant boring task, such as moni-toring a long string of quickly changing numbers for several minutes. Furthermore, the better their psi score the more erotic (and so more pleasant) were the pictures, whereas the worse that their psi score was the longer the boring task would last. This intrinsic reward or punishment was included as an unconscious incentive to do well on the psi task, such that utilising one's psi would lead to a more pleasant and therefore luckier outcome.

The results demonstrated that, overall, participants identified the correct target significantly more often than chance, which is interpreted as supporting the existence of psi. Also participants who perceived themselves to be luckier, and participants who believed luck to be more controllable, tended to score much better on the psi task, indicating that those who believe themselves to be lucky and those who believe that luck is controllable tend to do better on psi tasks with outcomes that work in their favour.

Evaluation: Although this experiment showed some promising results, two later replications (Luke, Roe & Davison, 2008) were unable to demonstrate the same relationship between luckiness, luck beliefs, and psi although they did continue to produce psi scores that were significantly better than chance. In conclusion, as much as there is some support for the notion that people who think they are lucky and can control luck are actually able to bend chance in their favour, the results of the experiments are not consistent, indicating that the initial success of this research was either *just lucky*, or that there are more complex factors involved in the relationship between luck and psi.

Summary

Concerning the development of superstitious beliefs, the hypothesis tested by some parapsychologists is that people who believe they are lucky are actually luckier than people who believe themselves to be unlucky because they are better able to use 'psi' in their favour. Usually psi in this sense is taken to be a subtle, unconscious, and automatic process driven by our desires. The experimental research testing psi under controlled laboratory conditions has so far demonstrated a generally positive relationship between perceived luckiness and psi ability, however only a few of these studies were actually significant, so the findings are currently inconclusive.

👁 When are people superstitious?

A rather different line of research into luck beliefs considers when and how people ascribe luckiness to an event outcome in certain situations. For instance, research by Teigen (1995) gathered volunteers' stories of lucky and unlucky events that were then rated by independent judges for the attractiveness of the outcome, the degree to which an alternative outcome was implied, and the attractiveness of the alternative. The results showed that unluckiness was more readily associated with unpleasantness than luck was associated with pleasantness. Additionally, lucky and unlucky events were characterised by the idea that events could have been dramatically different. Teigen (1995) interpreted these findings in terms of "counterfactual thinking", the idea of "what might have happened had things been different".

Follow-up research by Teigen (1996) manipulated factors of **counterfactual closeness** in a series of hypothetical stories, called **vignettes**. Counterfactual closeness refers to the activity of speculating about a more extreme outcome, which, counter to fact, did not actually occur but which nearly did, such as someone saying that they were lucky to only break their leg after falling out of a tree as they could have been killed instead. Factors manipulated in the vignette included physical closeness, temporal order, choice, how realistic was the alternative, and deservedness of the outcome. The results indicated that degree of luckiness could be manipulated and that judgements are consistent concerning who is the most or least lucky across varying situations.

More recently, Teigen (1998) reverted back to what might be called the more naturalistic and appropriate methodology of using an array of real stories, but this time concerning dangerous situations and careless behaviour. The stories were then rated and it was found that luck was related to the closeness, the aversiveness, and the estimated probability of the counterfactual outcome. Teigen (1998) asserted that luck is frequently a by-product of risk taking because it is primarily determined by counterfactual negative outcomes. Further real-world support comes from Janoff-Bulman (1992), who noted that trauma victims often perceive themselves to be lucky in light of the possibility of worse outcomes.

Finally, Teigen, Evensen, Samoilow, and Vatne (1999) conducted a series of real life stories and vignette studies with varying manipulations that led the researcher to conclude that good luck and bad luck are dependent upon certain situational factors and upon how a story is told. It was found that good luck involves downward comparisons to hypothetical outcomes, such as expressing luckiness for not having ill health, whereas bad luck involves upward comparisons. Good luck stories change from negative to positive abruptly at the end, often involving surprise and counterfactual closeness, whereas bad luck stories tend to begin normally and then slowly become increasingly more negative. Additionally, the reversal of the sequence of events is sufficient to warrant a change of evaluation from lucky to unlucky.

Summary

The studies outlined here demonstrate how the term luck is often used in conjunction with counterfactual outcomes, which Teigen (1998) asserted are primarily negative. Good luck is the avoidance of something negative, whereas encountering the negative is bad luck. In addition, the degree of luck or unluckiness is seemingly dependent upon various factors of the counterfactual outcome, such as counterfactual closeness, that is the relative physical and temporal closeness of the implied outcome. Stories of luck have also been demonstrated to vary in their delivery depending upon a good or bad outcome.

In evaluation, this line of research is useful in indicating when people ascribe luckiness to an event outcome but does not tell us anything directly about what people believe luck to be or why people engage in magical thinking and behaviour. Nevertheless the counterfactual element of luck that is expressed by demonstrating worse possibilities – in the case of good luck – *is* so apparent that there exists an entire children's book devoted to it. As Dr Seuss (1973, p. 3.) notes, "Just tell yourself, Duckie, you're really quite lucky! Some people are much more, oh, ever so much more, oh, muchly much-much more unlucky than you!" and "It's a troublesome world. All the people who're in it are troubled with troubles almost every minute. You ought to be thankful, a whole heaping lot for the places and people you're lucky you're not!" (p. 5).

👁 How do superstitions function?

A more direct and naturalistic avenue of investigation, compared with the use of vignettes, investigates how people in real situations consider luck to function. There is a wealth of research related to gambling that has proven to be important for understanding the psychology of superstition. This area documents various strategies used by gamblers who attempt to improve their success, and reliance upon luck is one of the major factors, of course. As Cohen (1960, p. 114) indicates, "it is impossible to divorce the practice of gambling from the idea of luck".

A survey of poker players conducted by Hayano (1978) revealed a number of beliefs about how luck functions. Luck was generally perceived to be either an agent to, or outcome of, the game, which could be negatively affected by pessimism. Additionally it was perceived to be an exhaustible resource in the short term, such that it could run out. Runs of bad luck could also be countered by superstitious activity, usually involving a change in the normal activities within the game setting to disrupt the bad luck, such as shuffling the deck or moving a seat.

Further research into the cognitive distortions made by gamblers indicates that luck is often perceived as being contagious, such that proximity and fellowship with apparently lucky individuals or places will also generate luck for those associated with them. This is closely linked to the concept of lucky mascots, which can be people or may come in the form of talismans, which confer luck upon the bearer. Toneatto (1999) also identified how luck can be seen to be a characteristic of the person. The perception of luck as a personality trait was also found in a pilot survey of students (Smith, Wiseman, Harris & Joiner, 1996). Respondents were categorised into three groups, with some viewing luck to be an innate characteristic and others viewing luck as a force bestowed upon them by a powerful other, such as God or fate. A third group was defined as perceiving luck to be a factor which could be controlled by superstitious behaviour, again echoing the findings of Hayano (1978) and Toneatto (1999). Superstition, in essence, is the name given to attempts at controlling luck, which is a function that some people believe they can achieve.

Summary

Research into the psychology of superstition, primarily with gamblers, has found that people ascribe various functional attributes to luck, such as its being an exhaustible resource, or a power that is accessible through the use of superstitious behaviour. It may also be affected by optimism or pessimism, and can be contagious, attached to people or objects, or a product of the environment. Luck can also be considered to be a force bestowed by a powerful other, such as God or fate, or it may be an innate characteristic.

◉ Further reading

Irwin, H. (2009) *The psychology of paranormal belief: A researcher's handbook*. Hatfield: University of Hertfordshire Press.
Pritchard, D., & Smith, M. (2004) The psychology and philosophy of luck. *New Ideas in Psychology, 22*, 1–28.

Summary of Section 1

We have covered a diverse range of explanations and correlates of anomalous experiences and beliefs in Chapters 2, 3, and 4, focusing on individual differences, cognitive deficits, and superstition and a need for control.

However, we have not addressed, here, any social or environmental factors. To some extent these are covered in relation to specific experiences in the final three chapters (on out-of-body experiences, near-death experiences, apparitions, and mediumship), such as the role of naturally occurring geomagnetism as a trigger of apparitions and the role of sociocultural factors in the development of a belief in ghosts.

Irwin (2009) proposes another hypothesis in addition to the cognitive deficits hypothesis, features of personality (the psychodynamics hypothesis), and the worldview hypothesis (where beliefs form an integral part of a religious or philosophical worldview, which are in part culturally determined), which is the social marginality hypothesis. We will briefly discuss this here.

This approach has examined demographics and sociological variables as predictors of a belief in the paranormal and anomalous experiences (such as age, gender, ethnicity, and socioeconomic status). Socially marginalised groups, it is reasoned, might have less control over their lives and as such might be more likely to resort to superstition and to hold religious and paranormal beliefs (see Irwin, 2009). Much of this research has achieved mixed and inconclusive results, somewhat undermining this hypothesis; for example, unemployment has been associated with low belief (Emmons & Sobal, 1981), which contradicts the social marginality hypothesis, while Wuthnow (1976) reported the reverse, thereby supporting it. However, women do tend to have a higher belief in some phenomena (e.g. ESP) and men in others (e.g. alien abduction), suggesting that gender is an important factor when considering anomaly-proneness (Blackmore, 1994). Irwin (2009) concludes that culture appears to affect not *whether* people hold anomalous beliefs, but *what* they believe.

In the next chapters we will evaluate another potential explanation for some anomalous experiences and a belief in the paranormal – based on the hypothesis that experiences such as that of telepathy might be veridical – the psi hypothesis. This postulates that certain cognitive processes and traits (such as fantasy-proneness) might lead people to be more sensitive to the acquisition of information by paranormal means.

Theoretical and Methodological Issues in Parapsychology

Chapter 5

Pseudoscience and the scientific status of parapsychology

👁 What is science?

Philosophers of science have not found it easy to distinguish science from non-science in general (Chalmers, 1999) and from pseudoscience in particular. Note that we would only consider referring to a doctrine as a pseudoscience if it claimed to be a science but failed to meet the standards required of a true science. If no claim to scientific status were being made, the label of pseudoscience could not apply. This, of course, requires that we have a clear notion of what defines a true science, a requirement which may sound simple but turns out not to be.

A widely accepted 'common sense' view of science, sometimes associated with the 16th-century philosopher Sir Francis Bacon, asserts that scientists discover universally true laws of nature by a process of induction. Putting it simply, they note any regularities that they observe in nature, for example, that water boils at 100 degrees centigrade. They then test this observation systematically by repeating it many times. If the water always boils at 100 degrees centigrade, they conclude that they have discovered another universally true law of nature. The problem is, of course, that even if one has observed water boiling at 100 degrees centigrade a million times, logically that does not guarantee that it will do so the next time you observe it. In fact, if you happen to be at the top of Everest when you make your next observation, the water will boil at a lower temperature due to the lower air pressure at higher altitudes.

Sir Karl Popper (1963) was concerned that no matter how many times observations appeared to support a hypothesis, one could never conclude that one had discovered a universally true scientific law. This meant that scientific theories could never be proved to be true in any absolute sense. Popper claimed, however, that it did follow logically that a single observation which contradicted a theory proves it to be false. Therefore, he argued, scientists should proceed by always attempting to falsify their own theories. If they could not, then they would be justified in tentatively accepting that their theory might be true, but they could never be sure of it. If they did manage to falsify their theory, they had to reject it and attempt to produce a better theory. In the case of our hypothetical observation that water did not boil at 100 degrees centigrade at high altitudes, we must reject our initial hypothesis and generate a new theory that can encompass all of the data collected up to that point and, ideally, generate interesting new hypotheses for testing. Thus, according to Popper, science proceeds by generating better and better guesses about the nature of the universe, but we can never be sure that any of its theories are true in an absolute sense.

According to Popper, if a statement is not falsifiable, then it cannot be scientific. It might appear at first glance that if a particular belief system can account for any outcome, this would indicate its strength. In fact, in scientific terms, such a belief system cannot be thought of as a scientific theory at all. If there is no turn of events that would falsify the belief system, then it clearly lacks any predictive power. It can only apparently account for events retrospectively. Popper viewed both Marxism and psychoanalysis as pseudosciences on the grounds of problems relating to falsifiability. There is no turn of events which the Marxist or Freudian would see as being incompatible with their belief system.

Although most scientists would agree that falsifiability is a critical feature of any truly scientific theory, it has simply not proved possible to produce a generally acceptable set of criteria or definition that would allow one to discriminate perfectly between science and non-science or between true science and pseudoscience in all cases. Instead, as we will see in the next section, there are benchmarks which characterise good science, as argued by Edge, Morris, Palmer, and Rush (1986). The degree to which a field meets all of these criteria will determine the degree to which it is viewed as being truly scientific, but there will be fields of human endeavour which clearly meet some of these criteria but are problematic with respect to others. Many would put the social sciences, including psychology, in this category of 'soft sciences'.

It is obvious that what we now accept as fully fledged sciences, such as chemistry, physics, and astronomy, did not come into the world that way. Modern chemistry can be traced back to alchemy, modern physics has its roots in the speculations of ancient philosophers, and some would claim that astronomy has its roots in the observations of astrology. There is no clear point at which a subject crosses the boundary from non-science to science, so it is sometimes useful to think in terms of protosciences. A protoscience might be defined as a field of investigation in its early stages of development, which is on the borderline between science and pseudoscience (Radner & Radner, 1982). Whether or not it achieves acceptance as a true science will depend upon how it develops.

The history of science includes cases where a revolutionary theory is rejected by the wider scientific community at the time it is proposed only to be subsequently shown to be true. Stent (1972) defines prematurity in science as follows: "A discovery is premature if its implications cannot be connected by a series of simple logical steps to canonical, or generally accepted, knowledge" (p. 84). For example, Alfred Wegener, a German meteorologist, was ridiculed by the geologists of the day for proposing the idea of continental drift in 1912. It was not until the 1960s that the idea was taken seriously and it is now universally accepted. The idea was premature when first proposed in the sense that it contradicted established beliefs of the time, but eventually it had to be accepted when new data accumulated which could not reasonably be accounted for in terms of the old theory. Many other cases could be cited.

Thomas Kuhn (e.g. 1962) has discussed such 'scientific revolutions' extensively. The concept of a 'paradigm' is important in Kuhn's work. This refers to the shared assumptions of workers in a particular field regarding not only which theories are likely to be correct, but also which issues are worthy of investigation, which methods of investigation are valid, and so on. Kuhn later uses the term 'disciplinary matrix' to refer to such shared background. He distinguishes between periods of 'normal science', when scientists work contentedly and productively within a paradigm or disciplinary matrix and 'revolutionary science' which occurs only when so many anomalous data have accumulated that the old paradigm is overthrown and a new paradigm, capable of accounting for the anomalous findings, becomes dominant as the new orthodoxy.

👁 What is pseudoscience?

At the most general level, 'pseudoscience' may be defined as claims and methods that are falsely presented as 'science'. As we have seen, however, there is no universally accepted definition or set of criteria that can be used to unambiguously characterise a domain of enquiry as a true science. This has not prevented commentators from proposing sets of criteria to identify pseudoscience, however, and it is reasonable to assume that the opposite of these criteria may be taken as being characteristics of good science.

Those who put forward these criteria differed in the degree to which they feel them to be absolute. Radner and Radner (1982), for example, felt that if a discipline displayed evidence of even one of their nine "marks of pseudoscience", that was enough to condemn that discipline as being irredeemably pseudoscientific. Lilienfeld, Lynn, and Lohr (2003), on the other hand, argue that "science probably differs from pseudoscience in degree rather than in kind. Science and pseudoscience can be thought of as [. . .] open [. . .] concepts, which possess intrinsically fuzzy boundaries and an indefinitely extendable list of indicators" (p. 5).

Here are some of the nine 'marks of pseudoscience' outlined by Radner and Radner (1982). According to the Radners, these features "are found only in crackpot work and never in genuine scientific work":

- *Anachronistic thinking:* the tendency to return to outmoded theories that have already been shown to be unworkable; for example, flat-earthers, creationists.
- *Looking for mysteries:* the assumption that if conventional theorists cannot supply completely watertight explanations for every single case that is put before them, then they should admit that the pseudoscientific claim is valid.
- *Appeal to myths:* the tendency to assume that ancient myths are literally true and that they can be explained in terms of hypothesised special conditions that held true at the time but no longer do so, then argue that the myth itself offers confirmation of the hypothesis. Such arguments have been used, for example, by Erich von Daniken (e.g. 1968) in support of his claim that the earth has been visited in its past by extraterrestrials. Another example would be creationists, who believe that the Bible is literally true.

- *The grab-bag approach to evidence:* 'the attitude that sheer quantity of evidence makes up for any deficiency in the quality of individual pieces of evidence'. For example, Charles Berlitz (1974) popularised the idea of the Bermuda Triangle, that is, that there was an area of ocean just east of Florida where ships and planes would mysteriously disappear without a trace. Erich von Daniken's (1968) claims relating to alien visitations in ancient times were, he claimed, supported by the existence of ancient artefacts that could not possibly have been produced by humans. In both of these examples, none of the numerous cases presented stood up to serious critical scrutiny.

- *Irrefutable hypotheses:* as already stated, Popper argued that any hypothesis that claims to be scientific must be, at least in principle, falsifiable.

- *Argument from spurious similarity:* the tendency to argue that the principles upon which a pseudoscience is based are already part of legitimate science when in fact any similarity is spurious and superficial; for example, astrologers often refer to perfectly acceptable research into biological rhythms as if the latter supported their claims.

- *Refusal to revise in light of criticism:* the tendency to argue that pseudoscientific beliefs (e.g. astrology, homeopathy) are better than conventional scientific beliefs, because conventional science is constantly rejecting or refining its theories in the light of new data.

James Alcock (1981, p. 117) presents the following summary of Mario Bunge's (1980) characterisation of pseudoscience:

- its theory of knowledge is subjectivistic, containing aspects accessible only to the initiated
- its formal background is modest, with only rare involvement of mathematics or logic
- its fund of knowledge contains untestable or even false hypotheses which are in conflict with a larger body of knowledge
- its methods are neither checkable by alternative methods nor justifiable in terms of well-confirmed theories
- it borrows nothing from neighbouring fields, there is no overlap with another field of research
- it has no specific background of relatively confirmed theories

- it has an unchanging body of belief, whereas scientific enquiry teems with novelty
- it has a worldview admitting elusive immaterial entities, such as disembodied minds, whereas science countenances only changing concrete things.

Scott O. Lilienfeld (2005) suggests that the following features distinguish science from pseudoscience:

- A tendency to invoke *ad hoc* hypotheses, which can be thought of as 'escape hatches' or loopholes, as a means of immunising claims from falsification
- An absence of self-correction and an accompanying intellectual stagnation
- An emphasis on confirmation rather than refutation
- A tendency to place the burden of proof on sceptics, not proponents, of claims
- Excessive reliance on anecdotal and testimonial evidence to substantiate claims
- Evasion of the scrutiny afforded by peer review
- Absence of 'connectivity' [. . .], that is, a failure to build on existing scientific knowledge
- Use of impressive-sounding jargon whose primary purpose is to lend claims a façade of scientific respectability
- An absence of boundary conditions [. . .], that is, a failure to specify the settings under which claims do not hold.

⊙ Problems in defining pseudoscience

It is immediately apparent that, although there are some common themes running through these representative sets of criteria, there is also a great deal of variation. The same could be said if other proposed sets of criteria had also been included in our sample (e.g. Gray, 1991; Mousseau, 2003). Clearly, this reflects the fact that science itself has proven to be impossible to define in terms of universally accepted criteria. It is also plausible to suggest that, at least in some cases, the choice of criteria put forward may have been influenced by the cultural background at the time (e.g. many of the Radners' [1982] criteria now look a little dated but they were proposed at a time when the ideas of Charles Berlitz and Erich von Daniken were extremely popular). The potential target for the 'pseudoscience' label is likely to have influenced the choice of criteria put forward.

In the limited space available in this chapter, we will not attempt to assess each of the criteria listed above but will briefly consider the problems associated with the criterion that is arguably most commonly put forward as a defining characteristic of pseudoscience: falsifiability. Although Popper's arguments were powerful and influential, they were subsequently strongly criticised and the limitations of falsifiability as a defining characteristic of science are now widely accepted. For example, it is obvious that in practice scientists do not behave in line with the Popperian recommendation that they should put all their time and effort into attempting to falsify their own hypotheses and then only tentatively accept those hypotheses if all such attempts at falsification fail. Instead, scientists naturally think in terms of confirming their preferred hypotheses and are delighted when the results of an experiment are consistent with their hypotheses. At best then, Popper's notion of falsifiability is prescriptive, in that it relates to an idealised version of how science should be practiced, and not descriptive. It is not unreasonable to suggest, however, that the falsifiability principle operates at the level of science as a collective enterprise even if it does not usually operate at the level of individual scientists.

Furthermore, it does not make sense in practice for scientific hypotheses to be abandoned following the first report of an apparent falsification. There are often plausible reasons why a particular experiment might not have actually been a fair test of a hypothesis, and it is not unreasonable for supporters of the hypothesis to point these out. In any but the simplest experiment, the experimental set-up will involve a large number of implicit supporting hypotheses in addition to the main explicit hypothesis being tested. It may be that the latter can be saved from falsification by proposing that one of the supporting hypotheses was actually invalid, for example, that the technique used to measure the dependent variable was inappropriate.

Alternatively, it may be that the theory from which the hypothesis was derived is correct but that an apparent falsification reflects factors of which the experimenters were unaware. For example, Newtonian physics was not abandoned in light of the observation that Uranus did not appear to follow the orbit that Newtonian physics predicted it should. Instead, it was hypothesised that a then-unknown planet must be causing the perturbations in Uranus's orbit and, based upon Newtonian theory, the position of this unknown planet was calculated and confirmed. Thus was Neptune discovered. Few would argue that this reflected pseudoscientific thinking. Rather, this is rightly viewed as an example of science at its best. Subsequently, a similar challenge was posed by apparently inexplicable perturbations in Mercury's orbit which did not correspond to the predictions of Newton's theory. This time, however, a paradigm shift from Newtonian to Einsteinian physics was required to account for the anomalous data. But even here, it would not be reasonable to accuse those who initially attempted to find explanations within a Newtonian framework of practising pseudoscience.

Does this imply that falsification is useless as a warning sign that we might be dealing with a pseudoscience? Probably not. There are at least two situations where the falsifiability criterion is useful. First, if a hypothesis is *in principle* non-falsifiable, then it seems reasonable to assert that it is not a scientific statement. Thus, many creationists believe that the earth is only around 10,000 years old whereas scientific evidence (e.g. the fossil record) suggests that it is much older than that. How do the creationists resolve this dilemma? They argue that when God created the earth, he created it with signs of a prior history already in place (e.g. he created rocks with fossils already in them). This means that any evidence that the earth is actually older than 10,000 years can simply be dismissed, making the original claim unfalsifiable. Secondly, if claimants resort to *ad hoc* excuses to explain away negative evidence relating to their favoured hypotheses to an excessive degree, especially if there appears to be very little compelling evidence that directly supports the hypotheses in question in the first place, we might also reasonably argue that we may be dealing with a pseudoscience. Inevitably, however, there will be a large degree of subjectivity underlying such judgments.

Apart from these problems of definition, there are other problems with the concept of pseudoscience that lie beyond the scope of this chapter. Richard J. McNally (2003) began a critical article on the usefulness of the concept of pseudoscience within clinical psychology with the memorable assertion: "Pseudoscience is like pornography: we cannot define it, but we know it when we see it." He then goes on to question whether, in fact, even this assertion is true, concluding as follows: "When therapeutic entrepreneurs make claims on behalf of their interventions, we should not waste our time trying to determine whether their interventions qualify as pseudoscientific. Rather, we should ask them: How do you know that your intervention works? What is your evidence?" Similarly, the late Marcello

Truzzi (1996, p. 574) argued that "there are good reasons to purge the term *pseudoscience* from our disputes. It may simply prove more useful and less incendiary to speak of *bad, poor,* or even *stupid* theories without entanglement in the demarcation problem".

While acknowledging the problems associated with any attempt to identify a universally acceptable set of criteria to distinguish science from pseudoscience, Lilienfeld et al. (2003, p. 5) argue that "[...] the fuzziness of such categories does not mean that distinctions between science and pseudoscience are fictional or entirely arbitrary. As psychophysicist S. S. Stevens observed, the fact that the precise boundary between day and night is indistinct does not imply that day and night cannot be meaningfully differentiated (see Leahey & Leahey, 1983). From this perspective, pseudosciences can be conceptualised as possessing a fallible, but nevertheless useful, list of indicators or 'warning signs.' The more such warning signs a discipline exhibits, the more it begins to cross the murky dividing line separating science from pseudoscience."

The scientific status of parapsychology

Having discussed the nature of science and pseudoscience, we are now in a position to consider the discipline of parapsychology with respect to the degree to which it meets some of the most commonly proposed criteria of pseudoscience. Space limitations preclude consideration of the discipline with respect to all of the criteria that have been proposed, but we can see how parapsychology measures up in terms of a representative sample of the most commonly cited criteria.

The type of parapsychology under consideration here is that exemplified by contributions to the *Journal of Parapsychology*, widely recognised as the highest quality journal within the field, and the research carried out by members of the Parapsychological Association which became an affiliated organisation of the American Association for the Advancement of Science (AAAS), amid much controversy, in 1969. The primary subject matter of parapsychology is limited to claims relating to extrasensory perception (ESP), psychokinesis (PK), and life after death. While such topics will inevitably be the subject of a huge amount of discussion in popular media such as books, newspapers, magazines, television and radio programmes, and on the internet, it would clearly be unacceptable to base an assessment of the scientific status of parapsychology upon these sources.

In the true scientific spirit, we will sometimes draw upon the empirical approach taken by Marie-Catherine Mousseau (2003) in addressing this issue. She compared the contents of a sample of mainstream scientific journals (e.g. *British Journal of Psychology, Molecular and Optical Physics*) with a sample of 'fringe' journals (e.g. *Journal of Parapsychology, Journal of Scientific Exploration*) with respect to several common criteria of pseudoscience. How then does parapsychology measure up as a pseudoscience?

(i) *Issues relating to falsifiability:* James Alcock (1981) presents an interesting list of postulated effects that he feels undermine the testability of paranormal claims, at least from the sceptic's perspective. First among these are *experimenter effects*. In conventional science, if two experimenters carrying out the same procedures consistently obtain different patterns of results, this is a cause for concern. It suggests that one or both are influencing the outcome, possibly by means of an unintentional bias of some kind. In parapsychology, however, the fact that only certain experimenters seem to consistently obtain results supporting the existence of paranormal phenomena is often seen as perfectly acceptable. Many parapsychologists argue that this is an indication of the lawful behaviour of paranormal forces insofar as they believe that the experimenters themselves may exert a paranormal influence upon the outcome of their studies. Thus, some experimenters are seen as being facilitators and some, especially sceptics, as inhibitors in this respect. The second example is the so-called *sheep-goat effect*. Parapsychologists generally accept that believers in the paranormal (often referred to in the parapsychological literature as 'sheep') are more likely to score at a level significantly above chance expectation on an ESP task compared to disbelievers (referred to as 'goats'), who may even score significantly below chance. However, in both cases, although such factors might reduce the possibility of sceptics directly observing paranormal phenomena for themselves, they are in fact both empirically testable (and therefore falsifiable), for example, by collaboration between pro-paranormal and sceptical researchers (e.g. Schlitz, Wiseman, Watt & Radin, 2006).

(ii) *Emphasis on confirmation rather than refutation:* Mousseau (2003, p. 274) reported that in her sample "almost half of the fringe articles report a negative outcome (disconfirmation).
By contrast, no report of a negative result has been found in my sample of mainstream journals". By this criterion then, parapsychology appears to be *more* scientific than the more mainstream disciplines.

(iii) *Formal background modest, little mathematics or logic:* Mousseau (2003, p. 274) reported: "All of the articles that aim to gather new empirical evidence, whether in fringe journals or in mainstream journals, use statistical analysis."

(iv) *Failure to propose new hypotheses and theories:* Mousseau (2003, p. 274) found that a healthy 17% of fringe articles deal with theory and propose new hypotheses.

(v) *Over-reliance on testimonials and anecdotal evidence:* There probably is more reliance on anecdotal evidence within parapsychology than within most other sciences. Testimonials are particularly common in relation to claims of psychic healing, for example, and anecdotal evidence is common with respect to reports of alleged haunting. But, as Mousseau (2003, p. 273) reports, "43% of articles in the fringe journals deal with empirical matters and almost one-fourth report laboratory experiments".

(vi) *Absence of self-correction:* Once again, Mousseau's (2003, p. 275) analysis would suggest that parapsychology actually fares somewhat better than mainstream sciences: "29% of the fringe-journal articles [. . .] discuss progress of research, problems encountered, epistemological issues. This kind of article is completely absent from the mainstream sample."

(vii) *Lack of overlap with other fields of research:* According to Mousseau (2003), in fringe-journals, 36% of citations were of articles in mainstream science journals (e.g. psychology, physics, neuroscience). In her sample of mainstream science journals, however, 90% of citations were of articles in the same field (99% in the case of physics). Once again, parapsychology appears to be more scientific than mainstream science by this measure.

(viii) *Use of impressive sounding jargon:* There is little doubt that many proponents of the paranormal, especially those promoting New Age therapies such as psychic healing, often use scientific-sounding terminology such as 'vibrations', 'energy', 'fields', 'harmonisation', and so on, in ways that bear little resemblance to the precisely defined meanings that such terms have when used by scientists. However, such imprecise usage is, by and large, not a feature of articles published in peer-reviewed journals within the field.

In general, parapsychology appears to meet the implicit criteria of science, to a greater or lesser extent, rather better than it meets the criteria of pseudoscience. There are a couple of the proposed criteria of pseudoscience that, arguably, parapsychology fully meets (e.g. it has no specific background of relatively confirmed theories; it has a worldview admitting elusive immaterial entities, such as disembodied minds) and some that quite clearly could not be directed at parapsychology at its best (e.g. evasion of the scrutiny afforded by peer review). With respect to the remainder of the criteria that are applicable, parapsychology fares reasonably well in terms of its scientific status, falling a little short on some of the benchmarks of good science but actually performing better than mainstream science on others.

Fraud in science

Fraud is a problem in all areas of science, as made clear in Broad and Wade's excellent (1982) book, *Betrayers of the Truth*. In the natural sciences, one need only worry about experimenter fraud, but in psychology and parapsychology, participants may also be tempted to cheat. Experimenter fraud may take numerous forms and have numerous causes. Furthermore, while we can all agree that some instances of data manipulation are clear cases of cheating, there are other situations where the issue is not so clear-cut. Suppose, for example, that an investigator fails to find a significant predicted effect when data are initially analysed but finds that the predicted effect does indeed reveal itself if a different statistical test is used to that originally planned. Or suppose that the elimination of one clear outlier from the data produces an effect, but that the investigator had not specified in advance that outliers meeting certain criteria would be eliminated. There are many other situations where the most honest of investigators might be tempted to give themselves the benefit of the doubt.

Fraud occurs in all areas of science. Even Mendel, in his seminal work on genetics, produced results which were simply too good to be true. Sir Isaac Newton fudged his results to make the data fit his theory better. Why should scientists feel this temptation? In some cases, such as those just mentioned, the scientists were so sure that their theories were correct that they wanted their results to reflect this as clearly as possible. As it happened, their theories were essentially correct and their data manipulation, rightly or wrongly, has largely been forgotten. In modern times, investigators often cheat simply to get publishable results. The top journals are not very interested in negative findings, and fame and respect depend to a large extent on producing positive results. On a more mundane level, pay and promotion may well depend upon the number of papers published, or even keeping your job. Within psychology, the most controversial case is that of Sir Cyril Burt, who is alleged to have invented participants, results, and even research assistants.

Fraud in parapsychology

There is no compelling reason to believe that fraud is any more common within parapsychology than within any other area of science, but it is certainly not difficult to find many examples of dishonesty on the part of both experimenters and subjects when one reviews the history of the field. Although people have believed in paranormal phenomena since ancient times, we can date the origins of modern interest in such phenomena very precisely. In March, 1848, in a house in Hydesville, New York, two young sisters by the name of Kate and Margaret Fox reported hearing strange rapping noises and eventually claimed that they could communicate with 'the other side' using a simple code. This marked the birth of the Spiritualist movement. Soon others also claimed to be able to communicate with the dead and séances spread like wildfire across America and Europe. The effects produced during séances became more elaborate, including movement of tables and objects, the playing of musical instruments by unseen hands and lips, strange lights in the dark, levitation of objects, the table or even the medium, the disappearance or materialisation of objects, the materialisation of hands, faces, or even complete spirit forms (ostensibly composed of 'ectoplasm'), disembodied voices, spirit paintings and photographs, and written communications from the spirit world. Unfortunately, it was a very rare medium indeed who was not caught red-handed in the act of using trickery to achieve their allegedly psychic effects (Hyman, 1985a). Indeed, in 1888, the Fox sisters confessed that the rapping sounds that had been heard 40 years previously in their little house in Hydesville were based upon nothing more than a practical joke that the girls had carried out in order to frighten their mother!

The most notorious case of fraud relating to experimental parapsychology is the data manipulation of S. G. Soal, a British mathematician, who claimed to have produced incontrovertible evidence of telepathy under well-controlled conditions (e.g. Soal & Goldney, 1943). Soal was trying to replicate effects that had been reported in the USA by J. B. Rhine, considered by many to be the founding father of experimental parapsychology. Rhine had reported highly statistically significant results in his own studies of ESP but his methodology had been severely criticised. Soal's meticulous methodology appeared to have eliminated the loopholes identified in Rhine's studies. Although rumours were circulating about possible cheating in Soal's studies almost from the outset, it took around 40 years to establish beyond reasonable doubt that he had indeed altered his results to produce the apparently impressive results reported.

Many other examples could also be cited. In the 1970s, Walter Levy, then director of Rhine's laboratory, was caught faking data in a study of precognition in rats (Rogo, 1985). Rhine immediately dismissed him. This came just months after Rhine had published a paper dealing with 12 cases of definite or probable fraud in his laboratories during the 1940s and 1950s (Rhine, 1974).

Subjects may be motivated to cheat for a variety of reasons. In the case of self-proclaimed psychics, receiving endorsement from scientists would do a great deal to further their reputations. In the case of ordinary people, the desire to win or to be mischievous or to 'show these stupid scientists that they are not so clever' or to be the centre of attention may all play a role. Also, it appears that pranks can sometimes get out of hand, as we saw in the case of the Fox sisters.

J. Fraser Nicol (1985) describes several other cases of children engaging in fraudulent activity in their attempts to pass themselves off as genuinely psychic. Some parapsychologists used to refer to the 'shyness effect', whereby it was found that many children who claimed to be able to psychokinetically bend metal like Uri Geller were curiously unable to demonstrate their powers when being directly observed. Some paraphysicists were so trusting that they would let the children take the metal home to bend and have them return it to the laboratory later. In one investigation, however, a group of 'Geller kids' was left unsupervised to achieve their psychic feats, but were filmed by a hidden camera. This revealed the use of distinctly physical forces to bend the metal.

Many parapsychologists object to the critics' claim that their studies are not properly controlled and that they are not sufficiently knowledgeable to detect fraudulent subjects. In 1980, James Randi set out to test the fairness of this claim directly, in an investigation which he called Project Alpha (Randi, 1983a, 1983b). Two collaborators, young conjurors named Steve Shaw and Michael Edwards, were instructed to present themselves to the McDonnell Laboratory for Psychical Research which had just been established at Washington University. The pair claimed to possess psychic powers and they were tested over a period of more than two years by laboratory staff. They appeared to be able to perform all of the standard paranormal feats: psychokinesis, telepathy, clairvoyance, and so on. However, they achieved all of their effects using simple tricks and they were never caught cheating. The McDonnell researchers described them as 'gifted psychic subjects'.

Here are a couple of examples of the ways in which they cheated. In one study of Edwards, he was left alone with a 'sealed' envelope containing target pictures. He simply removed the staples which constituted the seal, looked at the pictures, put them back, and put the staples back in without leaving any traces of his tampering – except that he had lost a staple! He got around this problem by asking the experimenter if he could open the envelope himself. He was allowed to do so!

The two were also investigated by parapsychologists independent of the McDonnell laboratory. One psychiatrist was very impressed by a mysterious 'swirl' that had appeared inexplicably on an eight-millimetre film which Shaw had shot. As Colman (1987) describes, the psychiatrist discovered many things hidden in this enigmatic swirl: "moving faces, a portrait of Jesus, a UFO, a woman's torso, a nipple, a breast, a thigh, and a baby being born" (p. 196). He must have been at least a bit embarrassed when it was revealed that the swirl had been produced by the non-psychic means of Shaw spitting on the camera lens. In fact, all of the investigators involved must have been a little put out when, after demonstrating their amazing abilities, the two were asked at a press conference how they achieved their incredible feats. "It's easy," they replied. "We cheat."

Parapsychologist Michael Thalbourne (1995) reviewed Project Alpha and was very critical of the way Randi had reported the affair. He claimed that Randi was more interested in showmanship than science and that he failed to take account of the distinction between exploratory research and formal research, a distinction which is particularly important in an area like parapsychology where subject-experimenter rapport may be all-important. It might be objected that parapsychologists themselves often blur this distinction, but there can be little doubt that Randi somewhat exaggerated the credulity of the McDonnell Laboratory investigators. Thalbourne accepted that one positive consequence of the affair was greater collaboration between parapsychologists and magicians in attempting to detect fraud. Somewhat ironically, however, there is probably not a parapsychologist in the world who would ask Randi to take on this role!

Summary

This chapter has discussed the nature of science and pseudoscience and, in particular, the problems associated with attempts to produce universally accepted definitions of either. Falsifiability is generally accepted as being a necessary feature of a scientific hypothesis or theory and non-falsifiability is a clear indication that a hypothesis or theory is pseudoscientific. However, problems arise if falsifiability is used as the sole criterion for distinguishing between science and pseudoscience.

Commentators have produced a variety of sets of criteria to identify pseudosciences which, although they share common themes, also show considerable variation. There are also disagreements between commentators with respect to the extent that these criteria should be thought of as absolute as opposed to merely indicative. When parapsychology is assessed in terms of a representative sample of these criteria, it appears to be better described as a science than a pseudoscience.

The problem of fraud in science generally and in parapsychology in particular was also discussed. Although there is no reason to believe that fraud is any more common in parapsychology than in other sciences, it is certainly of greater significance. There are two main reasons for this. First, acceptance of results supporting the existence of paranormal forces would require the rejection or at least major revision of many other generally accepted scientific theories across a range of disciplines. Secondly, the best argument against fraud in science is replication of the effects reported by independent researchers. Unfortunately, poor levels of replication has been a consistent feature of parapsychology since it began.

Further reading

Kurtz, P. (Ed.) (1985) *A skeptic's handbook of parapsychology*. Buffalo, NY: Prometheus.

Chapter 6

Methodological issues related to the study of psi

Parapsychologists take seriously the claim that extrasensory perception (ESP) and psychokinesis (PK) occur. This possibility is often overlooked by psychologists who assume that claims of anomalous experiences are by nature fallacious. Indeed, psychologists give less credence to the possibility of veridical ESP than other scientists (e.g. physicists) (Wagner & Monnet, 1979). There are good reasons for such caution: psychologists are aware of the susceptibility of the human mind to error, bias, and confabulation, as well as the foibles of statistical analyses and experimentation with human subjects (French, 2003). Nevertheless, the findings of parapsychology have important implications for our conceptualisation of everyday existence and consciousness. For example, might our minds be more interconnected than psychologists currently realise? Might consciousness directly interact with our physical surroundings? It has been argued that parapsychologists test extraordinary claims that consequently require extraordinary evidence to back them up (Truzzi, 1976). In pursuit of evidence, parapsychologists have developed controlled experimental designs to test for ostensible psi ability. These experimental protocols attempt to rule out normal explanations for apparent psi phenomena, such as sensory stimuli, logical inference, coincidence, or subliminal cues. The contentious nature of purported psi phenomena has instigated much debate and critical evaluation of the research methodologies and analyses employed. Such scrutiny has fuelled methodological refinements and developments in order to eliminate flaws that could lead to the making of a type one error (accepting as statistically significant something that was actually a chance occurrence). This attention to detail renders parapsychology a good area to consider potential problems in research more generally.

Methodological and analytical progression in parapsychology has a long history, from the observation of mediumistic séances in Victorian Britain to contemporary neurocognitive research (Beloff, 1993; Moulton & Kosslyn, 2008). Beginning in 1884 the French physiologist Charles Richet used randomisation and blind protocols as well as probability to evaluate ESP performance against chance expectation – all three of which are crucial elements of experimental research today (Hacking, 1988; Kaptchuk, 1998). These only subsequently filtered into mainstream psychology (Alvarado, 2005; Watt, 2005a). More recent advancements include the use of **meta-analysis**, a statistical tool that allows the outcomes of many studies to be combined in order to see whether or not there is a cumulative effect and, if so, what factors affect this, and assessment of the 'file-drawer' problem, the likelihood of there being enough unpublished and statistically non-significant studies languishing in the offices of researchers to negate any apparent cumulative effect (Bem & Honorton, 1994; Watt, 2005a). Indeed, there is a current debate, following the publication of a series of parapsychology experiments by Bem (2011), over how experimental psychologists should analyse their data; a Bayesian approach is advocated, which takes into account *a priori* beliefs about a phenomenon (Wagenmakers, Wetzels, Borsboom & van der Maas, 2011).

In this chapter we will consider some of the methodological protocols that parapsychologists have developed in order to test the 'psi hypothesis' that the anomalous transfer of information occurs. We will examine some of the criticisms of this work and some of the debates that have ensued between so called '*skeptics*' (or counter-advocates) and advocates of the psi hypothesis. For example, how might the data collected thus far be interpreted? Is there any evidence for psi? Are experiments riddled with errors, such as poor experimental controls or inadequate statistical analyses, and if so, might ESP be a better acronym for Error Some Place?

We will focus on current experimental protocols that are used for the testing of ESP and PK. For a more detailed history of research and trends in parapsychology the reader is referred to comprehensive texts such as Beloff's (1993) *Parapsychology: A Concise History* and Irwin and Watt's (2007) *An Introduction to Parapsychology*. We will pay particular attention to the experimental procedure referred to as the 'ganzfeld', because much debate and analysis has focused on this method, the most recent instalment of which was a new meta-analysis in 2010 (Storm, Tressoldi & Di Risio, 2010). We will also focus on design issues that are pertinent to ESP research – for guidance on general issues of experimental design the reader is referred to the many good texts on this topic.

Thinking scientifically

Richet (1884) tested for the occurrence of telepathy by having one person (an 'agent' or 'sender') attempt to telepathically transmit the information on an ordinary playing card to another person (a 'percipient' or 'receiver'). This was done repeatedly, resulting in a series of card guesses. In order to preclude guessing artefacts, each card was drawn randomly from a pack and, in order to reduce sensory cues, blinding protocols included shielding the agent and the percipient from each other and placing the cards in double envelopes (Kaptchuk, 1998). The probability of correctly identifying the playing card could be exactly determined and thus evidence for psi could be construed as obtaining more correct guesses over a series of trials than that which would be expected by chance. Variants of these three elements (blind protocols, randomisation, and inferential statistics) are regarded as essential in order to obtain valid results in contemporary research. For example, for the testing of the efficacy of drugs and medical treatments, people are randomly assigned to either a treatment or a control condition and their performance in each condition is compared. The participants should be blind as to which condition they are in and the experimenters who interact with participants should be blind (double-blind) as to the same.

Analyses in earlier ESP experiments had been qualitative in nature, such as comparing drawings to target images (Barrett, 1911). Further, rather than working with special participants, such as mediums or claimants with a vested interest in doing well on the task, which might motivate cheating, Richet worked with ordinary participants from the general population – as is typical in modern parapsychology research.

Let us begin by defining some terms. We have already defined ESP as the acquisition of "information directly, that is, seemingly without either the mediation of the recognised human senses or the processes of logical inference" (Irwin, 1999, p. 6). ESP may be divided into three types: telepathy, clairvoyance, and precognition. It is important to note that these are descriptive not mechanistic definitions, which are based on how they appear to experients only. Telepathy refers to the exchange of information without the use of the ordinary five senses, between two or more minds (Radin, 1997), "the paranormal acquisition of information concerning the thoughts, feelings, or activity of another conscious being" (Thalbourne, 1982, p. 18). Clairvoyance, which derives from the French for 'clear seeing', refers to the "paranormal acquisition of information concerning an object or contemporary physical event; in contrast to telepathy, the information is assumed to derive from an external physical source ... and not from the mind of another person" (Thalbourne, 1982, p. 11). Precognition refers to information received without the use of the ordinary five senses about future events, where this information could not be predicted or inferred by ordinary means (Radin, 1997). These three basic manifestations of ESP may overlap; in many cases there may be no way of isolating one descriptive type. Finally, psychokinesis (PK) is defined as "the direct action of mind on a physical system that cannot be accounted for by the mediation of any known physical energy" (Thalbourne, 2003, p. 98). It tends to be divided into two types: macro-PK, where the targets are observable objects such as tables (as in the 'table tipping' of séances) or pictures (that fall off a wall), and micro-PK where any effect is non-observable and is detectable by statistical outcomes in experiments (such as might occur in psychic healing in real life).

A brief history of ESP testing

Experimental tests of ESP share certain factors in common. A target is randomly selected from a set of alternatives for each trial and a participant (usually called a 'receiver') attempts to guess the identity of this target without the use of the five senses or logical inference. The receiver's response is recorded and is compared with the target. After all trials have been completed the number of correct guesses (where the receiver's response and the target match) are calculated and compared to what would be expected by chance alone.

Experimental laboratory-based research into ESP took off in the early 20th century. These early tests, to some extent, reflect the prevailing scientific and psychological zeitgeist of the time, behaviourism. Rhine (1934) is hailed as being the popularist of the experimental and statistical analysis of psi-outcomes (Mauskopf & McVaugh, 1980). He and his colleagues used forced-choice card guessing procedures in which the subject was aware of the possible target choices, and was asked to select a constrained response in a psi-guessing protocol. For example, Rhine, with the help of Dr Zener, created the iconic 'Zener cards', a pack of 25 cards, each depicting one of five symbols (circle, square, wavy lines, star, cross). A number of procedures were developed for using these cards experimentally to test for telepathy, clairvoyance or precognition, enabling the statistical significance of guessing the correct symbol above or below chance to be analysed (mean chance expectation [MCE] = 5 correct guesses in each trial of 25 guesses). For example, in the 'down through' method of clairvoyance, the shuffled, cut pack of Zener cards remained 'unopened' until after 25 'calls' were made, down through the pack, after which the accuracy of the recorded calls can be checked by an experimenter (Rhine, 1934, p. xi). This is an example of a forced choice design – where receivers' responses are limited to particular stimuli, in this case, five simple symbols. Two meta-analyses of clairvoyant and precognitive forced-choice studies from 1935 onwards have both obtained statistically significant effect sizes, indicating overall above chance scoring (Honorton & Ferrari, 1989; Steinkamp, Milton & Morris, 1998).

In the 1960s–1970s there was a drive towards developing an experimental procedure to study ESP that was more open-ended, spontaneous, and engaging for participants, attempting to increase ecological validity with a return to 'introspection' (e.g. Honorton, 1977). This reflected a general trend in psychology to rebuke the constraints of behaviourism, renewing interest in inner experience and human potential under the auspices of humanistic psychology. In 'free-response' paradigms, the percipient or 'receiver' usually makes a verbal report on the ongoing content of their consciousness (called a 'mentation') – there are no limits placed on what is reported. Simultaneously, in telepathy designs, a 'sender' will focus on a randomly selected visual image, the 'target', and attempt to transmit information about its content to the receiver, with whom non-anomalous communication is prevented. This is followed by the 'judging stage' where either the receiver or independent judges are shown a set of images (usually four), one of which is the target. Each image is given a confidence rating (a percentage) according to its similarity with the impressions that the receiver reported. This culminates in a ranking of images in terms of their perceived likelihood of being the target. To reflect reports of subjective cases of ESP, which appeared to occur more frequently in dreams, meditation and waking hallucination/hypnagogic states (e.g. Rhine, 1961), some free-response studies attempted to induce altered states of consciousness in receivers, through hypnosis, sleep, and sensory isolation. We have already discussed (in Chapter 2) one body of work in this vein – the dream ESP studies that were conducted at the Maimonides Medical Center between 1962 and 1978 (Ullman, Krippner & Vaughan, 1973).

The use of the 'ganzfeld' (whole field) in psi research was adapted from perceptual psychology in the 1970s (e.g. Honorton & Harper, 1974). "The impetus for this research involved converging evidence that anomalous communication effects were frequently associated with internal attention states characterised by reduced perceptual processing" (Honorton, 1995, p. 132). The ganzfeld paradigm attempts to reduce the threshold between imagination and reality, between waking and dreaming, and encourages free association. The ganzfeld environment consists of a 'homogenous perceptual field', reclining in a comfortable position, with halved ping-pong balls over the eyes which, being semi-translucent, enable an even pink glow from a red light to be perceived. The auditory analogue of this unpatterned visual field consists of listening to 'pink noise', randomised frequencies of audible wavelengths that sound like a gentle hissing. In an ESP trial a 'receiver' will rest in this environment, after a progressive relaxation procedure, for about half an hour. Meanwhile, a sender, in a different room, will attempt to send telepathically the content of a randomly selected image or video clip to the receiver. An experimenter, usually in a third room, listens (via an audio link) to the receiver's mentation and is blind as to the identity of the target. The experimenter will communicate with the receiver during the judging stage and will review their experience with them. With four clips, 25% of the time one would expect to get a 'hit' (correctly identifying the target clip) by chance alone. A typical ganzfeld experiment consists of about 40 trials with different sender-receiver pairs, and the overall scores are compared with chance expectation. Meta-analyses of psi-ganzfeld studies have been monitoring its ability to produce and replicate a psi effect for over twenty years. Discussions have proliferated at four key stages: the Hyman-Honorton meta-analyses (1985–86), the Bem and Honorton meta-analysis (1994), the Milton and Wiseman meta-analyses (1999), and the Storm et al. meta-analysis (2010). Not all of these analyses reach the same conclusion and thus there has been much debate over the differential treatment of data and interpretations.

Not all free-response ESP studies have attempted to induce an altered state of consciousness in receivers. Remote viewing, for example, involves a percipient attempting to obtain information from some source at a distance. The 'target' is usually a place or object in the environment, such as a building or landscape. The remote viewer may 'mentate', but may also draw sketches of this place or object. Two physicists, Russell Targ and Hal Puthoff, initiated remote viewing experiments at the Stanford Research Institute (SRI) in the 1970s. In a typical study, one experimenter would act as an agent and travel to a target location, randomly selected from 100 locations. Another experimenter would remain with the receiver who would describe their thoughts, as in the ganzfeld experiments. Remote viewers tended to be gifted subjects who took part in numerous trials. At the end of a series of trials, independent judges ranked the target and a set of decoys according to which most closely matched the information in the transcripts and sketches for each trial. A statistician, Utts (1995), assessed the evidence for anomalous cognition in remote viewing research at the SRI (1973–1988) and the Science Applications International Corporation (where the research programme moved to in 1990). She concluded that there was a statistically significant effect indicative of genuine psi.

Recent protocols have taken a cognitive or physiological approach, producing psi versions of well-known effects in psychology, such as the mere exposure effect (Bem, 2011) or the impact of emotional images on the autonomic nervous system (ANS) (Radin, 2004). These look for precognitive or time reversal effects where, for example, liking of an image precedes being exposed to it subliminally, or a peak in ANS activity occurs immediately prior to seeing a shocking image (compared with seeing a neutral image). For example, Bem (2011) reports on nine such experiments that obtained an overall significant precognitive effect. Bem's experimental protocol requires only a laptop, a computer programme that automates and displays the psi task, and a participant. It has been designed to be quick and easy to run, with the hope that it will attract replication studies. These designs measure a response (physiological or behavioural) which may have been unconsciously influenced by a target rather than eliciting conscious reports of a target.

Of course, this body of research has not gone without criticism; potential methodological problems have been aired which will be considered below (e.g. see Hyman, 2010). The results of the meta-analyses are open to interpretation of probable causation. Extreme interpretations ascribe the effect solely to unknown flaws and fraudulent/'sloppy' experimenters, or to 'proof of psi' (for recent debates refer to Krippner & Friedman, 2010). More common among parapsychologists is the position that the accumulated evidence for ESP phenomena is such that the occurrence of psi is a viable working hypothesis and that research seeking to uncover optimal conditions for this phenomenon is important. In the following section we will scrutinise the evidence more carefully, focusing on the ganzfeld research.

Methodological issues in psi research, focusing on the ganzfeld

The most frequent criticisms of psi research are that a replicable effect has not been demonstrated and that psi experiments have inadequate controls and procedural safeguards (Bem & Honorton, 1994). The ganzfeld experiment has been repeated many times since the 1970s and thus provides researchers with an ever increasing database of studies that can be submitted to meta-analysis in order to assess whether or not there appears to be a psi effect that is replicable across studies and different experimenters.

Meta-analysis involves a systematic review in order to find all independent published studies that have tested for a specific effect. The strength of the effect and its statistical probability are then calculated for all of these studies combined. Because meta-analyses include many participants or trials they have more statistical power, and are therefore more likely to find small, but 'real', effects than single studies. The systematic review also involves coding all studies according to their methodological quality. This enables flaws in protocols to be identified and the testing of whether these might explain any effect in the database. The relationship between other variables such as participant traits or variations in procedure and the effect can also be tested, in order to better understand and predict the phenomenon in question.

Meta-analytical reviews have spurred collaboration and debate between critics and parapsychologists in pursuit of a resolution to the question of whether or not there is any evidence for psi. For example, early analyses by both Hyman (1985), a critic, and Honorton (1985), a parapsychologist, led to a pivotal joint paper which scrutinised the

42 studies that then existed. Hyman (2010, p. 144) relates, when meeting Honorton for the first time in 1986, "I realized that we actually agreed about a number of issues regarding the evidential value of the original ganzfeld database." This revelation led them to join forces, drawing methodological guidelines with the hope of improving future ganzfeld research (Hyman & Honorton, 1986). In this 'Joint communiqué' they agreed that there was an overall significant effect in the ganzfeld database. However, they also both agreed that further research was necessary that adhered to a stringent protocol, in order to interpret this outcome meaningfully. These standards included strict security precautions against sensory leakage, the testing and documentation of randomisation methods for selecting targets and sequencing judging pools, statistical corrections for multiple analyses, advance specification of the status of the experiment, checking for recording errors, and full documentation of the experimental procedures and the status of statistical tests (planned or *post hoc*). We will discuss these methodological guidelines in more detail and will then consider subsequent meta-analyses of ganzfeld studies that have attempted to adhere to them. Has this helped to answer the question of whether or not psi occurs?

Sensory leakage

Sensory leakage is the transmission of information through normal means. For example, in early card-guessing experiments, a sender and receiver in the same room, even if separated by a screen, could have communicated through subtle cues such as changes in breathing rate. A rigorous ESP study must block all means of communication between the receiver and the target, the sender, and anyone who has knowledge of the target, at all stages of the experiment. Sensory leakage is perhaps the most insidious problem because it is difficult to completely rule this out of the question as it may occur in subtle or unexpected ways. For example, researchers have been warned that participants familiar with the layout of a laboratory could communicate through structural connections between the rooms of the sender and receiver that carry sound, such as pipes, ventilation shafts or the floor. Sensory leakage can be indirect and subliminal. For example, if the experimenter hears a low-level sound (e.g. of the target video or the sender vocalising about it) from the sender's room, even if the receiver is adequately shielded from the sender, this cue may unconsciously influence the experimenter in the judging stage when they communicate with the receiver, perhaps unknowingly using this information to steer them towards the target (Wiseman, Smith & Kornbrot, 1996). Ideally, senders and receivers will be kept in separate, sound attenuated, unconnected, electromagnetically shielded rooms, at some distance from each other, and no laboratory staff will be in contact with both the sender and receiver during the experiment.

Early ganzfeld studies were done manually. This presented numerous problems. For example, potential targets were printed images. If only one set of images was used in an experiment then, after a sender had looked at and touched the target (e.g. a postcard of Van Gogh's Sunflowers) and this was put with three decoy images and relayed to the receiver in the judging stage, the identity of the target might be communicated through cues such as a bent corner or mark on the target image. Improvements in sensory shielding were made following the Hyman and Honorton paper (1986) by automating much of the procedure. This essentially meant that the sender did not come into contact with anybody at all during the experiment as the target was selected, presented to them, and recorded by a computer program, and the identity of the target was withheld from both the experimenter and receiver until the end of the trial. The judging stage was likewise automated by the same program, presenting the receiver with four video clips on a computer screen and recording their ratings as to the likelihood that each was the target. This meant that an experimenter did not need to pass a target and decoy images to participants, thus improving blind protocols. Despite the advantages of the 'autoganzfeld', currently unknown sensory leakage might exist. However, despite such concerns, the criticism of sensory leakage in the current ganzfeld protocol is speculative.

Randomisation

Even if one is confident that effective sensory barriers were in place in a ganzfeld study, it is still possible that ineffective randomisation could lead to an artifactual 'ESP' outcome.

How a target is selected is important. First, the selection of a target needs to be independent of the proclivities of participants in any ganzfeld study. For example, if a sender chose a target image themselves from a wide selection of images, it might be that through familiarity with their habits, or shared taste, a receiver who knows them well could discern the target. To prevent this from occurring, each target is randomly selected from approximately 20 sets of four stimuli (the four video clips are chosen to be thematically different from one another), and then one of these four is randomly selected to be the target. Second, because ESP studies statistically compare a series of guesses to chance expectation, adequate randomisation of targets is essential. Systematic patterns in target selection need to be prevented in case these coincide with response biases of, or are detectable by, a receiver (or independent judge). This is less critical in a typical ganzfeld study as only one target is chosen per trial (there is therefore no pattern to detect at an individual level). It applies, however, when there is an independent judge who assesses all of the participants' mentations and compares these to the target and decoy video clips. When making a series of guesses, people typically respond in a non-random way; for example, by avoiding repetitions (e.g. avoiding the second image in a set of four because this was the target on the previous trial) (Brugger & Taylor, 2003). If target selection is also non-random, it is possible that the sequence of targets might coincide with that of a person's choice. Even with adequate randomisation, it is possible that such target selection patterns could occur by chance in a single study, but any such patterns should cancel out over a large number of trials because they are not systematic (Palmer, 2003).

Thinking scientifically

An example of a subtle flaw in a psi experiment comes from a critique by Marks and Kammann (1978) of the early remote viewing trials (Targ & Puthoff, 1974). While there may have been adequate precautions during the remote viewing part of the experiment, the consequent judging stage was criticised. Independent judges were given transcripts of the remote viewer's comments during the trial to match a set of potential targets. However, these transcripts included remarks about successes on previous trials which, it was argued, could have cued judges as to the identity of the target. In response, Tart, Puthoff, and Targ (1980) removed any statements from the transcripts that could act as a cue in this way and arranged for these new transcripts to be re-assessed by a different judge. They obtained, this time, an even higher psi score. However, from Marks (1981) came the rejoinder that this judge could have read the previously published study and retained knowledge of the targets.

It is also important that the order of presentation of the target and decoy video clips is randomised in the judging stage. For example, if there was a preference for all participants to give a higher rating to the first video clip that they see in the judging stage, and if inadequate randomisation meant that the target was always presented to the receiver first, then this would lead to an artificially inflated hit rate.

A range of methods have been used to produce random sequences, all of which have their unique flaws, including dice throwing and shuffling cards (which are most susceptible to bias), random number tables, electronic random number generators (which sample the output of a physical process such as thermal noise or radioactive decay) or pseudo random number generators (which are based on an algorithm) (Hyman & Honorton, 1986; Milton & Wiseman, 1997). Given that randomness is so important, care should be paid to how this is attempted, including by whom, and assessment made of whether or not it was achieved.

Statistical procedures and advance reporting

This reflects problems that are encountered generally in science. In case any statistical errors have been made in a paper, Hyman and Honorton suggested that full descriptive statistics and effect sizes are reported so that they can be recalculated if need be. However, more importantly, they remonstrated against fishing for statistically significant effects and not correcting for multiple analyses. To circumvent this they advocated the advance specification of statistical analyses that are planned for a study. This prevents researchers from experimenting with different analyses and tests until they find something that is statistically significant. It is also important to amend criterion levels for statistical significance according to the number of analyses that are conducted when testing a hypothesis. Each time one accepts a test as being statistically significant, with the usual criterion level of $p < 0.05$, there is a 5% chance that the effect was due to chance alone. Correction methods aim to keep the overall error rate at 5% irrespective of the number of tests done (Rosenthal & Rubin, 1989). This reduces the likelihood of making a type one error, in this case, of reporting a significant ESP outcome that might only have occurred when trying lots of different tests, thereby having a higher risk of being due to chance than might be acknowledged.

It is also important to report in advance how many trials will be included in a study. This prevents a problem known as 'optional stopping'. If an experimenter is aware of outcomes on a trial-by-trial basis, they might stop the study after a run of 'hits', anticipating further 'misses'. This could result in an artificially high hit rate.

The ganzfeld meta-analyses

The above potential sources of artefact concern single studies. However, science is cumulative in nature. Let us then consider how meta-analyses of the ganzfeld database since Hyman and Honorton's guidelines have fared. Is there a replicable psi effect? If there is a psi effect, is this attributable to study flaws? What problems arise when evaluating these issues?

Charles Honorton initiated the autoganzfeld protocol, and ten ganzfeld studies were conducted between 1983 and 1989 that complied with Hyman and Honorton's guidelines. These are often referred to in the literature as the PRL studies as they took place at the Psychophysical Research Laboratories in Princeton, New Jersey. Bem and Honorton (1994) subjected these to a meta-analytical review. There were 106 'hits' in 329 ganzfeld sessions, giving a hit rate of 32% (when 25% would be expected by chance). This was statistically significant, with a mean effect size of 0.16 (this effect size ranges from zero to one, like a correlation coefficient, with zero indicating no effect and 0.2 a small, 0.5 a moderate, and 0.8 a large effect) (Cohen, 1992; Storm & Ertel, 2001). Stouffer Z was 2.55, $p = 0.005$ (Stouffer Z tells us how many standard deviations the combined results are from that which would be expected by chance). While this outcome gives some support to statistical replication, any apparent psi effect needed to be replicated by other experimenters at other laboratories. This makes it less likely that some procedural error, self-delusion, bias or fraud is responsible for an effect.

Four later meta-analyses included studies by diverse experimenters, all conducted since those at the PRL (Bem, Palmer & Broughton, 2001; Milton, 1999; Milton & Wiseman, 1999; Storm et al., 2010).[1] However, these analyses did not concur, leading to disputes about meta-analytical procedures. The aim of meta-analysis is to present an impartial and factual overview of the efficacy of a treatment. However, decisions such as which studies to include, which outcome measure to use, and how to code flaws, introduce subjectivity into the process. For example, a major concern of meta-analysis is the heterogeneity of the database (whether the included studies are different from one another) which has implications for whether or not studies are 'combinable'. Heterogeneity can be defined in different ways, in terms of study protocols (whether there are any marked deviations) or the magnitude of the effect sizes of individual studies.

Milton and Wiseman (1999) identified 30 post-PRL studies conducted between 1987 and 1997 by ten different first authors from seven laboratories. They reported a mean effect size of 0.013 and a hit rate of 27.6%, which was not significant (Stouffer $Z = 0.70$, $p = 0.24$). Thus, it appeared that the apparent ESP effect was not replicable. Milton (1999) updated this analysis, finding another nine ganzfeld studies. Again, the cumulative effect was non-significant (Stouffer $Z = 1.45$, $p = 0.074$). However, she decided not to include one study by Dalton (1997) which obtained a very high hit rate (47%) and effect size (0.46), considering it to be an outlier. If included, this study, Milton reported, rendered the cumulative outcome statistically significant (Stouffer $Z = 2.28$, $p = 0.011$). In a further update, Bem et al. (2001) combined all of the then 40 studies in the post-PRL database, obtaining a mean effect size of 0.051 and a hit rate of 30.1%, which was statistically significant (Stouffer $Z = 2.59$, $p = 0.0048$). Finally, Storm et al. (2010) examined the cumulative effect of 29 studies (by 16 different first authors at ten laboratories) that had been conducted since Milton and Wiseman's review (1997–2008), again, reporting a significant psi effect, with a 32.2% hit rate and a mean effect size of 0.142 (Stouffer $Z = 5.48$, $p = 2.13 \times 10^{-8}$), thus they claimed the psi effect to be replicable.

What then are we to make of this contradictory set of outcomes? Milton and Wiseman explained the discrepancy between their meta-analyses and that of Bem and Honorton (1994) by suggesting that either the post-PRL studies were more methodologically rigorous or did not adhere to the same 'psi-conducive' protocol, thereby failing to replicate the PRL studies. In support of the latter explanation, Bem et al. (2001) found that ganzfeld studies that deviated from the original PRL protocol were less successful. Standard replications had an overall hit-rate of 31% (Stouffer $Z = 3.49$, $p = 0.0002$) and non-standard replications an overall hit-rate of 24% (Stouffer $Z = -1.30$, ns). There was a statistically significant difference in ESP scores between the two samples, suggesting that they might be different types of studies. Milton and Wiseman's database, then, might simply have included more of the non-standard studies. One example is a study by Willin (1996) that used musical rather than visual targets.

Might study flaws account for the ostensible psi effect in the ganzfeld meta-analyses? Hyman (1985b) and Honorton (1985) coded flaws in the pre-PRL database and agreed that neither selective reporting, sensory leakage nor statistical errors could account for the effect obtained. However, they did not concur over the coding of flaws for randomisation, which Hyman argued was correlated with the ostensible psi effect. Unfortunately, these flaw ratings were not made blind to study outcome, potentially introducing subjective bias into the process (Morris, 1991). Hyman (1994) also queried the adequacy of randomisation in the PRL database, but Bem (1994) rebutted this, performing statistical tests to check for randomisation artefacts. Milton and Wiseman (1999) speculated whether sensory leakage between the sender and experimenter could account for the PRL outcome, but this could not be tested as the laboratory no longer existed. In the most recent meta-analysis, Storm et al. (2010) reported that blind-rated study flaws (appropriate randomisation, blind protocols, adequate sensory shielding) were not correlated with the ESP effect they obtained, suggesting that experimental flaws were not responsible. Nevertheless, Milton (1999) points out that flaw ratings are poor measures of actual experimental error, in part, because the method sections of research papers do not include details of all that occurred throughout an experiment. As such, there is no definitive evidence that study flaws are responsible for the ganzfeld ESP effect, but this nevertheless remains a possibility that preys on the minds of researchers.

All of the ganzfeld databases are heterogeneous (Palmer, 2003). This has a number of implications. First, different treatments of this might account for the different meta-analytic outcomes. For example, both Milton (1999) and Storm et al. (2010) removed the Dalton (1997) study, due to its high hit rate, while Bem et al. (2001) did not. It has been suggested that the decision of which studies to remove can be subjective and inconsistent, with an unclear rationale; for example, Milton and Wiseman (1999) included Willin's (1996) study with its musical targets, but removed a study that used drumming noise in the ganzfeld (Schmeidler & Edge, 1999). Thus, some have suggested that no studies be removed and rather analysis be made of what factors contribute to any effect (Palmer, 2003). The technique of correlating variables with effect sizes across studies helps to identify whether an effect varies systematically with conceptually relevant variations in procedure. For example, might the fact that Dalton's (1997) participants were artists, as were those in another study with a high hit rate (50%) in the PRL database, suggest that the artistic creativity of participants is an important variable?

Second, unexplained heterogeneity (variation in outcome) suggests that unaccounted-for factors affect performance in the ganzfeld and thus, that the effect is not predictable, that researchers are not able to reliably reproduce it based on a 'recipe'. To rectify this it has been argued that 'process-' rather than 'proof-' oriented research should be conducted in order to build models of how psi might operate. The four meta-analyses considered in this chapter point to a number of psi-conducive factors. Bem and Honorton (1994) noted that the PRL sample scored very high on belief in the paranormal, having had prior psi experiences and having practiced meditation. They found a significant correlation between extraversion and the psi effect ($r = 0.18$, $p = 0.004$, one-tailed). Further, dynamic targets outperformed static targets. Milton and Wiseman found that novice participants did better if they had practiced meditation or some other mental discipline (Stouffer $Z = 2.24$, $p = 0.013$), but did not replicate the effects for dynamic targets or previous psi experience. Bem et al.'s (2001) research suggested that standard ganzfeld protocols are best. Storm et al. (2010) found that selected participants did better than non-selected participants ($t(27) = 3.44$, $p = 0.002$, two-tailed). Selected participants were those with prior experience of ESP studies, high belief in the paranormal, meditation practice or previous psi experiences. Nevertheless, such factors alone cannot account for the heterogeneity in the ganzfeld database. The 'ganzfeld psi effect' occurs in a rich matrix of variables, few of these being fully explored or understood.

Third, one might argue that the outcome is fragile and dependent on a handful of studies. The above meta-analyses might differ simply because they have included different studies, perhaps by particular experimenters. Storm et al. (2010) attempted to resolve this by analysing all ganzfeld studies that have ever been published in one meta-analysis. They created a homogenous database of 102 studies with similar effect sizes, removing six studies with extreme scores. This yielded a mean effect size of 0.135 (Stouffer $Z = 8.18$, $p < 10^{-16}$). However, their analysis has been criticised for including those pre-PRL studies that did not adhere to Hyman and Honorton's (1986) guidelines, and the removal of studies has been described by Hyman (2010, p. 486) in the following way: "they manufacture apparent homogeneity and consistency by eliminating many outliers and combining databases whose combined effect sizes are not significantly different". Thus, the process is seen as 'manufactured', motivated towards a specific outcome, and is not trusted.

This leads us to question whether meta-analysis, an inexact procedure with various subjective decisions to be made, is suited to proof-oriented questions such as 'is ESP real?'. For example, decisions must be made about what constitutes a study. In a process-oriented experiment that compares different ganzfeld conditions, such as those with and without a sender (Morris, Dalton, Delanoy & Watt, 1995) should all conditions be included or only those with a sender, following the 'standard protocol'? Or, which indicator of psi-success should be used, when more than one is available? Milton and Wiseman (1999) used z-scores and Bem and Honorton (1994) used direct hits. Indeed, it has been argued that the purpose of meta-analysis is not proof, but merely better understanding of a putative effect (Schmeidler & Edge, 1999). Hyman (2010) argues that replication in single, statistically powerful experiments is required – however, this would require an extremely large sample size for such a small effect (Utts, 1991). Direct replications are quite rare in psychology, most effect sizes being small to medium (Bem & Honorton, 1994; French, 2010).

Selective reporting

There is one final methodological issue that requires consideration. A meta-analysis is only as good as the studies that are included in it, but what if the collection of studies is biased? What if, for example, all published ganzfeld studies have been tracked down and included, but many unpublished ones exist that found no psi effect? In this case the sample of studies would be biased towards finding a statistically significant effect. This is known as the 'file-drawer problem' and is a widespread one. A related issue is what Hyman (1985) called the problem of 'retrospective studies'. In this case, a small exploratory study might be called a 'study' if it obtains significant results and a 'pilot study' if it does not. Being cognisant of the serious problem that selective reporting presents, the Parapsychological Association (1975) has a policy against the non-reporting of negative or non-significant results. But how effective is this policy? A statistical calculation can be performed to estimate how many non-published, non-significant studies are required to cancel out any statistically significant effect (Rosenthal, 1979). Honorton (1985) reported that 423 unpublished studies would be required, in comparison with the 42 studies in the pre-PRL database. Storm et al. (2010) reported that 293 null, unpublished studies would be required to negate the combined effect of the 29 studies in their meta-analysis. Is it likely that this many unpublished (non-significant) ganzfeld studies exist – ten times as many as all published reports? It is impossible to know for sure. Blackmore (1980) investigated the likelihood of this and found 19 unpublished ganzfeld studies, seven of which (37%) had significant effects. Selective reporting therefore seems to be a doubtful candidate for explaining the apparent ESP ganzfeld effect, especially given how time-consuming this type of research is (Palmer, 2003).

In summary, on balance the ganzfeld meta-analyses seem to support a psi effect and by extension the hypothesis that reported paranormal experiences may sometimes be veridical, rather than based on cognitive deficits. However, such an anomaly does not have to be paranormal. Indeed, it does not proffer any explanation, rather something that needs to be explained. Academics differ according to how they interpret the ganzfeld meta-analyses, as evidence for ESP according to standard statistical procedures (Utts, 1991), or as being weak, unreliable, and potentially due to artefact, not being 'extraordinary' or sufficiently convincing (Hyman, 2010). In the latter case, error and even fraud are given as more likely explanations. Nevertheless, at least, this debate illustrates instances of good practice when conducting research in psychology and highlights the subjective nature of the scientific process.

⊙ A brief history of research on psychokinesis and psychic healing

Experimental studies of PK have focused on micro-PK, effects which are only discernable through the application of statistics. In part this is because it is difficult to find willing mediums who claim to be able to produce large scale macro-PK effects, such as the levitation of objects, and who are willing to do so under controlled laboratory conditions. In part it is because of the spontaneous and contextual nature of reported experiences, such as the stopping of a clock when a relative dies or the crashing of one's computer during a stressful episode (Radin, 1997). In micro-PK experiments, participants attempt to influence the outcome of a random process to make it non-random, over a large number of trials. Thus, the source of randomness is crucial.

Taking inspiration from a gambler, in 1934 Rhine began the experimental study of micro-PK by asking participants to affect the roll of dice through mental intention (Beloff, 1993). A target number was specified and participants could 'will' this number to appear face up on the dice when thrown. This was repeated across numerous trials. In order to improve the randomness of this process, Rhine invented a mechanical dice-rolling machine. He made other methodological improvements, such as introducing a control condition where participants exerted no intention and reduced recording errors by having two experimenters note outcomes. Radin and Ferrari (1991) conducted a meta-analysis of 148 dice-throwing experiments and reported a very small but statistically significant effect, smaller than the ESP effect discussed above (but, importantly, no effect in the control conditions). This potential PK effect, they claimed, could be attributed neither to particular investigators or studies, nor to the file-drawer problem, nor to study flaws, issues that we discussed in the previous section (Radin, 1997). However, one flaw that raised concern was that not all of these studies had controlled for potential biases in the dice. The sides of dice have unequal weights; those with high numbers are lighter (they have more holes 'scooped out' of them), and so are more likely to appear face up. Radin and Ferrari (1991) did find an artefact in the data where hit rates were highest when the target was a number six! So, they did a separate analysis of 69 studies that had controlled for this bias, by counterbalancing high and low targets, for example. The putative PK effect remained statistically significant. However, this analysis has been criticised for not assessing whether any bias remained in the reduced sample (Bösch, Steinkamp & Boller, 2006). And of course, all experimental studies of PK have been criticised for lacking ecological validity, perhaps bearing little relation to how psychokinetic experiences are reported to occur in everyday life.

In the 1970s Helmut Schmidt, a German physicist, pioneered the use of random number generators (RNGs) in PK testing (Beloff, 1993). The use of RNGs has been the main source of randomness in subsequent PK research. As described earlier, RNGs sample the output of a physical process such as radioactive decay, which is thought to be 'truly random', and produce a binary output (0, 1) that can interface with a display. Displays provide ongoing feedback to participants. Schmidt used a display of light on a screen that participants could will to move in a particular direction, or a series of audible clicks that a participant could will into the right versus the left earpiece of a headset. More recent displays have been inspired by computer games, such as a greyhound racing game where a participant wills 'their' dog to win (Roe, Davey & Stevens, 2003). The use of RNGs and computers in this way has overcome many methodological criticisms of earlier work, for example, providing a better source of randomness and automatically recording data. However, researchers still need to adhere to the methodological recommendations we discussed in the previous section, such as specifying hypotheses in advance and optional stopping.

Three meta-analyses have been conducted on the RNG micro-PK research (Bösch et al., 2006; Radin & Nelson, 1989, 2003). As in the ganzfeld studies, these have reached different conclusions. Those of Radin and Nelson (1989, 2003) support the psi hypothesis (including 515 studies by 91 different first authors), while that of Bösch et al. (2006) reach a more parsimonious interpretation (including 380 studies by 59 different first authors). All three meta-analyses report a very small but statistically significant effect. However, Bösch et al. (2006) found that this effect was vulnerable and dependent on the inclusion of particular studies. They also found a relationship between effect size and the sample sizes of studies, such that studies with fewer participants obtained larger PK effects. They suggested that this could indicate a publication bias, where in some cases large-scale follow-up studies may have not been published due to null findings (even though many such unpublished studies would be required, 1500 in fact). Overall, the putative PK effects are so weak that Bösch et al. prefer to err on the side of caution and attribute them to potential methodological errors.

Psychokinesis clearly has implications for the interaction of mind with living (rather than inanimate) systems. Biological PK has also been explored experimentally, a major proponent of which has been William Braud who developed the Direct Mental Interactions with Living Systems (DMILS) protocol. Research in this area has worked with a variety of living systems, seeking to influence, for example, the swimming direction of fish (Irwin & Watt, 2007). However, a common contemporary protocol is for one person to attempt to influence the physiology of another person at a distance. Adequate sensory shielding is essential, as in the ganzfeld experiments. Typically, one participant takes the role of an 'agent' and is asked at randomly selected intervals (by an automated system) to either activate or calm the 'receiver' (or to rest). The activity of the receiver's autonomic nervous system is continuously monitored by measuring their electrodermal activity (the amount of sweat on the tips of the fingers, which is indicative of arousal or the 'flight or fight' response). Fluctuations in electrodermal activity are then compared across the control (rest), activate, and calm conditions to see if there is a statistical difference across them. The psi hypothesis would predict that the agent increases the autonomic activity of the receiver in the 'activate' conditions and decreases it in the 'calm' conditions. A meta-analysis of DMILS studies has found evidence for a small but significant effect (Schmidt, Schneider, Utts & Walach, 2004). However, Schmidt et al. suggest that the drawing of conclusions regarding the implications of this effect be postponed until further data, by researchers outside of the parapsychological community, is collected.

Psychic healing

Psychic healing is a variant of biological PK (Irwin & Watt, 2007). As with other subjects covered in this textbook, belief in psychic healing is fairly high among members of the general population, at 58.6% (Rice, 2003). In addition, the healing practice Reiki has become increasingly popular among members of public and healthcare providers (Miles & True, 2003).

'Psychic' or 'distant healing' refers to several practices in which there is conscious willing or intention for the improved well-being of another individual, without the use of normal physical or social mechanisms (Leder, 2005, p. 924). Healing is claimed to occur as a result of an anomalous process, which cannot be explained conventionally. Healing occurs in a variety of contexts and forms across cultures and there are at least 19 variants (Krippner & Achterberg, 2000), including 'spiritual healing', prayer, faith healing, divine healing, and what is known as 'bioenergy' healing (many healing traditions have considered healing as involving energy; see Levin & Mead, 2008, for a review). Better known examples of psychic healing practices include Reiki and Johrei (Gruzelier, in press), but there are many others.

Despite these differences, consistencies are often observed in the phenomenology. These include a 'pre-healing' state of consciousness (this may be akin to a state of psychological absorption, that is, attention is completely focused on mental imagery which seems vivid and realistic). The state of consciousness arises as a result of a variety of strategies which result in either low arousal (including meditation and prayer) or high arousal (such as vigorous dancing). Some healers may be able to enter the 'healing state of consciousness' at will, without the need for such rituals. Healers often engage in practices to connect with the healee, which seems to result in some form of knowledge about the ailment the person is suffering from, and how to treat the ailment. There is also a blurring of boundaries between the healer and healee. Many healers report that 'healing energy' is transmitted to the healee, which is either derived from an external source (for example, the universe) or from the healer himself or herself.

Winkelman (1992) noted that there are several categories of healer; those who accessed spiritual entities to assist them in the healing process, those who directed the healing practices of the society they are working within (e.g. rituals), and those who employed special powers, including the casting of spells.

There are several alternative explanations for the healing effects which can occur as a result of psychic healing practices. Firstly, they may result from placebo effects – very powerful healing effects which occur when patients believe that they are receiving treatment for a given physical condition. If there is no psychic effect, placebo effects derived from belief in psychic healing may have their own health benefits (Easter & Watt, 2011; Lyvers, Barling & Harding-Clark, 2006).

As such, these effects are assumed to result from belief or expectation activating certain neural circuits (in particular the prefrontal cortex and limbic areas of the brain) set off a biological chain of events that results in a physiological outcome. Placebo effects can also occur when recipients of treatment are informed that they are receiving a placebo (Kaptchuk et al., 2010), implying that belief in a treatment does not have to be very strong. Secondly, they may result from the use of mental imagery and (self) hypnosis/relaxation which may enable physical healing to manifest. For example, Gruzelier (in press) has undertaken several studies with students imagining a shark, and later friendly dolphins, consuming 'invaders' in the immune system, and found that this had positive outcomes on physical and mental health. Healing may also take place due to imagery and beliefs that are shared with others in the social world. Such shared imagery may work as metaphors which are concrete versions of an ailment or elimination of that ailment. This may then allow for healing via placebo mechanisms.

In recent years, there have been several studies which have explored whether psychic or distant healing are genuine phenomena, that is, whether mental intention (e.g. that of a healer) can impact on the physiology of a healee, ruling out all normal physical interactions between healer and healee (Schwartz & Dossey, 2010). Overall, the findings have been mixed in terms of their outcome, with some studies finding evidence for the existence of psychic healing, while others do not (Leder,

2005). For example, one study found a distant healing effect for sufferers of chronic fatigue syndrome (Walach et al., 2008), while another recent study examined the effects of distant healing alongside expectation effects for arthritis sufferers, and found no effects of distant healing (Easter & Watt, 2011). However, a later study found a definite health benefit associated with expectation effects; that is, thinking that one is receiving distant healing intention had a positive impact on physical health measures (Easter & Watt, 2011). More recently, a meta-analysis undertaken on prayer, did not find an overall effect (Masters, Spielmans & Goodson, 2006). However, Astin et al. (2000) evaluated a variety of distant healing studies, and although it was not possible to undertake a meta-analysis due to the studies being too heterogeneous, they found that 57% of all the studies demonstrated significant effects. They concluded that this presents a clear case for the further study of distant healing phenomena. Given the significant DMILS meta-analysis discussed above, it may be that some types of psychic healing may be more efficacious than are others.

Psi wars

Finally, we will consider issues in the wider debate about psi, focusing on criticisms of research in parapsychology. For more in-depth analyses of conceptual issues the reader is referred to the Special Issue of the *Journal of Consciousness Studies*, 'Psi Wars' (Alcock, Burns & Freeman, 2003) and the recent book *Debating Psychic Experience* (Krippner & Friedman, 2010).

Alcock (2003) presents us with a number of reasons for remaining doubtful about the psi hypothesis, some of which are more powerful than others. These concerns include the negative definition of psi, replicability across many (and sceptical) experimenters, unpredictability, unreported methodological weaknesses, reliance on statistics, and a lack of theory. First, Alcock argues, psi being defined in terms of what it is *not*, when information about the target is not attainable by known means, it is not clear what psi is. When (and if) all normal means of communication are ruled out, what are we left with? With no positive definition of psi we do not know when it might occur and how to prevent it from occurring. This makes the effect dependent upon adequate sensory shielding, and methodological flaws may be difficult to discern if they are unreported, as discussed above. Second, Alcock laments parapsychology's reliance on statistical procedures in order to identify whether psi has occurred – any psi effect is not directly apprehended. The effect sizes are so small as to be theoretically inconsequential and possibly easily accounted for by a number of experimental flaws. Further, statistical significance alone tells us nothing about causality, and, given the negative definition of psi and a lack of a comprehensive, positive theory to explain the effect, Alcock (2003, p. 43) comments that "the significant outcome would provide as much support for my hypothesis that Zeus exists as it does for the psi hypothesis that the human subject's volition caused the results". Third, Alcock has concerns about the heterogeneity of the ganzfeld database, which suggests to him that the effect is not easy to replicate or predict. Further, the meta-analyses themselves have not replicated each other. The putative psi effect does not appear to be robust like some other effects in psychology, such as the Stroop effect, which is commonly used in student practicals due to the high likelihood of it being observed (French, 2010). Further, the 'experimenter effect', discussed by parapsychologists as being one factor that impacts upon the psi effect (where, for example, certain individuals appear to create a warm ambience that elicits a psi effect [Smith, 2003]), seems to Alcock to be a get-out clause for a lack of replication across all experimenters. Rather than such heterogeneity, he argues, "one would normally expect that continuing scientific scrutiny of a phenomenon should lead to stronger effect sizes as one learns more about the subject matter and refines the methodology" (2003, p. 36).

Of course, these criticisms have been rebutted and assuaged. For instance, an important point is that replication is not as straightforward, or as commonly achieved, as many psychologists believe (Utts, 1991). A real effect, if it has a small effect size, requires extremely large sample sizes to enable replication in an experiment (because bigger studies are more likely to detect small effects). Small effects are common in psychology and despite their magnitude can impact upon our lives in a crucial way. A commonly cited example is the evidence for the efficacy of aspirin, the effect size for which is analogous to that for psi (Bem & Honorton, 1994). In terms of predictability, there do appear to be some predictors of psi performance, for example, the individual difference factors of extraversion (Honorton, Ferrari & Bem, 1992) and belief in psi (Lawrence, 1993). Nevertheless, further experimentation needs to take into account the complexity of the system; for example, the role of experimenter behaviour. Parapsychology experiments are not alone in being sensitive to contextual factors; indeed the 'experimenter effect' has been well documented in social psychology – for example, experimenters can introduce expectation effects in participants that might create bias across conditions (Rosenthal, 1966).

Parapsychology does not lack theories, but no single one has been accepted and consistently tested. With this lacuna, psi can be but defined negatively. This may reflect the relative immaturity of parapsychology as a discipline. The 'two-month argument' is sometimes given by parapsychologists in support of this, after Schouten (1993) computed that the time given to parapsychology research in the last one hundred years equates to two months of research in mainstream psychology in the United States. On a final note, it has been suggested that the evidence for psi be evaluated in relation to prior beliefs about its possibility. For this, Utts (1991) argues, Bayesian statistics could be helpful. Bayes's theorem considers how likely an event is when considering events occurring prior to it. It has been used to examine how belief affects the likelihood of new scientific evidence being accepted. Indeed, Alcock (2003, p. 30) himself writes that:

> Arguably, the only significant differences that distinguish the proponents from the sceptics in this collection of articles are in terms of their *a priori* subjective weightings of the likelihood that psychic phenomena exist, which in turn may influence their evaluations of the adequacy of the research protocols that have been employed in parapsychological research and the quality of the data thus obtained.

Concluding comments

This chapter has focused on methodological issues in experimental parapsychology. However, experiential, qualitative research also has an important role to play, as demonstrated through the work of Louisa Rhine who, in the 1950s, collected and analysed case studies of paranormal experience and classified them into different types (intuitions, hallucinatory, realistic dream and unrealistic dream psi experiences) (Rhine, 1961). In recent years, in part perhaps due to frustrations with the inconclusive nature of statistical outcomes, there has been a return to qualitative work (see for instance a special issue in *Qualitative Research in Psychology* [Murray & Wooffitt, 2010]).

Phenomenological approaches focus on accounts of real-life experiences and thus allow us to gain an understanding of the detail, context, richness, and meaning of anomalous experiences. This approach enables us to identify the core characteristics of a type of experience, the typical features of an 'out-of-body' experience, for example, as we will see in the final three chapters of this book. Qualitative approaches are particularly important in the study of anomalous experiences, which can be spontaneous, dramatic, and infrequent. It can be difficult to study these experimentally; for instance, it is almost impossible to capture and record correlates of an apparition or an out-of-body experience in the laboratory, as they do not usually occur upon demand. Even if this is attempted (e.g. in the ganzfeld research there are attempts to produce a genuine psi experience), the experiences had in a laboratory may differ from real-life cases and lack ecological validity (for example, there are not likely to be intense emotions or life-threatening events, as in the case of Agnes Paquet described in the introduction).

However, qualitative work also has its problems, due to the subjective and private nature of consciousness. D. Chalmers (1999) described a number of problems with introspective methods: it is not possible to gain 'pure' access to the first-person experiences of another; introspection changes the experience that is the focus of observation; access to the contents of consciousness is selective (it can't all be accessed or reported at once); reports may be susceptible to 'grand illusions' (introspective experience may not concur with objective reality); and experience is difficult to report linguistically. Foibles of introspection additionally have been noted to include: forgetting; confabulations and errors based on reconstruction; reporting based on beliefs about experience rather than experience itself; reporting based on inference rather than observation; censoring sensitive details; social desirability (reporting in a way that portrays oneself in a good light); deception; demand characteristics (being influenced by the aims and setting of the research study, such as acting in line with the experimenter's expectations); and experimenter effects (for example, where the unique characteristics of experimenters bring about different responses in participants) (see Pekala & Cardeña, 2000; Wooffitt & Holt, 2011). For these reasons Wooffitt and Holt (2011) advocate discursive methods that study naturalistic talk of anomalous experiences, without assuming access to anything 'inner' or creating artificial scenarios, such as a recorded interview.

Some of the above issues are of import in experimental work in anomalistic psychology more generally, such as in expectation effects. For example, the work of Michael Persinger (1993) has applied weak electromagnetic currents above participants' temporal lobes, using the so-called 'god helmet', which he reports induces anomalous experiences such as a sense of presence or a spiritual experience (we have already met Persinger in the chapter on individual differences in relation to temporal lobe lability). As we will discuss in the chapter on apparitions, this work has been criticised for not employing a **double blind** design – the participants *know* that electromagnetic fields are being applied to their skull. This knowledge comes with expectations about what might occur, to which people who are suggestible might be more susceptible. Thus, it has been argued that any unusual experiences encountered under the 'god helmet' might be attributable to suggestion and expectation rather than to the effects that the weak electromagnetic fields might have on the temporal lobes (Granqvist et al., 2005). Other work in anomalistic psychology – for example, the effect of haunted locations on persons – must also control for expectation effects (e.g. French, Haque, Bunton-Stasyshyn & Davis, 2009).

Note

1 In addition, other meta-analyses have been conducted on the entire database of ganzfeld studies, which support the psi hypothesis, but these will not be considered here because they include protocols that were criticised by Hyman and Honorton (1986) (Schlitz & Radin, 2003; Storm & Ertel, 2001).

Further reading

Alcock, J., Burns, J. & Freeman, A. (eds.) (2003) Psi wars: Getting to grips with the paranormal. *Journal of Consciousness Studies, 10*(6–7), 1–246.

Krippner, S. & Friedman, H. (2010) *Debating psychic experience: Human potential or human illusion.* Oxford: Praeger.

Milton, J. & Wiseman, R. (1997) *Guidelines for extrasensory perception research*. Hertfordshire: University of Hertfordshire Press.

Pekala, R. & Cardeña, E. (2000) Methodological issues in the study of altered states of consciousness and anomalous experiences. In E. Cardeña, S. Lynn & S. Krippner (eds.), *Varieties of anomalous experiences* (pp. 47–82). Washington, DC: American Psychological Association.

Summary of Section 2

In the previous two chapters we hope that we have illustrated the thorny and difficult nature of research in parapsychology and the methods that have been used to evaluate it, as well as giving insights into what science is and the way that science is conducted.

Of interest here is work by the sociologists Collins and Pinch (1982) who took a step back from this debate and analysed the processes that occur in the construction of scientific meaning and scientific controversies, focusing on the marginal field of parapsychology. They argue that the scientific process is much messier than is acknowledged by scientists and that decisions about 'what is true' are often made for a variety of reasons other than analysis of the data alone. For example, the data might be ambiguous and lend itself to a variety of interpretations. Both advocate and counter-advocate positions tend to be supported by a community of researchers who share constructs and meanings. Collins and Pinch argue that it can be difficult to reach a shared criterion for how proof should be established for a controversial phenomenon. For example, in what they call 'the experimenter's regress', it is not clear what a successful outcome might be, which makes interpretation vulnerable to cognitive bias, attributing support, or otherwise, to a theory, for which the evidence might not be direct or sufficient. This position is usually rectified through negotiation and social processes.

Whatever one makes of the research in parapsychology it is undeniable that people report having had anomalous experiences. In the next section we will focus on three particular types of experience: out-of-body and near-death experiences, apparitions and mediumistic experiences. We consider these from a wide variety of perspectives, applying the approaches that we have evaluated thus far in order to illustrate how psychology (and in some cases sociology) has sought to explain and understand these phenomena. As is the case in botany, psychologists often begin by seeking to understand the nature of a phenomenon (what its constituent features are) and collect cases of it. Then, researchers may move on to attempt to understand the mechanisms that might explain why such experiences occur, what their correlates are, and what the implications of having them are for the persons involved.

Research into Specific Anomalous Experiences

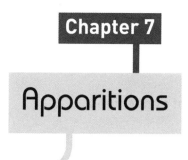

Chapter 7

Apparitions

In this chapter we will define and explore the experience of apparitions, with reference to case studies, phenomenology, and precipitating factors, and then look at several paradigms that have been adopted to explain them. We will then attempt to summarise and evaluate the merits of these approaches.

👁 Defining apparitions

Apparitions are the subjective experiences of a figure or being, when no real figure is physically present and when normal means of communication are ruled out (Irwin & Watt, 2007). These experiences are felt to be very real. The definition shares commonalities with that of hallucinations, which are perception-like experiences that occur without a corresponding appropriate stimulus but have a similar impact to the equivalent 'real' perception. Hallucinations are also characterised by their autonomy; that is, they seem to occur outside the control of the experient (Slade & Bentall, 1988). Apparitions can therefore be considered to be one type of 'hallucination' (broadly defined, and neutral in terms of pathology), although Irwin and Watt (2007) note several qualitative differences that exist between the two types of phenomena. In contrast to the hallucinations associated with drugs or **psychosis**, there are examples of apparitional experiences which seem to provide veridical information (e.g. that another living person is undergoing a crisis or is dying, as we saw in the case of Agnes Paquet in the introduction). Secondly, apparitions often relate to a genuine (living or deceased) person, while hallucinations are often of unknown figures. Finally, apparitions may be shared experiences (there are reports of people experiencing similar imagery at the same apparently haunted location), while hallucinations are typically (but not always) experienced by one person.

Case examples of apparitions

It might have been an hour or so that I had been asleep, when suddenly awaking, I observed at the foot of the couch a sort of bluish vapour, which seemed to fill up the end of the room, and what seemed to me a shadowy form appeared to come out of it, which gradually took the form of a female; the features bore the exact likeness of my intended. I was now fully awake and exclaimed 'Louisa is that really you? What has happened?' I received no answer and in a few seconds the apparition was gone, and seemed to melt away into the vapour, which also disappeared. I still supposed I had been dreaming but could not shake off the impression this apparition had made upon me.

I wrote to my friends in England, saying that I feared my intended was dying or dead. I received an answer that my fears were too well founded, and that the poor girl had died of inflammation of the brain, on the same day and about the same time as I mentioned seeing the apparition.

(Gurney, Myers & Podmore, 1886, pp. 449–450)

It was around ... three-thirty in the afternoon, and I was setting up for dinner. And I heard someone calling me – just my name ... I heard this three or four times. But I was so engrossed in setting up the table ... I turned to say – I was getting a little angry too – and I turned to say, 'What do you want?' ... I saw this man ... He was a man standing on the stairs, and he had this uniform on ... a Revolutionary War soldier, only to me he was like a general. ... And he looked so startled when I said, 'What is it?' And, just like that, he disappeared. I would say it was three-dimensional .... The figure that I saw on the stairs was not transparent. I couldn't see through the figure, and that's what startled me so. ... The bartender ... looked at me and he said, 'What's the matter? You look like you saw a ghost'. And I said, 'Well, I think I did'.

(Maher, 2000, p. 4)

My mother lived in California and I lived in Wichita, Kansas. At 9:40 a.m. on February 17, I was sitting in my bedroom at my dressing room table, brushing my hair in front of the mirror. Suddenly the room was illuminated with the strangest light, one I can't fully describe. I then felt a rustle of wind across my shoulders, and a faint sound like the brushing of birds' wings. Then I looked in the mirror.

My mother was standing behind my chair.... She just stood and smiled at me for a full thirty seconds. I finally said, 'Mom!' and rushed for her, but she disappeared, light and all. I was so upset by this that I shook for an hour. When my husband came home for lunch, I told him about it and got myself ready for a phone call that mother was dead.... Sure enough, about one p.m. that same day, the call came that my mother was gone.

(Feather & Schmicker, 2005, pp. 261–262)

Varieties of apparitional experiences

The term 'apparition' is often equated with the term 'ghost'. However, ghosts are only a subset of apparitions, which actually occur in a variety of contexts and refer to different types of figures (that are not just human in form). To include the full range of apparitional experiences, some psychologists (e.g. Lange & Houran, 2002) have employed '**entity encounter experiences**' as a wider term. These include religious visions (including those of the virgin Mary, called 'Marian apparitions') and seeing such figures as fairies or little people, demons, black dogs, shamanic 'power animals', witches, unidentified flying objects and extraterrestrials, and 'Men in Black', as well as apparitions of deceased individuals (ghosts). These different types of experience share several core components (Evans, 2001) and statistically correlate with one another, suggesting that they may be psychologically similar (Houran & Thalbourne, 2001).

Types of 'ghosts'

Evans (2001) notes that within the apparitional category of 'ghosts' there are a number of sub-categories. Firstly, there are traditional ghosts or revenants, apparitions of individuals who were once alive (and are now discarnate, literally meaning without a body) and who appear to be associated with a particular person. Secondly, there are 'haunters', apparitions of individuals associated with particular locations, who are dressed in clothing from a previous era, and who appear to behave in a manner that does not interact with the observer. These include examples of figures who appear to walk through walls at the location of an old door. The third category is 'crisis apparitions', the experience of observing a figure at the point of their death, or while they are undergoing an accident or traumatic event. The fourth category is 'phantasms of the living', apparitional experiences of people who are living. Evans's final category is the 'doppelganger', experiences where two forms of a person are perceived at the same time – a real person and an image of that person (at a different location).

Haunting experiences pertain to apparitional experiences associated with a particular location, traditionally an old building. Haunting experiences are complex and multisensory, and incorporate auditory phenomena such as footsteps, voices, knocking, doors creaking, music, and furniture being moved. They also include temperature-related phenomena (e.g. feelings of cold) and the perception of a sense of presence, alongside the visual experience of seeing a ghostly figure (McCue, 2002; O'Keeffe & Parsons, 2010). Hauntings are often accompanied by other anomalous experiences, including doors opening (without someone physically opening them) and bedclothes being mysteriously disturbed. Although we are primarily concerned with the apparitional experience *per se*, some of the theories to be explored in this chapter will touch on other experiences that often co-occur with the experience of an apparition.

⊙ Phenomenology

Unlike the stereotypical notion of a ghost as a transparent figure, apparitions are mostly perceived to be solid and lifelike (Williams, Ventola & Wilson, 2010). However, they vary in terms of whether they have shadows and reflections. Consistent with the stereotype, apparitions can appear or disappear, cannot be touched, and at times appear to walk through doors and walls (Williams et al., 2010). Apparitions of figures are experienced in a variety of positions and heights, and although most are stationary, a quarter of apparitions reported in a recent survey (of afterlife apparitional experiences) were mobile (Arcangel, 2008).

Apparitional experiences of the living are more likely to be of close family members than strangers (Williams et al., 2010). McCreery (2006) notes that the apparitional figure is often perceived to stand alongside and occasionally interact with objects in the perceiver's environment. As such, theories of apparitions must account for the unified nature of the perceptual field (room + apparition) and not merely a figure in isolation.

In this chapter we will explore apparitional or entity encounter experiences from a wide-ranging perspective. We will consider the simpler experience of a sense of presence at one end of the spectrum and the more complex perception of a full-blown visual (and other sensory) experience of an identifiable figure at the other end of the spectrum.

Theories should attempt to provide explanations for this rich variety of apparitional experiences.

Incidence and occurrence

Apparitional experiences are reported by 17–30% of the population (Irwin & Watt, 2007) and are therefore a significant aspect of human experience which warrants further exploration and understanding. Hallucinatory experiences are also reported among members of the normal population in the absence of psychopathology (Johns, 2005).

Apparitions are reported in a variety of contexts and have been reported across recorded history. Apparitions are reported when people expect them to occur; for example, at locations which are significant for certain religions (Marian apparitions) and old buildings which have a reputation for being haunted (Wiseman, Watt, Greening, Stevens & O'Keeffe, 2002). Sense-of-presence experiences can also occur during creative writing, and can be experienced as the 'muse' (Persinger & Makarec, 1992).

If we look to the case examples of apparitions given above, it is clear that apparitions can occur when one is either awake or asleep. Systematic research has indicated that apparitions are associated with being extremely stressed or upset, but paradoxically, they also occur when people are extremely tired, and are commonly experienced when people are just falling asleep or just waking up (the hypnagogic and hypnopompic states, respectively; see the later section on sleep) (Gurney et al., 1886).

The majority of apparitional experiences are reported around the time of death (Gurney et al., 1886; Persinger & Koren, 2001). These include reports of apparitions of the person who is about to die, a few days prior to their death (Alvarado, 2008a), apparitions of the dying person on the deathbed itself, and also apparitions of the deceased following death. The latter type of apparition is called the 'bereavement apparition' when it refers to apparitional experiences of a loved one who has recently died. The film *Truly, Madly, Deeply* explored this theme, with Juliet Stevenson's character experiencing a bereavement apparition of her deceased lover, who was played by Alan Rickman.

Many experiences occur spontaneously. However, apparitions can sometimes occur as a result of intentionally seeking to interact with a deceased loved one or communicate with other deceased or otherworldly figures (e.g. in mediumship and shamanic rituals respectively). It has also been claimed that some are the result of intentional out-of-body projections of one person (A) whose apparition is viewed by another person (B). In shamanic rituals, spirit animals may be perceived as part of a shamanic journey, which includes relaxation, guided imagery, drumming and sometimes the ingestion of mind-altering drugs such as ayhuasca (Luke & Friedman, 2009).

In addition, a technique called the 'psychomanteum' has been developed by Moody (1994) that involves focusing on a particular deceased individual, then sitting in a darkened chamber and gazing into a mirror. After some time this procedure appears to be conducive to apparitional experiences of deceased individuals. The third stage of the procedure involves discussion and reflection on the experience, which has been employed with some success in the context of bereavement counselling (Hastings et al., 2002).

Summary

Apparitions reflect a range of perceptual experiences of figures that are not physically present. These experiences include the traditional idea of the ghost alongside a range of other figures. Within the category of ghosts, there are several sub-types, including the traditional idea of a deceased spirit trapped on earth and apparitional experiences of living people. Apparitions occur in a variety of contexts, and are often associated with religious and paranormal themes. The majority of apparitions are reported in association with death, often of close family members. Apparitions can occur in a variety of states of consciousness and can result either spontaneously or from intentional procedures (out-of-body projections, shamanic rituals, the ingestion of mind-altering drugs, and the psychomanteum).

Biological approaches

Michael Persinger has argued that apparitions, or their more rudimentary form, the 'sense of presence' may be explained neurologically. Most people are right-handed, and have a representation of their sense of self in the left hemisphere of the brain. Occasionally, the right hemispheric 'homologue' of the sense of self might be experienced by the dominant interpreting left hemisphere as another human (or other alien) presence. This might occur under circumstances of extreme tiredness or stress. Indeed, Shermer (2010) provides several examples of the sense-of-presence experience occurring at times of extreme physical exhaustion (including hypoxia, a lack of oxygen to the brain) and social isolation (e.g. a lone mountaineer climbing Everest).

Persinger considers that the sense of presence may be experienced artificially if one stimulates the area of the brain responsible for the representation of the sense of self (usually in the right temporal lobes) with a magnetic pulse. This part of the brain houses the limbic system, which include structures associated with sense of self, reality monitoring, and memory access, and emotionality and meaningfulness. Researchers at Persinger's lab then usually expose both hemispheres of the brain to a different pulse – designed to encourage the intrusion of right hemispheric representation into the left hemisphere (which is thought to *interpret* the experience).

There have been several examples of the artificial induction of a sense of presence in the laboratory (e.g. Cook & Persinger, 1997). In addition, Persinger reports a study with a man who had previously experienced a ghost. In a fascinating experiment, mild magnetic pulsations were presented to the right temporal lobe of the brain. After ten minutes of this stimulation, the man reported a ghost-like presence, which subjectively felt like his prior spontaneous experience (Persinger, Tiller & Koren, 2000). Drawing from their brain stimulation research, Persinger and Koren propose that some of the phenomena associated with hauntings may result from the activation of the right temporal and **parietal lobes** and other limbic regions.

Thinking scientifically → **Evaluating Michael Persinger's research**

Persinger's theory is an intriguing one. However, the evidence provided in support of this theory has mostly been provided by Persinger's own laboratory. The benchmark of a good scientific theory is replication, and a finding is more convincing the more often it is found. In addition, there is greater support for a theory if it is found by different, *independent* researchers. To date only one brain stimulation replication study has been undertaken outside of Persinger's own laboratory, by Granqvist et al. (2005). In contrast to Persinger's findings, this study found no differences between the treatment and control conditions. These authors proposed that Persinger's effects might reflect **suggestibility**, rather than a neurological effect. Persinger (Persinger & Koren, 2005) has defended the neurological interpretation, and suggests that this effect would have been found if Granqvist et al. had exposed participants to a longer period of magnetic stimulation (15 minutes). However, the participant who experienced a ghost in the laboratory did so after only ten minutes, and it is not clear what his expectations were about the experiment. If this participant knew about Persinger's research before he came into the laboratory, this could act as a confound, leaving open the expectation and suggestibility explanation. In addition, as the temporal lobe structures are also implicated in memory and emotion processing, the laboratory ghost experience could also reflect a memory (rather than reconstruction) of the prior experience.

Other research has also challenged Persinger's model. Houran, Ashe and Thalbourne (2003) investigated the relationship between personality variables, brain laterality, and entity encounter experiences in a survey investigation. In contrast with Persinger's theory, they did not find a relationship between brain laterality and encounter experiences, or that there was a bias toward experiencing apparitional phenomena on a particular side of the body. Arcangel (2008) also found that afterlife apparition experiences were not restricted to one side of the physical body of the perceivers. As such, these findings challenge the proposal that entity encounter experiences reflect the awareness of the right-hemisphere equivalent of the sense of self (thus appearing on the left side of the body).

Persinger and Koren (2001) have noted that, for some people, the hemispheric direction is reversed or not as clear-cut due to laterality differences, and that other people experience an oscillation of cerebral dominance (approximately every 90 minutes). As such, there may still be a role for projections between hemispheres in the aetiology of apparitional experiences.

What can we conclude? Laboratory brain stimulation studies often seem to induce a sense of presence and apparitional experiences; however, we should remain open about the exact mechanism by which this occurs – the temporal lobe structures may or may not be implicated in these experiences.

Luke and Kittenis (2005) recently found that participants who had ingested the drug DMT (N,N-Dimethyltryptamine) were particularly likely to report encounter experiences. This is a core component of the hallucinogenic drug ayhuasca, employed in South American shamanistic traditions. Hill and Persinger (2003) consider that DMT may be implicated in the neural aetiology of the sense of presence as prior research has found that DMT was associated with entity encounter experiences (Strassman, 2001). Hill and Persinger suggest that the brain may produce DMT from the pineal gland, which has been found to be affected by naturally occurring electromagnetism.

Persinger (1993) has also found that reduced **melatonin** levels (produced in the pineal gland) are associated with the reporting of bereavement apparitions. He suggests that melatonin is affected by an increase in **geomagnetism** in the environment. In turn, this interacts with the effects of grief on the brain, which causes an increase in a brain chemical that is implicated in epileptic effects (corticotrophin-releasing factor). Persinger suggests that these factors interact with the sleep–wake cycle, particularly nocturnal REM (rapid eye movement) sleep which is associated with strong dream imagery. The results are sudden nocturnal awakenings, which are followed by the experience of a sense of presence or apparition.

Summary

Biological approaches to apparitions have explored the idea that the temporal lobes of the brain may be strongly implicated in the aetiology of apparitional experiences. It is proposed that under certain circumstances, namely stress, tiredness, and grief, the non-dominant hemisphere's homologue of the sense of self may be perceived by the dominant hemisphere as a sense of presence and at times as a full-blown apparition. Brain stimulation studies have frequently resulted in sense-of-presence experiences in the laboratory. Other biological approaches include the observation that certain drugs may be implicated in the aetiology of sense of presence and apparitional experiences.

◉ Special topic: Sleep and apparitions

Apparitions commonly occur when one is not quite asleep and not quite awake. When one is falling asleep there is an interesting state of consciousness known as the hypnagogic state, which is associated with a tendency to have a lot of dream-like mental imagery which seems to be subjectively real and appears to derive from an external source (i.e., is hallucinatory) (Mavromatis, 1987). At the opposite end of sleep, there is another interesting state of consciousness known as the hypnopompic state. Both states of consciousness appear to be associated with reports of ghostly figures and other apparitions (Sherwood, 2002).

McCreery (1997, 2006) has argued that apparitional (and out-of-body experiences) can be explained by the invasion of hypnagogic 'micro-sleeps' (short bursts of this brain state) into waking consciousness. He also notes that this is particularly the case among those who score high on the anomaly-prone personality type, positive schizotypy. Green and McCreery (1975) argued that a '**metachoric' experience**, a hallucinatory experience which is perceptually real and seems to be continuous with previous waking reality, may be a good explanation for at least some, if not all, apparitions, and that this may be associated with the hypnagogic state. Indeed, there is evidence that hypnagogic sleep states can occur during the daytime while people feel awake (Foulkes & Fleisher, 1975). It is of note that Persinger's (e.g. Persinger & Koren, 2001) neural stimulation studies work better during the evening or early morning hours, which indicates an interaction with circadian rhythms.

Sleep paralysis also appears to be associated with apparitional experiences. There are two components: the incubus experience and the intruder experience (Cheyne & Girard, 2004). The incubus is a particular form of apparition which appears in many cultures with different names, including the Canadian 'old hag' (witch) and the Anglo Saxon 'Mara' (Cheyne, 2002; Hufford, 2001). This experience includes the perception of being pinned down, being unable to move, alongside breathing difficulties, choking, strangulation, bodily pressure, and thoughts of dying. The intruder experience consists of a numinous sense of presence alongside other (visual, auditory, and tactile) hallucinatory experiences, which are usually interpreted as a threatening sense of presence in the room. These two experiences have been argued to be based on different neural systems, with the intruder experience emerging from a threat-activated vigilance system. Together, they instigate subjective experiences of witches, aliens, and other threatening presences. Sleep paralysis is a paradoxical state of consciousness whereby the person is conscious, but unable to move. This occurs at sleep onset and offset, and during the night (prior to or emerging from periods of rapid-eye-movement sleep, the sleep stage that is highly correlated with dreaming). Paralysis is associated with confusion between the physiological processes associated with waking and sleeping, as the person is usually paralysed during nocturnal sleep, to prevent people from acting out their dreams. Such confusions may arise from micro-arousals (due to stress or sleep problems such as apnea, stopping breathing during sleep) and sleeping on one's back (what psychologists call the supine position, Cheyne, 2002). It is of note that those who report one type of encounter experience (that of aliens) are more likely to report experiences characteristic of sleep paralysis (French, Santomauro, Hamilton, Fox & Thalbourne, 2008).

A recent analysis of two collections of ghost stories in Japan (Furuya et al., 2009) concluded that 17% of one collection of tales were sleep-related (including those associated with hypnagogia and with REM disorder), while 43.9% were what they defined as non-sleep-related. In a second collection of stories, 36.6% were sleep-related while 31% were non-sleep-related. In the non-sleep-related category, the authors included what they describe as 'highway hypnosis experiences', experiences associated with becoming drowsy and falling asleep while driving a car, as well as those associated with vivid waking hallucinations. It is clear that sleep processes are strongly implicated in personal apparitional experiences as well as in those which are recorded as 'ghost stories' in a particular culture.

Summary

Several sleep-related states are implicated in the aetiology of apparitional experiences. These include hypnagogic and hypnopompic states and sleep paralysis. Sleep seems to have a key role in the aetiology of apparitional experiences.

Cognitive–perceptual approaches

A pre-existing mindset that ghosts exist or that a building may be haunted appears to be involved in the aetiology of unusual experiences. This reflects a top-down influence on experiences, whereby people see and experience what they expect to see and experience, at least to a certain extent. For example, those who were told that a property was haunted were much more likely to report a range of unusual experiences while walking through that building than those who were simply told that the same property was being renovated (Lange & Houran, 1997). Wiseman et al. (2002) found that people who believed in ghosts had more unusual experiences than those who did not believe in ghosts when walking around Hampton Court Palace. A laboratory study also found that the expectation that one might experience an apparition increased the likelihood of having both visual and auditory apparitional experiences in the psychomanteum (Terhune & Smith, 2006).

Belief in the paranormal may also be implicated in a general tendency to see apparitions (Houran & Thalbourne, 2001) and have alien encounter experiences in particular (French et al., 2008). Houran and Thalbourne (2001) found that a tendency to have entity encounter experiences was particularly associated with paranormal beliefs that relate to experiences in one's own life (personal beliefs, such as in psi and astrology) rather than to cultural beliefs (such as the devil and ideas of heaven and hell). Thus, Houran and Thalbourne proposed that entity encounter experiences may arise when they are psychologically needed, and may be associated with an increased sense of personal control over life events.

Lange and Houran (2002) argue that context (personal beliefs and culturally available beliefs) drives the perception of ambiguous stimuli. This can occur in a manner akin to a prime, priming a paranormal interpretation of an ambiguous stimulus, or after an experience, through reconstructing an encounter in line with paranormal beliefs. They also suggest that once an ambiguous event has been labelled this will heighten attention to other similar anomalies, and bias attention toward interpreting phenomena as being anomalous in a similar manner.

Another cognitive theory which crosses over into neuroscience is the proposal that at least some apparitional experiences could result from apophenia, the tendency to find connections between random events and meaning and significance in random events (Brugger, 2001). Interestingly, apophenia is more likely among paranormal believers and personality types who are more prone to experiencing apparitions. Being more prone to this cognitive bias may play a key role in shadows being perceived as human or animal figures (in the half-light) and certainly in the perception that anomalous shadows, blurs, and orbs in digital photography are 'ghostly' figures.

Summary

Cognitive approaches include the role of expectation and pre-existing belief in the aetiology of an apparition. These include personal beliefs; individuals' expectations (suggestibility) may encourage the experience of anomalies, particularly under ambiguous circumstances (e.g. in dark buildings). These also include cultural beliefs, as people tend to expect more unusual phenomena when they are told that a building is old or haunted compared to when they are told that a building is under construction. The tendency toward apophenia – seeing meaningful shapes when none are present – may explain some apparitional experiences.

Personality approaches

The cluster of personality types associated with strong mental imagery and entering altered states of consciousness (e.g. fantasy-proneness and absorption, which were discussed in Chapter 3) is associated with reports of apparitions. In particular, those who are fantasy-prone are very likely to report having had apparitional experiences (Wilson & Barber, 1983). Other related variables, being prone to dissociation, and to a slightly lesser extent, hypnotisability (an increased likelihood of being hypnotised), are also associated with apparitional experiences (Kumar & Pekala, 2001). Parra (2006) found that people who reported both apparitional and sense-of-presence experiences scored significantly higher on absorption and fantasy-proneness. Finally, people who report experiences of encounters with a particular type of entity – aliens – also score high on dissociation, absorption, and fantasy-proneness (French et al., 2008).

Scoring high on transliminality is also associated with the propensity to experience entity encounter experiences (Houran & Thalbourne, 2001). Houran and Thalbourne suggest that high scorers on transliminality may be particularly likely to experience entity encounter experiences (apparitions) during times of psychological need. A related variable, boundary thinness (Hartmann, 1991), is also associated with having more entity encounter experiences (Houran et al., 2003). In addition, those reporting both apparitional experiences and experiences of the sense of presence have scored significantly higher on a measure of positive schizotypy than those who do not report these experiences (Parra, 2006). (These three personality constructs, transliminality, boundary thinness, and schizotypy were discussed in Chapter 3.)

A later study (Houran, Wiseman & Thalbourne, 2002) found that transliminality also appears to facilitate the relationships between expectation (paranormal belief) and the number of experiences actually reported in a haunted location and also between expectation and **hyperaesthesia** (extreme perceptual sensitivity) and the number of different categories of experience reported in a haunted location. Transliminality (and related variables) are therefore very important in terms of understanding the tendency to experience apparitions.

In the previous section, the role of apophenia was noted in the perception of stimuli as apparitions. As such, it should be noted that those who score high on positive schizotypy (and related variables) are more prone to this tendency (Brugger, 2001).

The idea that perceptual sensitivity may be involved in the perception of apparitions has recently been explored directly by Jawer (2006), who has found that displaying a 'sensitive' personality profile – being prone to allergies and being chemically and electrically sensitive – is associated with reporting apparitions (and other anomalous experiences). His study also found that apparitions are more likely if one is female, a first-born or only child, single, ambidextrous, imaginative, and introverted, as well as able to recall traumatic events in one's life.

Summary

Apparitions are more likely among people who are prone to fantasy and to experience altered states of consciousness (dissociation and absorption), those whose minds and brains are more likely to have information-crossing boundaries (transliminality and boundary thinness), and those who exhibit perceptual sensitivity. Together, these factors imply that apparitions may result from sensitivity to subtle environmental factors (or other subtle or ambiguous factors), which are experienced as ghosts or apparitions.

Environmental approaches

There is some evidence that houses which are perceived to be 'haunted' have certain environmental characteristics which may be implicated in the perceptual experience of ghosts. For example, locations where many apparitional experiences are reported often appear to be associated with unusual electromagnetic activity. Indeed, Persinger and Koren (2001) summarise that haunting phenomena are associated with increased geo-magnetic activity, tectonic strain – areas of the earth which are prone to earthquakes – and thunderstorm activity. For example, Persinger and Derr (1989) reported an example of a shared hallucination of the Virgin Mary above a church in Egypt (seen by thousands of people), which turned out to be the result of misperceptions of the luminous phenomena which arose from tectonic strain.

Wiseman et al. (2003) explored the experiences of participants in two haunted locations – Hampton Court Palace and a haunted vault in Edinburgh – and found that unusual experiences were more likely to be reported in locations which were renowned for being 'haunted'. The authors were able to rule out an expectation effect, and found that these effects were associated with the variance of the local electromagnetic field and lighting. The authors propose that some lighting effects may impact on the perception of a ghost due to shadows (which could be misperceived as ghosts in a haunted location); this dovetails with cognitive explanations explored earlier in this chapter.

Apparitions may be particularly likely when electromagnetic activity is complex in nature. Unusual electromagnetic activity may interact with neurophysiology and personality (for example, if one is a high scorer on

Persinger's temporal lobe signs scale) and result in hallucinatory experiences. For example, Persinger (1993) has proposed that geomagnetism may interact with the brain via its production of melatonin, which may affect the sleep–wake cycle and result in apparitional experiences among those whose brains are sensitised (in terms of their neural wiring, as personality, or under circumstances whereby the brain has been sensitised via stress or grief as in the case of bereavement apparitions).

In addition, haunted locations may exhibit features that interact with the physical presence of a moving human being and result in magnetic fluctuations that may then have an impact on subjective experiences (Braithwaite, 2004).

It has also been suggested (Tandy, 2000; Tandy & Lawrence, 1998) that locations where many apparitional experiences are reported are associated with very low frequency sound (sound that cannot be audibly perceived, at around 19Hz) or 'infrasound'. It has been hypothesised that this induces apparitional experiences due to a combination of physiological effects alongside the expectation that one might encounter unusual experiences in haunted environments. Physiological effects may include vibrations of the eyes which may cause blurring of vision. This may be implicated in the perception of shadowy forms which could be perceived as ghostly figures. Another effect is hyperventilation which may cause a slight light-headedness that may result in a fear response, characteristic of many subjective experiences of ghosts.

Tandy (2000) found evidence that a standing wave resonating at approximately 19Hz was associated with subjective anomalous experiences in a reportedly haunted 14th-century cellar in Coventry, and that the peak of the wave was at the entrance to the cellar. This is of interest as several anecdotal reports provided by a local tour guide, Colin Cook, described experiences as visitors entered the chamber. It may well be that haunted locations are those which are conducive to the resonance of sound in the infrasound range.

Claims relating to electromagnetism and infrasound have been questioned, as experimental research to date has not often included the simultaneous measurement of electromagnetic activity and infrasound in a haunted and in another baseline location (Braithwaite & Townsend, 2006; French, Haque, Bunton-Stasyshyn & Davis, 2009). However, Braithwaite's own research (2004) did undertake this methodology, and found evidence supporting electromagnetic anomalies in the aetiology of apparitions.

A recent study by French et al. (2009) attempted to investigate whether being exposed to complex electromagnetic fields, infrasound, or both together might lead to more anomalous experiences than a baseline condition by constructing a 'haunted room'. They wanted to ascertain whether the environmental effects reported to date are genuine, or rather, the result of suggestion. Their results found some evidence for anomalous experiences in the haunted room, but these were not associated with either electromagnetic fields or infrasound. The authors conclude that anomalous experiences were more likely to have been the result of suggestibility, given that all participants were informed that they might experience unusual sensations while in the chamber.

Persinger, Koren and O'Connor (2001) have argued that there may be interaction effects between the environment and personality such that those who score high on a scale measuring temporal lobe lability (Persinger & Makarec, 1987) are more sensitive to electromagnetic anomalies in the environment. It is of note that temporal lobe lability correlates with transliminality (Thalbourne, Crawley & Houran, 2003). In addition, the temporal lobes appear to be implicated in **cross modal mapping** (where information from different sensory sources are joined together) and some synaesthetic thinking (Rouw & Scholte, 2007). Some apparitions could result from synaesthetic-like perceptions of environmental factors, to which people with transliminal traits are more sensitive.

Summary

Several environmental factors have been proposed to be important in the aetiology of apparitional experiences. These have mainly focused on geomagnetic factors and infrasound, but other environmental factors (e.g. lighting) may also come into play. It may well be that environmental factors are better understood in conjunction with personality factors, as sensitive people may be more likely to detect weak stimuli and perceive them as apparitional figures.

👁 Sociocultural approaches

The ghost is a culturally popular image and regularly features in movies, television shows, and tourism. This is clearly seen in the popularity of television shows such as *Most Haunted*, alongside the presence of ghostly narratives in many popular films (Edwards, 2001). Ghost mythology has also been woven cleverly into the heritage industry in Scotland (Inglis & Holmes, 2003) which has a long recorded history of ghosts. As such, the ghost has a role within the history and popular culture of the Western world. In addition, ghosts and apparitions play a role in folklore and in the development of (religious) belief systems. For example, Marian apparitions have been cited as evidential for the Christian faith (Horsfall, 2000). McClenon (2001) has applied a sociological perspective to apparitional phenomena. He argues that haunting experiences (including the perception of an apparition) can be studied neutrally, using survey techniques, the content analysis of the narratives deriving from first-hand experiences and observation of participants. He presents an argument for the experiential source theory. This argues that there are universal features in anomalous experiences of the haunting type which may have a physiological basis. He also argues for the ritual healing theory, which is a social–evolutionary perspective on the generation of anomalous experiences (including those of the apparitional type). The propensity to experience anomalous phenomena (in general) is associated with a genotype that predisposes one to dissociate or become hypnotised. This tendency is particularly associated with experiencing apparitions. Being able to dissociate may have been selected by evolution because access to altered states (in rituals) enabled healing via hypnosis or the reduction of pain. Beliefs pertaining to ideas of spirits, souls, and life after death may have developed as a result of these first-hand experiences. Such beliefs are then propagated socially, even among those who are not personally wired to experience anomalous phenomena, as vicarious observation of anomalies can also serve to generate beliefs, in a manner similar to many other socially generated ideas (social learning theory). This is further instantiated through rituals held at the group level which may inspire beliefs in more structured belief systems that impact on the usefulness of beliefs in rituals associated with healing. McClenon notes that although his theory begins with the experiences of a given individual, the group processes may be "particularly conducive to generating robust anomalous perceptions" (p. 81) of the apparitional variety.

Summary

Socio–cultural perspectives on apparitions include those on the role of the apparition within a particular social group. Traditional ideas of the ghost are used by the tourist industry around the globe. Apparitional experiences are employed as evidential in some religious groups (in particular, Marian apparitions in Catholicism). McClenon has applied experiential source theory and ritual healing theory to the development of belief systems pertaining to ideas of life after death and the soul. It is suggested that there is an interaction between an individual's tendency to experience anomalous phenomena and group (ritual-based) experiences, which can serve to generate and propagate beliefs via social learning.

Psi approaches

Some theorists consider that apparitions actually exist as a different energetic form, while others have asserted that apparitions are mental projections resulting from a telepathic influence. If apparitions are a different energetic form, then they may be measurable. Research on apparitions has therefore attempted to determine whether apparitions are subjective phenomena or if they have some kind of objective existence. McCue (2002) discusses four hypotheses pertaining to the psi hypothesis and apparitions: the traditional spiritualist view of the ghost, the perceptual hypothesis, the telepathic hypothesis, and the psychokinetic hypothesis.

The traditional spiritualist view is that apparitions reflect the earthly presence of discarnate spirits who are unable to make the transition to an afterlife. This is the ghost hypothesis and implies that apparitions are genuine independent entities that can be directly perceived or indirectly detected as anomalous energetic effects. A different version of this idea is that of Denning (described in McCue, 2002), where haunting/apparition events are associated with the energy that persists after a traumatic event (a pseudo-haunting). As such, this fits with the idea of a place having some form of memory or trace, which was originally proposed by Harry Price in 1939 (Williams et al., 2010).

Ghost-hunting research has explored apparently haunted buildings and attempted to measure the presence of ghosts by a variety of assessment tools, including infrared cameras, temperature gauges, random number generators, and Geiger counters. Recent research has also employed digital cameras in an attempt to capture spirits on camera, and has recorded on blank tapes or onto digital voice recorders in an attempt to record **electronic voice phenomena**. One intriguing example of this research was undertaken by William Roll in his investigation of the apparently haunted Queen Mary cruise ship. Roll left a voice-activated tape recorder on the boat overnight, which had apparently recorded a series of strange noises consistent with traumatic events in the history of the ship (Williams et al., 2010). Smith and West (2002) report a more spontaneous example of an anomalous human image which was captured on a CCTV camera at Moor Lane Mill in the UK. After investigation, these authors concluded that the most likely explanation was that this was not an apparition, but rather an image of a living person who worked at the Mill.

Other researchers (see Maher, 1999, for a summary) employed two groups of individuals (one group of psychics and mediums and one control group which sometimes comprised sceptics) who were blind to the apparitional experiences reported in a given building. These people were brought into the haunted location and asked to record their experiences, using checklists and floor plans of buildings. Experiences were then compared between areas in which many apparitions had been observed and areas where no apparition had been observed. Maher's meta-analysis indicated that the group claiming to be psychics tended to do better than control participants at matching the claims of experients. However, controls also matched some of the apparitional experiences, indicating that some experiences may result from stereotypes associated with the rooms or other environmental cues.

The perceptual hypothesis proposes that there are interaction effects between anomalies in the environment (i.e. electromagnetic fluctuations) and neural functioning which allows people to perceive phenomena that are really there but not usually perceptible, including the perception of genuine ghosts of discarnate spirits.

The perceptual hypothesis is supported by observations from the environmental and personality approaches toward understanding apparitional experiences that we discussed above. People who are more likely to experience subjective paranormal phenomena (including apparitions) are more likely to be influenced by electromagnetic anomalies (Persinger et al., 2001). In addition, they are more likely to be affected by weak stimuli (Crawley, French & Yesson, 2002; Evans, 1997) and perform better at some experiments testing for extrasensory perception in the laboratory (Parker, 2000). As such, some people could be more likely to perceive phenomena which are present but usually imperceptible.

The telepathic hypothesis does not necessarily require a discarnate spirit for the manifestation of the apparitional experience and is therefore parsimonious in terms of apparitions of both those who are living and deceased. It is suggested that apparitions may result from an intense tele-pathic connection with another person which affects brain functioning and causes the telepathic communication to be perceived as projected outside of the body as an apparition. This may occur when someone is undergoing a traumatic experience or crisis, but could also include information from a deceased loved one. As such, an apparition reflects a different way of experiencing information which was actually acquired from a psi source. This is an interesting idea, but difficult to empiri-cally evaluate. There is indirect support from research into telepathy, as ganzfeld findings indicate that there is better ESP performance among people who are biologically or emotionally close to one another (Dalton, 1997) and among those who score high on variables related to positive schizotypy (Parker, 2000).

The fourth hypothesis is the psychokinetic hypothesis, which suggests that intense subjective experiences sometimes intrude upon our physical world. Experiences which occur in poltergeist cases (objects and events move anomalously, but seem to derive from a focal person who is often extremely psychologically disturbed) and research on macro-PK (that mind may have an impact on larger matter) may support this idea. How-ever, it is generally agreed that laboratory studies on micro-PK (effects of human intention on probabilistic systems) are more convincing than studies of macro-PK (Steinkamp, 2002).

Radin and Rebman (1995) undertook an experiment to explore whether apparitions are the result of psychology, or if they might reflect the existence of an independent entity, using the psychomanteum pro-cedure. They monitored a series of variables (the psychophysiology of the participants, electromagnetic activity, electric and magnetic fields, ionising radiation, temperature, and the output of a random number generator). The study used seven participants who all underwent a psychomanteum procedure. The experimenters monitored the electro-magnetic spectrum inside the psychomanteum chamber. Four out of the seven participants reported some form of mild apparitional experience, but no one reported sustained life-like apparitions. None of the monitor-ing equipment detected the presence of an anomaly, although there were correlations between physiology and environmental measures. There was also a suggestive relationship between physiology and random number generator scores. The authors suggest that apparitions may be the result of a bi-directional process with the environment affecting physiology and with the person affecting the environment as a PK-induced apparition. This is a unique and interesting study, which is in need of replication.

As it stands it has small sample size and methodological weaknesses that could be improved in a future study.

The early psychical researchers undertook a census of hallucinatory experiences, including apparitional experiences, particularly occurring around the time of death and including the perception of the deceased as a ghostly figure. These researchers took great pains to apply probability theory to the apparently veridical experiences which suggest that these do occur more than might be expected by chance (Gurney et al., 1886; James, 1895). Other case study research has explored the psi question and focused on cases where people had recorded that they saw an apparition of a person while the person was subjectively out of their body, or felt that they were visiting people in dreams or in their imagination (see Williams et al., 2010).

Summary

Psi hypotheses pertaining to the question of apparitions include the classic idea of the ghost as a discarnate spirit: the perceptual hypothesis which suggests that environmental factors interact with personality to allow people to perceive things that are really there but not usually perceptible (e.g. ESP or actual ghosts); the telepathic hypothesis suggests that apparitions reflect a telepathic perception which is experienced as an apparitional projection; and the PK hypothesis suggests that some apparitions may result from the emotional experiences of the observer. Research has explored these questions by measuring haunted areas, by exploring the experiences of psychics and controls in haunted locations, by understanding more about telepathy in the laboratory, and by trying to create apparitions both in the real world (as out-of-body projections, in case studies) and under laboratory conditions (by using the psychomanteum).

Thinking critically about apparitional experiences: Evaluating research approaches

Apparitions may well be a particular sub-category of the umbrella category 'hallucinations' – as they refer to the perception of something which is not physically there. However, they are a fascinating sub-category of hallucinations which may at times refer to information about a place or a person that the experient should not have access to (if all normal routes of information transfer are ruled out). As such, apparitions are an interesting and complex type of hallucination. In addition, even if it turns out that some apparitions are purely hallucinatory, this does not mean that experiences equate to pathology. Indeed, many healthy people report pleasant or adaptive experiences and Hasting et al.'s (2002) work indicates that apparitions are useful in the therapeutic setting.

In this chapter we have explored apparitional experiences from a variety of perspectives. What should we conclude about the nature of apparitions? At times, apparitions may merely be the product of apophenia or expectation or prior belief when faced with a darkened chamber or a room which is purported to be 'haunted'. However, apophenia in particular may well apply to shadowy figures and the orbs in photographs, but it is potentially problematic for explaining the richer apparitional experiences, for example, of ghostly figures wearing old-fashioned clothing, and the fact that many people report similar apparitions at one given location.

At other times, apparitions may reflect a synaesthetic perception of other subtly available environmental cues, which may include electromagnetic fluctuations. They may also occasionally be the result of the intrusion of the right hemisphere homologue of the sense of self into the left brain (and vice versa), which could result from a sensitivity to electromagnetism (temporal lobe lability and related personality variables). They may also result from strong imaginary and creative capability, which is a key component of personality types that are prone to these types of experiences. However, cases where people experience an apparition of a close person in distress at the same time as that person is going through a trauma or crisis or dying are intriguing, particularly where the person appears to obtain knowledge to which they should not have access (recall the case of Agnes Paquet).

At times it is difficult for apparitional experiences to be accommodated by any one of the approaches described in this chapter. Perhaps some (particularly simpler) experiences are better explained by neurological and cognitive theories, while others require a more interactionist approach, that is, some apparitions might be best explained by a combination of various explanatory models. At times this could also include a psi explanation, where environmental conditions drive the perception of a usually imperceptible stimulus in sensitive people. Environmental cues (or psi information) may both be consciously experienced in a different (perhaps synaesthetic) way.

Unfortunately, many models and research studies have not examined multiple theories in one study (with a few exceptions – e.g. French's creation of a haunted chamber and Radin and Rebman's psychomanteum study). Research like this, which has aimed to create an apparition under laboratory conditions, may be the most promising way in which many hypotheses might be evaluated. Unfortunately, this type of study is rare, but hopefully future studies will continue to adopt a multidimensional approach.

◉ Further reading

Houran, J. & Lange, R. (2001). *Hauntings and poltergeists: Multidisciplinary perspectives.* Jefferson, NC: McFarland.

Chapter 8

Out-of-body experiences and near-death experiences

This chapter explores out-of-body experiences (OBEs) and near-death experiences (NDEs). These are related but distinct phenomena, but they are considered together here because the latter often encompass the former. We will define both with reference to case studies, phenomenology, and precipitating factors, and then look at several paradigms which have been adopted to explain the experiences. We will then attempt to summarise and evaluate the merits of these approaches.

Defining out-of-body and near-death experiences

Out-of-body experiences

Where are 'you'? Usually, a person's sense of self is **embodied** – it feels as though we are inside our bodies – in particular, the head – and are looking out at the world through the eyes. When people have OBEs, the sense of self feels as though it has been separated from the body. Such an event has also been described as 'astral travel', projection (Muldoon, 1936), the ecsomatic (this literally translates as outside of the body) experience, travelling clairvoyance, and psychic excursion. It can be broken down into three phenomenological (what it feels like) components:

1 feeling disembodied (the sense of self is not located in the body);
2 observing the world from an elevated and distanced perspective;
3 sensing that one can observe one's own body from the elevated perspective (known as **autoscopy**) (Bünning & Blanke, 2005).

The person experiencing an OBE usually feels wide awake and the subjective experience is as though one has really left the body. The next section presents two examples of OBEs.

Case examples of OBEs

This event occurred some years ago when I was in my twenties. I was in bed and about to fall asleep when I had the distinct impression that 'I' was at ceiling level looking down at my body in the bed. I was very startled and frightened; immediately I felt that, I was consciously back in the bed again.

(Irwin, 1985, p. 1)

[Louise] began a meditation for health course in an attempt to relax and de-stress herself after leaving a long-term relationship with a violent partner. She found the course difficult and struggled for the first few weeks to relax and let go of her thoughts and feelings and enter the meditative state. Her instructor encouraged her to continue and she eventually went into a meditative state in her sixth class. Her instructor was guiding the class through a Jungian meditation that described a journey to a forest. She felt very relaxed prior to leaving her body and very aware of the instructor's voice. After a while she realised she could not hear the instructor's voice anymore and felt that she really was in the place that was being described in the meditation. She felt disembodied and disconnected and experienced some very powerful emotions. She recalled seeing her physical body curling up on the floor below her. She came out of the OBE when roused by her instructor, who had also noticed her curling up on the floor and crying. Although she enjoyed being in the OB state, she was profoundly upset at the vulnerable condition she perceived herself to be in. She went back to the class the following week and during that evening's meditation session she felt as if she was 'moving off' to have another OBE. This frightened her and she terminated the experience and the meditation. She never went back to the class again. Although she was very frightened by the experience, she also remembered the peace and tranquillity of being in the OB state and said she would like to try meditation again, but only if she thought she could feel safe.

(Wilde & Murray, 2009, p. 99)

Phenomenology of OBEs

The subjective experience of being out of the body can vary greatly. For instance, there are differences in the nature of the experience of the separated self, with some people reporting the perception of a full 'double', while others do not report the experience of another body at all. Events that include a double may actually be a distinct or separate phenomenon from those which do not. Cheyne and Girard (2009) have proposed that the sense of being separated from the body might be labelled as an 'out-of-body feeling', while seeing the body from a different visual perspective might be labelled as an 'out-of-body autoscopy'. The latter may develop from the former; that is, being 'disembodied' may lead to the richer forms of OBE.

Alvarado (2000) has noted differences in how people experience the sense of self in the absence of a body double. These include the feeling that one is 'pure consciousness', a 'ball of light', and other shapes (for example, clouds). Early writings suggested that the separated self was connected to the body via a cord (Muldoon, 1936), but there is little empirical support for this (Alvarado, 2000).

While some people experience the sense of self as simply out of the body (e.g. on the ceiling and looking down at their body), others experience imaginal 'journeys'. For example, Blackmore (1996a) describes an OBE in which she left her body and embarked on a journey in which she left the room and flew across rooftops. Interestingly, this subsequently inspired her to undertake research in parapsychology. In addition, Hélène Smith (Irwin, 1985) is famous for reporting OBEs which included visits to Mars. Visual and perceptual experiences are more common than the simple experience of being separated from the body. A recent survey found that 70% of these episodes included visual and perceptual features, while 30% described many of the core aspects of being out of the body but without any visual features (Terhune, 2009).

It is clear that OBEs are complex and occur in a variety of forms. As such, they should be considered to be 'polymodal' (Braithwaite &

Dent, 2011). Unfortunately, much research to date has explored OBEs as though they are one unified phenomenon.

Incidence of OBEs

Alvarado's (2000) review of the OBE literature suggests that these events are reported by approximately 10% of the population, compared with 25% of those in student groups and 48% of those in groups interested in parapsychology. As such, these experiences are unusual but not uncommon (particularly among particular types of personality – see the later section on personality approaches) and they therefore warrant academic attention.

Near-death experiences

NDEs first came to public attention when Raymond Moody published the book *Life after Life* in 1976. Since that time the phenomenon has been studied by psychologists and those working in psychiatry and medicine, as well as those working in the field of parapsychology. NDEs have been defined as "profound psychological events with transcendental and mystical elements, typically occurring to individuals close to death or in situations of intense physical or emotional danger. These elements include ineffability, a sense that the experience transcends personal ego, and an experience of union with a divine or higher principle" (Greyson, 2000a, pp. 315–6).

Case examples of NDEs

The first example of an NDE is a schematic experience constructed by Moody, based on his case collection (1976):

> A man is dying and, as he reaches the point of greatest physical distress, he hears himself pronounced dead by his doctor. He begins to hear an uncomfortable noise, a loud ringing or buzzing, and at the same time feels himself moving rapidly through a long dark tunnel. After this, he suddenly finds himself outside of his physical body, but still in the immediate physical environment, and he sees his own body from a distance, as though he is a spectator. He watches the resuscitation attempt from this unusual vantage point and is in a state of emotional upheaval.

After a while, he collects himself and becomes more accustomed to his odd condition. He notices that he still has a 'body', but one of a very different nature and with very different powers from the physical body he has left behind. Soon other things begin to happen. Others come to meet and help him. He glimpses the spirits of relatives and friends who have already died, and a loving, warm spirit of a kind he has never encountered before – a being of light – appears before him. This being asks him a question, nonverbally, to make him evaluate his life and helps him along by showing him a panoramic, instantaneous playback of the major events of his life. At some point he finds himself approaching some sort of barrier or border, apparently representing the limit between earthly life and the next life. Yet he finds that he must go back to the earth, that the time for his death has not come. At this point he resists, for by now he is taken up with his experiences in the afterlife and does not want to return. He is overwhelmed by intense feelings of joy, love, and peace. Despite his attitude, though, he somehow reunites with his physical body and lives.

(Moody, 1976, pp. 23–24)

The second example is taken from a recent qualitative study by Wilde and Murray (2008):

She was having an operation, which was going smoothly until at some stage her heart rate and blood pressure began falling. The surgical team fought to restore her vital signs, including using a defibrillator to restart her heart. In the midst of this, she found herself floating on the operating theatre ceiling. She was in a state of pure bliss and could see the theatre, the equipment, the staff, and her own body below her. She recognized her friend, the anaesthetist, and tried to communicate with her by tapping her on the shoulder, but her friend did not acknowledge her presence. She then found herself leaving the hospital and flying peacefully along a tunnel towards a blue light. She saw a hand descending out of the light and reaching towards her. She felt that if she had taken the hand she would have died. At this point she began a short dialogue with what she believed was the voice of God: "As I got there, I turned round and said, I don't want to go yet ... My baby's a couple of months old and I was still feeding, I can't leave my children, I want to see them grow old ... I want to be a grandmother ... and, in answer to this, 'ok, you can go back,' and ... I had made promises ... cos that power to me is God ... and I'd said to him ... I'll go and do your work for you." At this point she returned to her body and awoke from under the anaesthetic.

(Wilde & Murray, 2008, pp. 8–9)

Phenomenology of NDEs

The NDE may be summarised as including the following features: peace and joy, an OBE, a sense that any previously experienced pain has stopped, the perception of a dark tunnel (or void), the perception of a bright light (often felt to be a being comprising light, which is a loving presence and may communicate with the experient), the experience of meeting other beings including deceased people, memories, a sense of judgement, having the experience of another realm, the perception of a border (beyond which the person is unable to go), and finally, returning to the physical body (often experienced against the will of the person). Some near-death experients also report a 'flashforwards' experience, which appears to predict their future. Sometimes NDEs include prophetic visions that have a wider focus and relate to the world's future (Lundahl, 1999). Those who have NDEs are more likely to report subjective paranormal phenomena after the event, and sometimes they report an awareness of events which occurred while they were 'dead' or when they should not have been able to perceive the world in the normal manner. As such, the NDE has been of particular interest to those working as parapsychologists.

NDEs can differ widely from individual to individual in terms of the order of events and presence of some of the above components but not others (Moody, 1976). These events have been measured and distinguished from other similar experiences by use of a 16-item scale (Greyson, 1983), whereby a score of seven or above indicates that one has had an NDE. It is also possible to ascertain the 'depth' of the NDE, whereby a deeper experience includes more components. Contrary to the idea that NDEs might be embellished over time with false memories (French, 2003), there is evidence that experiences are actually remembered very accurately and do not change significantly over a long period of time (Greyson, 2003). The majority of NDEs are subjectively blissful; however, there are also a minority of cases that are subjectively distressful (Bush, 2010). They are often highly meaningful and transformative events which alter the sense of self and outlook on life of the experient following the event (Wilde & Murray, 2008).

Incidence

NDEs occur cross-culturally (Blackmore, 1993) among about a third of individuals who come 'close to death', which is equivalent to approximately 5% of the general population (Greyson, 2000a). For example, in a prospective study of those in a cardiac unit, 6.3% of people who had had a cardiac arrest (heart attack) experienced phenomena which met the criteria for an NDE (Parnia, Waller, Yeates & Fenwick, 2001). As such, although these are relatively rare, they are part of the conscious human experience.

Antecedents

A variety of precipitating factors can lead to the feeling of one's self being separated from the body. These include being very relaxed; in a sleep state; meditating; under extreme stress; feeling awake, active, and alert; alongside less common triggers such as being in an accident, ingesting drugs, undergoing childbirth, suffering pain or cardiac arrest, or even having an orgasm (Blackmore, 1984; Twemlow, Gabbard & Jones, 1982). OBEs may also be associated with migraines or headaches (Alvarado & Zingrone, 2008; Blackmore, 1984; Blanke & Arzy, 2005) and can occur via intentional induction (Palmer, 1978). A recent survey (Zingrone, Alvarado & Cardeña, 2010) found that they are more likely when people are inactive, and especially when they are lying on their back. OBEs which arise from this position also include a larger variety of features than those arising from other static and waking positions.

NDEs can arise when one has physiologically died, when one is close to physiological death or when one perceives one's self to be close to death (Greyson, Williams Kelly & Kelly, 2010). They are often reported following cardiac arrest (heart attacks) and while patients are under general anaesthesia. They have also been reported following ingestion of the recreational drug ketamine.

The list of antecedents for OBEs strongly suggests a role for being in a state of consciousness that differs from the waking state, and includes states related to sleep and states associated with the ingestion of certain drugs and meditation (see Wilde & Murray, 2009, for a review). OBEs and NDEs may both be examples of *dissociative* experiences, which occur when there is a separation of thoughts, feelings, and subjective experiences from the normal stream of consciousness and memory (Greyson, 2000b).

Summary

OBEs and NDEs were defined as related but distinct. The former are more common than the latter. A variety of factors appear to precipitate an OBE, and NDEs often occur when people are physically or psychologically close to death, and are often reported under general anaesthesia or following heart attacks. Both appear to be associated with altered states of consciousness, in particular those which are dissociative in nature.

Perspectives on OBEs and NDEs

In the following sections we will present an overview of some of the key theoretical approaches towards understanding both of these events. For more details the student is referred to Alvarado (2000) and Greyson (2000a).

Neuroscientific approaches

The cognitive-neuroscience approach to OBEs has dominated the academic literature in recent years, with a plethora of studies supporting the idea that these episodes result from a) problems in the neural pathway from the **prefrontal cortex** to the temporo-parietal junction of the brain and b) problems in the integration of the multisensory inputs associated with the representation of the embodied self at the temporo-parietal junction (Blanke & Arzy, 2005). The prefrontal cortex has a role in the creation of the representation of the sense of self (Easton, Blanke & Mohr, 2009), and a disconnection in the information transfer between the prefrontal cortex and the temporo-parietal junction appears to be implicated in the aetiology of OBEs.

Usually, the brain aims to create one coherent representation of a unified sense of body and self. However, sometimes proprioceptive (awareness of the body's position in space), tactile (touch), vestibular (balance), and visual information about the body is not adequately integrated. This lack of integration can result in more than one representation of the sense of body and self, and result in the feeling that the sense of self has separated from the body. The sense of separation between body and self is enhanced by problems in the vestibular (balance) system, as this causes further disintegration between the sense of personal space and visual space (outside the person).

The perception of an additional body arises neurologically in a similar way to the perception of a phantom limb in some amputees (Bünning & Blanke, 2005).

There have been several studies which support the idea that these areas of the brain are implicated in the OBE. These have included brain stimulation studies, neuroimaging studies, and recent cognitive-neuroscience studies which have explored people's 'mental own body transformation ability' (designed to tap the neural pathways relating to the prefrontal cortex and temporal parietal junction). These studies have asked people to make a decision about the left or right location of a grey highlighted hand on a schematic figure.

Easton et al. (2009) asked people to make decisions under two circumstances: when they were in the position of a figure presented on a screen, or when they imagined that images on the screen were a mirror reflection of themselves. Those who reported prior OBEs had longer reaction times when the task type 'switched' but not when the same type of trial was repeated (that is, when they had to switch imagined orientation). This indicates that there is some difficulty in representing the self in space among those who had experienced OBEs.

Many physiological explanations have also been directed towards understanding NDEs (Greyson et al., 2010). These include the influence of altered blood gas levels (oxygen and carbon dioxide), the release of endorphins and other opioids at times of extreme stress, Jansen's n-methyl-d-aspartate (NMDA) model, limbic models, and the REM intrusion model (see the 'special topic' on sleep). We will explore some of these explanations in this section.

Anoxia (lack of oxygen to the brain) may explain many of the phenomenological features of the NDE. However, anoxia cannot explain all such events because not all people experience a lack of oxygen prior to the episode. Alternatively, it may be that carbon dioxide build-up in the brain may be implicated in NDEs (Blackmore, 1996b; 1998). Blackmore has proposed that anoxia may be indirectly implicated in NDEs, as this may cause cortical disinhibition, which may explain many visual features of the event (a computer model of the progress of cortical disinhibition in the visual cortex would mimic the perception of a dark tunnel with bright light at the end of it) (Blackmore & Troscianko, 1989).

As with our earlier discussion of OBEs, the temporal lobe structures of the brain are strongly implicated in NDEs. These structures are associated with multisensory integration, and the limbic structures are implicated in memory access (the hippocampus), the attachment of meaning and significance to human experiences (the amygdala), and 'gating' or working out the source of incoming information (that is, whether information is from an external or internal source and whether it is imaginary or real [hippocampus]).

In support of a temporal lobe explanation for these experiences, people with temporal lobe epilepsy report experiences which sometimes mimic NDEs. In addition, people who report having an NDE exhibit brain activity similar to that found in temporal lobe epilepsy and subjective experiences which indicate greater lability of the temporal lobes compared with those who do not report having an NDE (Britton & Bootzin, 2004).

The ketamine model (Jansen, 1997) arose from observations that the altered state of consciousness induced by this drug (50–100 ml) is associated with several features which are reported in NDEs (including the dark tunnel, light, the sense of being dead, the sense that one is communicating with a God-like presence, OBEs, and mystical states). Ketamine was originally used as a tranquiliser for horses but has recently become popular as a recreational drug. It may work at the site of the receptors, which are located in the temporal and **frontal lobes** for a neurotransmitter (NMDA) in the brain. A flood of the chemical glutamate is assumed to over-activate these receptors, which results in neurotoxicity (i.e. neurons begin to die). Ketamine (and a hypothetical equivalent chemical in the brain) blocks these receptors to protect them, which results in an altered state of consciousness. This is interesting because glutamate flooding may also result from other precipitating biological factors for the NDE (e.g. temporal lobe epilepsy). However, a protective brain chemical which floods the NMDA receptors is yet to be found, presenting a challenge to the hypothesis.

The ketamine model for the out-of-body component of NDEs was supported in a recent study (Morgan et al., 2011), where the drug's ingestion was related to an increased tendency to perceive a rubber hand as belonging to the self. The authors suggest that this may have resulted from an increase in cross-modal binding of incoming sensory information and possibly a shift to the dominance of the visual input (top-down processes) over other (bottom-up) sensory inputs. This dovetails with cognitive theories, which will be discussed in the next section.

◉ Special topic: The sleep hypothesis

A key theoretical perspective on both OBEs and NDEs is that both are associated with sleep processes intruding into wakefulness (and vice versa). McCreery (1997; 2006), for example, has argued that apparitional experiences and OBEs may result from hypnagogic microsleep interjections into waking consciousness. The hypnagogic state is an intriguing and paradoxical state of consciousness that is traditionally associated with falling asleep but may occur at other times during the waking day (Foulkes & Fleisher, 1975). Hypnagogia is closely associated with hallucinatory experiences (imaginary experiences can seem to derive from an external source and seem perceptually real) and with many subjective paranormal experiences (Sherwood, 2002). McCreery proposes that OBEs are particularly likely among those who score high on positive schizotypy as these individuals exhibit a lot of lability in their **arousal systems**, such that they are highly prone to rapid changes in their state of consciousness. Green and McCreery (1975) proposed that such experiences may relate to OBEs as another example (alongside apparitional experiences) of a metachoric experience, a hallucinatory episode which seems continuous with waking reality.

Palmer's (1978) theory also suggests that the OBE is fundamentally hypnagogic in nature. He proposed that it is one of several possible results of a body image change, triggered by a threat to one's personal identity, that prevents the threat from reaching conscious awareness (other possible responses include fainting or lucid dreaming). Murray (2010) has criticised this approach on the grounds that it does not adequately explain why some people are more likely to experience an OBE than are others, given similar precipitating circumstances, but the answer may lie in an interaction between personality and those circumstances, given that positive schizotypy in particular is associated with greater susceptibility to hypnagogic experiences (see the later section on personality).

The experience of sleep paralysis is associated with both out-of-body feelings and out-of-body autoscopy experiences (Cheyne & Girard, 2009).

Sleep paralysis occurs when one feels as though the body is paralysed while awake, and it is associated with the traditional dream state (the, rapid eye movement [REM] stage of sleep). During sleep paralysis, REM sleep intrudes into the waking state of consciousness, resulting in a mixed and paradoxical state of consciousness. The phenomenon is associated with illusory (body-self) movement experiences comprising vestibular experiences (e.g. floating, flying, falling, spinning, and elevator sensations) and motor hallucinations (e.g. illusory limb movement, sitting, standing, and locomotion). In agreement with the earlier discussion, Cheyne and Girard (2009) consider that the sense of being out of the body results from false and conflicting information about the location and movement of the body in space, when the various representations of the body and self (proprioceptive, tactile, vestibular, motor, and visual) fail to become integrated. Vestibular anomalies may lead to the sense of disembodiment, which may in turn lead to the perception of the self as separate from a perceived body double. This is particularly likely during sleep paralysis, as the REM sleep state is associated with reduced blood flow to the prefrontal cortex and temporo-parietal regions of the brain, which are important in the generation of a representation of the sense of self. Interjections of 'sleep' processes into the waking mind may cause the generation of more than one representation of the sense of self.

Sleep-related theories have also been applied to the NDE, in particular that these events may arise from REM intrusions into the waking state (Nelson, Mattingly, Lee & Schmitt, 2006; Nelson, Mattingly, & Schmitt, 2007). This argument derives from observations regarding the aetiology and phenomenology of the NDE – namely that they often occur in response to danger or crisis, and exhibit a real sense that the person is unable to move and is 'dead'. Nelson et al. note that REM intrusions can occur during the hypnagogic and hypnopompic states in particular, and include visual and auditory components alongside sleep paralysis, which they suggest could "reinforce a person's sense of being dead and convey the impression of death to others" (2006, p. 1004). They argue that an REM explanation can explain many features of the NDE, including the sense of detachment, the perception of unusual light, autoscopy (feeling outside of the body), pleasant/euphoric feelings, and sensed presence. However, NDEs and dreams do differ fundamentally in terms of the extent to which the two experiences are felt as 'real' – as one of the key features of the former is that they are often felt to be more real than reality.

There is evidence for altered sleep patterns among those who are near-death experients. In particular, Britton & Bootzin (2004) believe that they experience shorter sleep duration and delayed REM sleep compared with a group of non-near-death experients. These authors suggest that the temporal lobe anomalies may be implicated in the NDE and sleep anomalies, and that near-death experients are a neurologically interesting group of participants.

Summary

Biological approaches currently dominate the literature on OBEs and NDEs. Recent research in cognitive neuroscience implies that problems in the fronto-parietal network (the neural structures implicated in the generation of the representation of the self) may be implicated in the aetiology of the OBE. In particular, it is assumed that the representation of self is usually the result of a coordinated neural fusion of sensory inputs and that this is not the case in those who have experienced OBEs. Several biological theories have been proposed to explain NDEs, which indicate a clear role for the temporal lobe structures.

Both experiences may be associated with sleep processes (hypnagogic and REM states) interjecting into wakefulness and vice versa (waking states interjecting into nocturnal sleep states).

Thinking scientifically → **Evaluating the biological perspective**

There is a lot of evidence supporting a biological role in both OBEs and NDEs. In our current dominant paradigm (or way of seeing and interpreting the world), finding a biological component to an experience is often used as a causal explanation – that is to say, an experience arises *due to* the activation of a given area of the brain. However, the neurological perspective should be considered critically. Firstly, if biological models (e.g. anoxia) are correct, then all people who undergo a similar antecedent (e.g. cardiac arrest) and clinically die should hypothetically have an NDE (van Lommel, van Wees, Meyers & Elfferich, 2001). This is simply not the case.

Secondly, it should be borne in mind that no correlation is equivalent to causality. As such, a physiological correlation cannot completely explain the subjective experience. Likewise, the subjective experience itself is not equivalent to the neural level of explanation. Correlations such as these should be considered neutrally – that there is a relationship between physiological activity and subjective experience, but they are not one and the same thing (**reductionism**). Long and Holden (2007) have asserted that researchers should be cautious in interpreting the causality of brain-based theories (including the sleep hypotheses), because, even if there is an association between neural functioning and subjective experience, this is correlational and not necessarily causal.

Some NDE researchers have thought about the relationship in a different way. For example, Long and Holden (2007) and van Lommel et al. (2001) have both proposed that the brain might function as a receiver and transmitter of consciousness, rather than causing it. In addition, Jansen (1997) has argued that ketamine may act like a 'mental modem' which allows the person to perceive a different reality and that NDEs are associated with the experience of another reality, and not merely a hallucination. The same argument might be applied to the idea that NDEs and OBEs are associated with 'sleep responses'. Rather than saying that the NDE is 'just a dream', another view might be that the dream state could allow for the perception of other realities.

Another problem with the biological perspective is that it is very easy to move towards a pathological interpretation of anomalous experiences. On the contrary, even though some people with neurological problems are prone to OBEs, this should not pathologise all OBEs, which may actually have a variety of different causal pathways.

Likewise, Neppe and Palmer (2009) note that biological theories cannot explain all NDEs, and that researchers should be aware that there is not one NDE to be explained but rather a collection of them, with potentially different aetiologies and components.

Cognitive–perceptual approaches

Several cognitive approaches have been proposed to explain OBEs. For example, the idea of the self being 'in' the body may actually be one of several possible models of reality (Metzinger, 2005); other models of reality are possible, including a model from an imaginal source with a 'bird's-eye' view (Blackmore, 1987). Blackmore proposed that the OBE is a cognitive construction based on a shift in the usual model of reality (where the self is in the body) to an imagination-driven 'observer' perspective, which is caused by an alteration in sensory input, which arises under situations of stress, sensory deprivation, and so on. She found that OBEs are more likely among people who are better able to perceive the world from an 'observer' or 'bird's-eye' perspective, particularly for their dream imagery, which also lends support to the sleep hypotheses. In addition, Cook and Irwin (1983) also found that out-of-body experients were better able to imagine a scene from other perspectives. In contrast, recent research has found that these individuals are actually slower at undertaking a 'perspective taking' task (trying to see the world from an alternative viewpoint) (Braithwaite & Dent, 2011). Braithwaite suggests that this conflicting finding might be due to differences in the recent task which might be tapping 'what' as opposed to 'how' another person perceives the world. Differences in research findings may also result from the existence of varied phenomenology of these types of experiences, which may have been lumped together in many empirical studies.

Irwin and Watt (2007) note that other imagination-based explanations of the OBE fail to explain *how* one feels that the sense of self is physically separated from the body. Irwin's (1985) own theory attempts to answer this question. His theory incorporates absorption, being out of touch with bodily sensations, inwardly directed attention, and synaesthetic processes. In this theory, absorbed states of mind can arise from both very low and very high arousal states, and he has elsewhere asserted that there are individual differences in absorption and the need for absorption (see the personality section). Being in a state of absorption interacts with a sense of being out of touch with one's body (what Irwin calls the **'asomatic'** factor), which may result from relaxation *or* repetitive motor actions. This model is based on an interaction between absorption, attention, and the 'asomatic' factor. There are times when it is easy to lose awareness of one's bodily sensations and become absorbed in one's mental imagery. This can occur with a variety of precipitating factors. The perception that there is an actual separation of self from the body, and/or an actual body double, may result when there is a persistent lack of feedback that the person is in the body. The cognitive system then develops an idea of a separated self, which becomes represented as a floating self. Synaesthetic processes may then 'fuse' the representation of the separated self with visual components, which can seem perceptually very real (Irwin, 1985; Irwin & Watt, 2007).

Irwin (2000) has recently added that dissociation from the body is more likely among those who are prone to OBEs, which is an important underlying factor in their aetiology. In support of Irwin's model, Terhune (2009) found evidence for synaesthesia in visual OBEs but not in experiences which do not include visual and perceptual components. He considers that visual content during an OBE may arise from a general facility for cross-modal binding; for example, of representations of the body and visual perceptions which are a unified conscious experience during the episode.

Sagan's (1979) proposal that the tunnel experience in the NDE reflects a 'birth memory' can also be considered to be cognitive (as well as psychodynamic) as it implies that the person actually relives a particular memory. However, there is little support for this idea as there are no differences in tunnel experiences between those who were born naturally compared with those who were born via caesarean section (Blackmore & Troscianko, 1989).

Summary

Cognitive perspectives on OBEs and NDEs indicate that there are alterations in the usual representation of the sense of self as *embodied*. Some imagery abilities associated with perspective-taking may be enhanced, while others are deficient among those who have OBEs, although it is not clear that all such events are equivalent. However, being very absorbed combined with a continued reduced sense of being embodied can result in the sense of being out of the body, which with synaesthetic perception may combine to produce classic OBEs which include visual components, such as a body double.

◉ Personality approaches

Interestingly, not everyone reports OBEs and NDEs under similar conditions, which supports the idea that there are individual differences in who is likely to report these experiences. A cluster of variables relating to the tendency towards being hypnotised – absorption, fantasy-proneness, hypnosis, and dissociation – are consistently associated with the tendency to have OBEs (and were discussed in relation to general anomaly-proneness in Chapter 3; see Alvarado, 2000, for a review).

Dissociation is particularly implicated in these experiences (Irwin, 2000; Murray, 2010). This is the case both for questionnaire measures (Dalton, Zingrone & Alvarado, 1999; Gow, Lang & Chant, 2004) and for empirical measures of dissociative experiences. For example, Murray (2010) has argued that those who are more likely to have OBEs exhibit a reduction in their everyday experiences of feeling 'embodied'. This was supported in two laboratory studies, where out-of-body experients had more body dissatisfaction and body-based dissociation, less awareness of the body during a virtual reality session (Murray & Fox, 2005), and more dissociative alterations in body image during a mirror-gazing task (Terhune, 2006).

Another recent survey found that those who have OBEs score higher on absorption, dissociation, fantasy-proneness, and hallucination-proneness, and they have stronger visual imagery than those who have not had OBEs (Parra, 2009). In addition, those who score high on the personality dimension of positive schizotypy are particularly prone to OBEs (McCreery & Claridge, 2002; Parra, 2009). Parra notes that the hypnotisability cluster of variables also correlates with positive schizotypy, and that these variables support a dissociation model for OBEs.

Others have proposed that there are anomalies in the sleep–wake cycle/arousal system of positive schizotypes and those who score high on dissociation, which renders them more likely to experience rapid shifts in their state of consciousness (in the daytime and at night). This biological predisposition may underpin both nocturnal sleep anomalies and diurnal anomalous experiences (Koffel & Watson, 2009; Mahowald & Schenck, 2001) and may be precipitated by stress or trauma (Koffel & Watson, 2009), one of the precipitating factors associated with OBEs.

Positive schizotypy is associated with a greater tendency to experience more 'in-between' states of consciousness, such as hypnagogia (Parra & Espinoza Paul, 2009), which may 'interject' into the waking state (McCreery, 1997).

Greyson (2000a) notes that there are very few personality characteristics which distinguish near-death experients from non-experients. However, those who have had NDEs also tend to score higher on scales tapping dissociative experiences than other people who have also come close to death (Greyson, 2000b; see also Holden, Long & MacLurg, 2010, for a discussion).

Noyes and Kletti (1976, cited by Holden et al., 2010) proposed that the NDE is an example of depersonalisation (a type of dissociation) which emerges to protect the self from the threat of death by instigating a sense of unreality – a sense that the person is not 'really there'. However, there are differences between depersonalisation and NDEs, a key one being that NDEs appear *more* (rather than less) real, and often pleasant (Gabbard & Twemlow, 1984; Holden et al., 2010). Interestingly, those who have NDEs are more likely to report abuse or trauma in their life histories. As dissociation is a natural response to trauma, having more trauma may have contributed to the likelihood of having an NDE, although not all research has found that near-death experients are more prone to dissociation (Holden et al., 2010). Holden et al. suggest that childhood trauma may add something to the aetiology of the NDE, but given that not all experients report such a life history, an alternative perspective might be that the NDE may be a healing experience and that it may potentiate a greater openness to disclose early childhood events. There is also evidence that the personality variables absorption and fantasy-proneness (Holden et al., 2010), and scoring high on the personality variable temporal lobe lability (Britton & Bootzin, 2004), also contribute to NDEs, supporting a role for the temporal lobes in the generation of these types of experiences.

Summary

Not everyone has OBEs and NDEs under similar conditions. There is a cluster of personality variables that are associated with a greater likelihood of these events (absorption, dissociation, and fantasy-proneness). In addition, scoring high on positive schizotypy is associated with OBEs. This may be due to a tendency towards rich imagination, including absorption and a biological predisposition (including anomalies in the arousal system and temporal lobe lability), which renders people more likely to experience dissociative states of consciousness, particularly in situations of stress or trauma. Dissociative experiences are important in the aetiology of both types of experiences.

◉ Social and cultural approaches

The OBE appears to be a universal phenomenon, described by Metzinger (2005) as a 'neurophenomenological archetype' which has the potential to occur among all human beings. This supports McClenon's (1990) assertion that the 'experiential source theory', a human tendency for a certain experience, may be a better explanation than the 'cultural source theory', the existence of specific belief systems within cultures, in driving these types of experiences. In fact, anomalous experiences (including the OBE) are found at similar incidence rates in countries where religious experiences are actually discouraged (e.g. in China, see McClenon, 1990). This may have impacted upon rudimentary belief systems, as the OBE clearly lends itself to the idea that a human being has a metaphysical component, or *soul* (Metzinger, 2005). Cheyne and Girard (2009) also note that soul beliefs are universal and appear across many different cultures.

There is an equivalent lack of relationship between prior religiosity and NDEs (Greyson, 1991). As such, NDEs are also likely to reflect a universal archetype, which may have been influential in the development of religious ideas, supporting the experiential source theory.

Social approaches to the OBE and NDE have also explored how these events are expressed and integrated within a social group or culture. It is of interest that the dominant paradigm for understanding the OBE is pathological (at least in the West) and, as such, the experiences continue to hold a fringe position in our society. This was highlighted by a recent qualitative study with out-of-body and near-death experients, where participants noted the awkwardness of discussing these types of experiences among colleagues (Wilde & Murray, 2010).

Summary

Social and cultural perspectives on OBEs and NDEs suggest that both transcend culture, and belief systems related to the soul may derive from experiences (the experiential source theory) rather than culturally present beliefs. Social approaches also explore the phenomenology of these events, and how they are interpreted and integrated into the social life of the person.

Psi approaches

Psi approaches towards understanding OBEs and NDEs have explored the idea that a metaphysical or spiritual aspect of human nature actually leaves the body, asking whether consciousness can exist independently of the body and also whether OBEs and NDEs are conducive to extrasensory perception.

OBEs

There is an intriguing collection of cases of apparitional experiences in which a person who is having an OBE is observed by another witness or witnesses *at the same point in time* (this is known as an 'OB apparition', see Alvarado, 1989; Gurney, Myers & Podmore, 1886), which support the idea that some aspect of human consciousness can separate from the body. However, even if such cases appear to be convincing, the only way to really explore possible veridicality of the projection model of the self is via experimental research. A series of experiments have attempted to detect the presence of a double (Alvarado, 1982a, 1989; Blackmore, 1983). Several studies have employed special claimants as participants (people who are regular out-of-body experients and can reliably induce an OBE under laboratory conditions) and have attempted to measure the presence of a double at a particular location. 'Detectors' have ranged from people, animals, and an array of physical apparatus, including magnetometers, ultra-violet and infra-red detectors, strain gauges, thermistors (devices which detect minute changes in temperature), and detectors of magnetic and electrical effects. Irwin and Watt (2007) note that detector studies have generally found null results, with the occasional exception where there have been unusual recordings from detectors (Osis & McCormick, 1980). Taking these experiments as a whole, Blackmore (1983) has argued that these attempts to demonstrate that the OBE is evidence for something metaphysical leaving the body do not provide strong evidence that anything *actually* leaves the body and, as such, OBEs are probably better explained by a psychological model. There are several other studies which support the idea that being out of the body is associated with extrasensory perception (Dalton, Zingrone & Alvarado, 1999; Osis & McCormick, 1980; Tart, 1998). For example, Tart (1997) asked participants to perceive a randomly selected five-digit number, placed on a high shelf. One participant, Miss Z, got the number exactly correct, at odds against chance of 100,000 to one. Other similar experiments found that participants got the number wrong as well as right. More recently, Dalton et al. (1999) found that those who reported a prior OBE performed better at a laboratory extrasensory perception (ESP) test than did other people. However, this body of research is small.

In addition, despite the existence of some intriguing findings, Alvarado (1982b) considered that on the whole, there is only weak evidence for a relationship between OBEs and ESP performance (under laboratory conditions).

NDEs

In terms of NDEs, early researchers attempted to explore whether there was something metaphysical which leaves the body at the point of death by weighing the soul (Macdougall, 1907). It has been argued that these events provide evidence that consciousness can function separately from the physical body (van Lommel et al., 2001). In support of this, some NDEs are associated with physiological death (sometimes for long periods of time) and are called 'strong NDEs'. Greyson et al. (2010) have argued that although some (residual) activity is possible in cases of death, consciousness and information processing should not occur. This is a challenge to the dominant materialist paradigm for consciousness, which maintains that consciousness is fundamentally tied to physiology (and to life). Greyson (2010) has argued that these NDEs might only be explained by new non-materialist models of mind (e.g. quantum models). This perspective has been criticised as it is not clear *when* exactly the memory for experiences reported during such episodes is actually formed – the memory might occur when consciousness is regained and not while the person is physiologically dead or under anaesthetic (Nelson et al., 2006). However, this criticism does not hold up for 'veridical NDEs' where experients are aware of information pertaining to events which occurred *during* the period in which they were classified as clinically dead. Research into these claims includes anecdotal reports, systematic studies of the reports of near-death experients (by comparison of descriptions of veridical components with medical and other records), and prospective studies (which have included perceptual targets, selected such that all living people are blind to their identity) (Holden, 2010). There are approximately 150 cases in the history of NDE research in which there has been some attempt to corroborate information obtained during the experience. However, Holden notes that 100 of these may be associated with errors, which raises a question mark with regard to the validity of at least some of them. Despite the remaining number of cases being small, normal explanations have been ruled out and some experiences are very impressive (Sabom, 1983, 1998, cited in Greyson, 2000a, p. 339.).

Prospective controlled experiments (which have placed randomly selected ESP target materials in hospitals) have thus far been unsuccessful in eliciting above-chance results for those having NDEs. However, there have only been five such studies to date. There is an ongoing collaborative project run by 25 hospitals and medical centres around the globe (AWARE: awareness during resuscitation study) which will investigate the extent to which those who have NDEs are able to accurately perceive ESP target information. The question of awareness of information during periods of death/prolonged unconsciousness may thus be resolved in the near future.

Summary

Overall, experimental evidence for the projection model has resulted in many null results, with notable exceptions for one or two intriguing studies. There is stronger experimental evidence for an association between being 'out of the body' and ESP performance, although this literature is also mixed in overall outcome. For NDEs there are a minority of intriguing corroborated cases of 'veridical NDEs'. To date there have only been five controlled **prospective experiments** in hospitals, which do not support a psi hypothesis. The most striking implication of NDEs is the observation that people appear to have conscious awareness during brain states which cannot sustain consciousness.

◉ Thinking critically about OBEs and NDEs: Evaluating research approaches

OBEs and NDEs are complex phenomena, which may have influenced religious thought and the development of the concept of the soul (Metzinger, 2005), and possibly the content of religious texts (Lundahl, 1999). They are experiences that are often life-transforming, and many experients become more spiritual and content with life as a result (Greyson, 2000a; Wilde & Murray, 2008).

As is the case with other anomalous events that are explored in this book, the reader should remain cautious and sceptical of accepting any *one* approach over others to explain all examples of these experiences. It is also becoming increasingly clear that there are a variety of sub-types of

OBEs and NDEs and that some research may have combined all phe-nomenological sub-types and treated them as one unified phenomenon. It is clear that there are individual differences in the tendency to expe-rience both types of phenomena, given that not everyone has an OBE or NDE under similar circumstances. Both appear to be dissociative, which may be more likely under altered states of consciousness and among cer-tain personality types. However, some experiences also appear to emerge from a waking state of consciousness. The sleep hypothesis may allow for some **parsimony**, particularly if a 'sleep response' is possible as a result of extreme stress as well as under-arousal, and that sleep is not an all-or-nothing event (we fall asleep in several stages, and it is reason-able to assume that parts of the mind-brain might be asleep while others are awake, leading to experiences which are hallucinatory but apparently continuous with waking reality). In addition, the observation that a per-sonality type that is particularly prone to sleep anomalies, dissociative experiences, and OBEs also fits this model. However, the sleep theory as applied to NDEs may not fully explain *all* of the features of this experi-ence, in particular the sense of extreme reality and the fact that NDEs are often profound, spiritually transforming experiences. Other brain-based theories do have excellent explanatory value for at least some of the com-ponents of OBEs and NDEs, but it is not clear that they can explain all aspects (as discussed in the 'thinking scientifically' box). Cognitive per-spectives contribute to an integrated explanatory model, which is based on physiology and dissociative processes combined with imagination and a role for synaesthesia, at least for visual OBEs.

However, the existence of case studies and some experiments challenge a merely reductionistic view of both experiences. Although the existence of a metaphysical double is not on the whole convincing, the idea that the OBE and NDE reflect interesting states of consciousness *is* supported. For both experiences, although the overall evidence must be considered to be weak, at times laboratory studies indicate that people may have access to information that they should not have access to under the exist-ing model of reality. In addition, strong examples of NDEs may present something of a challenge to a purely physiological account for human consciousness given that conscious experience is being reported under circumstances whereby consciousness is assumed to be impossible.

What should we conclude? A recent article (Fingelkurts & Fingelkurts, 2009) attempted to weigh up the pros and cons of the neuroscience ver-sus theological perspective on religious experiences, which would include the NDE, and considered that the best way to move forward may be to adopt an "integral view where the human is seen as a psycho-somatic entity consisting of the multiple levels and dimensions of human existence (physical, biological, psychological, and spiritual reality), allowing consciousness/mind/spirit and brain/body/matter to be seen as different sides of the same phenomenon, neither reducible to each other" (p. 1).

Further reading

Alvarado, C. (2000) Out of body experiences. In E. Cardeña, S. Lynn & S. Krippner (eds.), *Varieties of anomalous experiences* (pp. 183–218). Washington, DC: American Psychological Association.

Holden, J., Greyson, B. & James, D. (Eds.) (2010) *The handbook of near-death experiences: Thirty years of investigation.* Santa Barbara, CA: Praeger.

Online resources

- International Association for Near Death Studies (includes examples of NDEs): www.iands.org
- Susan Blackmore's website (includes many of her research articles on OBEs and NDEs): www.susanblackmore.co.uk
- Charles Tart's website (includes many of his research articles on OBEs and NDEs): www.paradigm-sys.

Chapter 9

Mental mediumship

Mental mediumship reflects the subjective experience of communicating with a discarnate (deceased) personality. This communication is either experienced directly with a discarnate personality or indirectly, via an intermediary personality known as a 'spirit control'. Mental mediumship is more commonly known as 'psychic mediumship' in lay terms, but the term 'mental' is used to distinguish this practice from 'physical' mediumship which involves physical demonstrations, such as the levitation of objects and the production of ectoplasm. Mental mediumistic experiences often occur when the medium is in a state of 'possession trance', in which a deceased or otherworldly being apparently takes control of the behaviour of the medium, including their speech and bodily movements (Hageman et al., 2010). Mediums have existed throughout the ages and across most cultures, and can appear in a variety of guises, including shamans, oracles, and priests (Roll, 2006), as well as the archetypal Spiritualist medium of the late 19th century and the television and entertainment mediums of the modern era.

The practice of mental mediumship in Europe emerged and became popular during the Spiritualist era (late 19th and early 20th century), and in fact the topic of mental mediumship was instrumental in the inauguration of the Society for Psychical Research, whose members began extensive research into the claims of mediums, which were tantamount to a claim for survival of human consciousness after bodily death. Mediumship has persisted into the modern era and is a common practice in Brazil (Krippner, 2011). In the West, it may well be one of the most accessible forms of interaction with 'the paranormal' (Wooffitt,

2007). Indeed, a significant proportion of the general population report consulting psychics or mediums (Roe, 1998). At the turn of the 21st century it was possible to watch mediums (such as John Edward and Derek Acorah) on the television in one's own home. In addition, with growing use of technology, mediums are now personally available for consultation over the internet and telephone, as well as at psychic fairs and stage demonstrations which are held for members of the public. One may also attend Spiritualist churches, in which mediums pass messages to the congregation from spirits (Wooffitt & Gilbert, 2008). This availability of mediumship may be one of the reasons why the topic has received increased academic attention in recent years, with a variety of research approaches that focus on both the experiences of the medium and the person who receives purportedly paranormal information from that medium being employed.

Phenomenology of mediumship

Irwin and Watt (2007, pp. 14–15) provide a synopsis of the phenomenology of Spiritualist mediumship. They note that mediums in the Victorian era were mostly female. The medium would sit in a darkened room with her eyes closed. Following some deep breathing, she would appear restless before calming down. Following this, the medium would whisper to herself in a voice which was uncharacteristic of her usual (waking) voice. The voice was claimed to be the voice of the spirit control (or spirit guide), whose role was to act on behalf of the medium in the spirit world and converse with people attending the séance (the sitters). Irwin and Watt note that the spirit guide would often claim to be the spirit of a deceased person from another culture, and would speak in broken English, often making derogatory remarks about the medium during the séance. After some time there would be messages about members of the spirit world, or the appearance of a new spirit personality (characterised by a different spoken voice of the medium), who would speak directly from the spirit world and provide information to the sitters. Several such 'communicators' may have appeared during a séance. The séance would end with a similar transition for the medium, with visible restlessness and deep breathing as they returned to their usual state of waking consciousness. The medium would often claim to have little or no memory of what occurred during the séance. Sometimes the communicators would speak in a different language, which was unknown to the medium in her waking life (an ability known as xenoglossy) (Roll, 2006). At other times, information might be communicated through automatic writing (writing which seems to be produced without the conscious effort of the medium, but is driven by some 'external agent').

In her autobiography, the famous medium Eileen Garrett (2002) describes her psychic experiences. This includes the first time she encountered her own spirit control, 'Uvani', who was purported to be of Oriental descent. She notes that Uvani appeared when she was in an 'autohypnotic' state (which she describes as being similar to sleep but with some continuing level of awareness). She says that she had little memory of the conversations that Uvani had had with living people present in the room, nor of the information apparently provided from discarnate spirits. But she also describes direct experiences of deceased personalities communicating through clairvoyance (psychic 'seeing') and clairaudience (psychic hearing), seeing 'light' imagery which changed rapidly in her mind's eye, and hearing voices.

Are mediumistic experiences the same the world over? The Candomblé, Kardecismo, and Umbanda mediumship practices of Brazil are also characterised by a belief in spirit agents with whom human beings can interact. The mediumship experiences are induced by a range of practices, including drumming, dancing, singing, and the ingestion of mind-altering drugs. Ritualistic behaviours are also conducted in line with the mythology of their religions, including offering gifts to deities. This mythology proposes the existence of a 'sky god' and other intermediary gods, called orixás, who symbolise the forces of nature (Krippner, 2011). It is understood that mediums can interact with the orixás and that other 'lower' spirit entities (including ancestors) can occupy the bodies of living beings. The term 'incorporation' is employed to describe the voluntary experience of mediums becoming 'taken over' by a spirit, while the term 'possession' is used to describe an equivalent but involuntary experience (Krippner, 2011). It is believed that by channelling the spirits of the orixás, and also through precognition with the help of the orixás, it is possible to obtain information about future disasters and to diagnose and prescribe treatments for illnesses within the community (Hageman et al., 2010).

Summary

Mediumship is a distinctively human experience, which has existed across different eras and persists into the modern era. To date, it may be one of the most visible and accessible ways in which members of the public can seek a paranormal experience. As such, it is a valid topic for psychologists to explore, in terms of the experiences of both the medium and the sitter who is provided with purportedly psychic information.

There are commonalities between the phenomenology of 19th-century Spiritualist mediumship and modern Brazilian mediumship. Both are characterised by a transition into a different state of consciousness, during which state it is considered possible to interact with discarnate spirits who are assumed to be in the 'spirit world'. Such spirits sometimes embody them and speak through them. In the trance state, mediums claim to be able to obtain information paranormally, from deceased spirits.

Cognitive explanations

Cognitive explanations for the phenomena observed in mental mediumship have particularly focused on those interpreting the information provided by mediums. One such explanation hinges on the idea that most people are wired to find meaningful connections between unrelated events and see patterns where none actually exist. This is known as apophenia, or the tendency to make the type one error (Brugger, 2001).

Apophenia can be applied to the 'cross correspondences', one of the more convincing pieces of evidence from mediumship research for the survival of human consciousness (which we discuss in the later section on psi explanations). These are records of the claimed communication of deceased members of the Society for Psychical Research (particularly Frederic Myers), which appeared in the transcripts of several mediums. The information only made sense when all of these transcripts were considered together, hence the name 'cross correspondences'. Moreman (2003) has proposed that these correspondences may be explained by chance coincidence – that the apparently related and meaningful information that seemed to emerge from examining these scripts was actually due to random events, rather than being directed by some discarnate intelligence that hid messages in their communications with mediums. Moreman assembled a group of postgraduate students in

English literature (in an attempt to mimic the classical knowledge of early SPR members). He asked them to look at a series of scripts that were created by combining five randomly selected passages from books. Their task was to find as many correspondences and coincidences as possible. A series of 'cross correspondences' were found, leading Moreman to conclude that people may see meaning in randomness in the communication of mediums.

Cognitive explanations for mediumship have also focused on the use of Barnum statements in psychic readings. Barnum statements are generalised statements that apply to a large proportion of the population. For example, many of us can agree with statements such as 'you are about to come into some money' and 'you have a friend who is unwell'. Roe (1996) notes that Barnum statements may be used in psychic readings, so that people may readily agree with the statements that a medium makes.

O'Keeffe and Wiseman (2005) found that the type and length of statements produced by mediums is related to the extent to which that information is endorsed by a client or sitter. For example, longer, more generalised statements were given a higher mean accuracy rating by participants (who acted as sitters) than for short and specific information. Interestingly, Roe (1995) notes that people *are* aware that the information provided by psychics is often of a general nature, but that they still continue to be impressed by other information provided during a reading.

Roe (1991) has presented a hierarchy of 'cold reading' strategies that are used by pseudopsychics (e.g. fake mediums) to convince a client or sitter that they are providing information psychically. The hierarchy has a number of basic strategies upon which other strategies are built. The first level reflects the use of Barnum statements, which are presented to the client to be responded to either positively or negatively. Other filler statements are also included, which reflect trivial information, and 'cradle to the grave' information, which relates to the various life stages that most people go through. The second level is pigeon-holing, the generation of stereotypical statements about the client, based on age, gender, or occupation (which may have been provided at the start of the reading), the type of clothing worn, their manner of speech, and so on. Level three reflects 'cold reading', where the pseudopsychic employs non-verbal feedback (how the client responds to information) to generate more specific information about the client. Finally, level four is 'warm reading', which employs open questions or statements to which the client responds or direct 'fishing' for information, encouraging them to talk about themselves. This information is then re-presented to the client as though it came from the psychic.

Summary

Cognitive explanations focus mainly on the psychology of those interpreting the information provided by mediums. Finding meaningful connections between unrelated information (chance coincidence/apophenia) may explain some paranormal claims. Pseudopsychics (and some mediums) employ a hierarchy of strategies when providing information to sitters. This includes the use of Barnum-like statements (statements designed to apply to many members of the population), which may be particularly convincing when more information is provided, and information is general rather than specific. The use of general 'filler information', stereotype-driven pigeon-holing, cold reading strategies, and warm reading strategies, may also contribute to a reading being considered to be more convincing.

◉ Personality explanations

When adopting a personality approach to mediumship it is important to consider that mediumship incorporates both the experience of the medium him- or herself and the experience of the sitter. Indeed, there may be personality components which predispose certain people towards becoming a medium or to mediumistic experiences. Likewise, there may be personality characteristics which predispose certain people towards a meaningful interpretation of the messages provided by mediums.

◉ Mediums

We will begin by exploring the personality profiles of mediums, with special consideration of the extent to which the experiences associated with mediumship equate to psychopathology.

Some research indicates that mediums display high levels of dissociation (Laria, 2000; Reinsel, 2003). Dissociation encompasses "a broad spectrum of experiences ranging from common experiences in normal populations (e.g. transient experiences of absorption or imaginative involvement while driving, reading or watching television) to more pathological forms (characterized by dissociative amnesia, derealization, depersonalization and altered self-perception)" (Pérez-Fabello & Compos, 2011, p. 44). Dissociation may be measured psychometrically (using the Dissociative Experiences Scale [DES]), with people displaying individual differences in their proneness to dissociative states. It is related to the traits of fantasy-proneness and imaginative absorption that we discussed in Chapter 3.

The history of thinking on dissociation may be traced back to writing and research on mediumship (Alvarado, 2008b). Indeed, the trance states, automatic writing, and experiences of other entities which are associated with mental mediums might all be associated with these dissociative states. Neppe and Palmer (2009), for example, consider that the mediumistic trance is a dissociative state in which the medium experiences mental processes, including voice phenomena, which *seem* to derive from a source outside of the self, and that in the context of a séance these externally derived perceptions are labelled as discarnate spirits.

Several authors have explored the commonality between mediumship and the extreme form of dissociation, dissociative identity disorder (DID) (Braude, 1995; Moreira-Almeida, Neto & Cardeña, 2008; Reinsel, 2003). Braude (1995) notes that there are superficial similarities between the two experiences. For example, the personality of the medium and 'primary' personality are bland in comparison to the personalities of the alternative personalities and spirit visitors; experients are often unaware of what has taken place during the time that an alternative personality/spirit is in control; the switching between different personalities seems similar to the experience of being visited or taken over by different spirit communicators; and there is evidence that mediums and those with DID are engaging in some form of 'role play' (at an unconscious level). As these patterns are not consistently present, he notes that comparing the phenomenology of DID and mediumship does not provide strong evidence that mediumship is the same as DID. Other research has undertaken more direct comparisons between DID and mediumship and found that mediums display very good mental health, in contrast to those suffering from DID (Moreira-Almeida et al., 2008; Reinsel, 2003). Other research has found health differences between younger and older mediums. This implies that the (dissociative) experiences associated with mediumship may become healthier as the medium develops (Negro, Palladino-Negro & Louzã, 2002). Seligman (2005b) has argued that within Brazilian Candomblé mediumship, rather than being a pathological experience, dissociation can act as a beneficial therapeutic mechanism which is learned as a result of religious participation. Indeed, Roxburgh (2010) found that mediums scored higher on measures of mental health than non-medium controls (as well as scoring higher on openness-to-experience, extraversion, and neuroticism, correlates of anomaly proneness that were discussed in Chapter 3).

Dissociative experiences may also be placed into the realm of normal experiences, enhancing human potential and creativity (Pérez-Fabello & Compos, 2011). As such, this presents a challenge to the pathological perspective on dissociative mediumship experiences. Cases exist in which mediums were apparently able to produce great creative works while in a dissociative trance; for example, Mrs Curran's mediumship experiences as 'Patience Worth' produced writing that she would not have been able to achieve in her usual waking state (Braude, 1995; Cory, 1919). Thus, Braude considers that there are psychological advantages to the perception that information is coming from *outside* the self, even if it actually derives from an unconscious part of the self.

Summary

The altered state of consciousness experienced by the mental medium may be an example of a dissociative state of consciousness. This does not imply that mediumship is pathological, however, as mediums actually display very good mental health. Mediums may be prone to enter dissociative states. The dissociative state accessed in mediumship may reflect an awareness of information which actually derives from the self, but appears to derive from another, external source (labelled as a discarnate spirit).

The sitters

We will now consider the personality profiles of the sitter/interpreter. It has been claimed that those who believe in the paranormal are less able to think critically as compared with sceptical individuals. However, as we noted in Chapter 3, this is an over-simplistic hypothesis.

Although Barnum statements are designed to appeal to *all* people, some personality types are more likely to apply them to themselves. For example, Furnham and Varian (1988) found that those who score high on the personality dimension of neuroticism are more likely to accept Barnum statements as describing their own personality. This was particularly the case when statements had a high 'base rate' (this means that there is a greater statistical likelihood of an event actually occurring) and if the statements were positive in their nature.

Recent research has found that scoring high on positive schizotypy and cognitive disorganisation (two aspects of the personality construct of schizotypy that was discussed in Chapter 3) is also associated with the tendency to apply Barnum statements to the self (Claridge, Clark, Powney & Hassan, 2008). Likewise, Mason and Budge (2011) explored how schizotypy and self-referential thinking related to the endorsement of four different types of Barnum statement (favourable and unfavourable personality descriptions, computer-generated readings, and horoscope-based readings). They found that both self-referential thinking and positive schizotypy predicted the extent to which people endorsed these statements.

It seems then that scoring high on questionnaires designed to tap neuroticism and the cognitive–perceptual aspects of schizotypy is associated with the tendency for information to appear to be personally meaningful. It is clear to see how this applies to mediumship, as generalised statements generated by a medium are more likely to be seen as being personally relevant to people who score highly on these traits, even if the statements could be equally applied to anybody.

Summary

People who are more likely to apply general statements to themselves and to be impressed with the readings of mediums display personality profiles indicative of high neuroticism, high positive schizotypy, and high cognitive disorganisation. It may be that those who seek out mediums are motivated to receive information from deceased friends and relatives, and also, they may be primed to consider information that derives from a medium to be more accurate.

Biological explanations

Despite the dominance of the biological paradigm, there has been surprisingly little research undertaken on biological correlates of mediumship. However, a recent chapter by Hageman et al. (2010) presents an excellent review of biological theories as well as describes the results of some research on mediums in Brazil. They suggest that certain areas of the brain – in particular the limbic system – underpin the state of dissociation which is associated with mediumistic trance. Winkelman (2000) has proposed that dissociation may be biologically explained by several brain areas. Firstly, there is a shift towards right hemispheric dominance (in people who are right handed, the left hemisphere usually dominates). Dissociative states are also characterised by a dominance of the **parasympathetic nervous system** – high-voltage slow theta waves which originate in the limbic system. The limbic system (the hippocampal-septal region of the brain and the amygdala) may precipitate a dissociative state of consciousness as it modulates the survival drives and the release of neurotransmitters and opiates from other areas of the brain – in particular, the hypothalamus and pituitary gland. The hypothalamus is particularly implicated in dissociation, hallucinations, analgesia, and amnesia, which were noted earlier as phenomenal features of the mediumistic state of consciousness. It is also the case that the hypothalamus is responsible for the control of the sympathetic and parasympathetic nervous systems.

Hageman et al. note that practices which induce a dominance of parapsympathetic activity are employed as part of mediumistic rituals in modern Brazil. This is often achieved by excessive sympathetic activation, for example, as a result of drumming, chanting, and dancing. In the Spiritualist era this may have been achieved via the use of breath, for example, via hyperventilation. Indeed Grof (ND) has explored how breathwork may induce altered states of consciousness. Altered states of consciousness may also arise in a more traditional manner via arousal – being in a relaxed and sleep-like, perhaps hypnagogic state of consciousness (McCreery, 1997).

Two in-depth physiological studies have recently been undertaken with Brazilian mediums. The first study explored the psychophysiology of two mediums. Both mediums were asked to *imagine* being incorporated by a spirit entity (rather than undergoing the actual mediumship procedure). Different and incongruent/paradoxical psychophysiological outcomes were apparent for both of these mediums. In particular, there was an incongruence between the central nervous system and the autonomic nervous system. Specifically, there was a reduction in sympathetic vaso-constriction and increased muscle tension during the imagination. There was also an increase in alpha activity of the brain. Muscle tension is consistent with intrusive cognitions, but in contrast these mediums felt calm rather than agitated.

The authors note that this pattern is consistent with other physiological studies with mediums, and that this fits with character observations of mediums who exhibit conflicting characteristics: being critical, rational, and practical at the same time as deepening their fantasy and emotional reactivity.

The second study found a lack of consistency across the EEG readings of nine mediums whose EEGs were monitored while they went into a trance during the study. The findings ranged from a normal EEG pattern to some EEG slowing (in different areas of the brain). As such, this research does not support the idea that there is one brain state characteristic of mediumistic trance. Mediums may therefore each enter slightly different types of altered states of consciousness. Or, it may be that biological factors do not necessarily match the subjective state of awareness. It is also the case that, to date, there has been no research addressing how psychophysiology differs from waking to trance states in mediums.

Summary

Biological approaches towards mediumship have explored the psychophysiology behind the mediumistic trance as a dissociative state. With advancing technology it has been possible to explore a variety of psychophysiological indices while mediums are in the trance state. Research indicates that mediums may exhibit an interesting paradoxical biological pattern while they are in a trance, such that they are simultaneously calm and stressed. Other research indicates that other biological measures were not found to be consistent across different mediums, implying a dissociation between subjective state of consciousness and their biology.

👁 Social explanations

Mediumship occurs within different cultural contexts. This may be classical Spiritualism or modern Spiritualism which occurs within the context of the Christian church or in other religious contexts, such as the Candomblé religion of north-eastern Brazil. Or, it may be secular. Research has explored the role of the medium within different cultures (Edge, 1993; Seligman, 2005a; 2005b). These include the role of healer, whereby mediums work to obtain diagnoses and treatments for those who are physically and mentally unwell (Hageman et al., 2010). In the more secular culture of the West mediums provide psychological counselling for bereaved people (Roxburgh, 2010; Walter, 2008) or may play the role of an entertainer (Roe, 1998).

Other social perspectives on mediumship have explored how the social medium of language performs social actions; for example, how mediums communicate with their audience in stage demonstrations (Wooffitt & Gilbert, 2008). Other work has explored the language interactions between the medium and the sitter in dyadic (two person) interactions (Wooffitt, 2001; 2007). This work has employed conversation analysis to explore how language is used to create a shared understanding that psychic ability has been demonstrated. This approach is neutral in terms of the ontological reality of spirits. Wooffitt (2001; 2007) notes that mediums tend to employ a series of three-part 'turns', whereby information is presented, responded to (by the sitter) and then an attempt is made to demonstrate that it derives from a paranormal source. More specifically, the first turn reflects a question or statement which implies or hints at knowledge pertaining to the sitter, the second turn reflects some (minimal) acceptance of that statement by the sitter, and the third turn often includes descriptions of deceased beings and information portrayed as deriving from a spirit, in order to demonstrate that information actually derives from a paranormal source. Wooffitt (2007) notes that similar turns also appear in other demonstrations of apparent psychic ability.

Recently, Wooffitt, and Gilbert (2008) explored the interaction between a medium and a larger audience and how this is choreographed in a secular context. They were interested in the mechanisms that led people to believe that the medium is indeed communicating with spirits. As spirits are invisible to the audience, it is through language that their presence is 'made visible'. As with the dyadic interactions, they found that the medium employs reoccurring language sequences. This includes a question about a deceased person, a request that audience members should respond to his impressions quickly (with a yes or no response), and an attempt to demonstrate that the information is derived paranormally. It is argued that these patterns of language use can manage the audience and render them more likely to participate in the event, in addition to encouraging people to accept events as genuinely deriving from a discarnate source.

Further work, taking a phenomenological approach, has illustrated the importance of the social context for interpreting anomalous experiences as being indicative of mediumship; for example, growing up in a family that endorses this view. Social networks play a supportive role, helping potential mediums to interpret anomalous experiences (such as hearing voices after the death of a loved one) in the framework of mediumship, and as being healthy rather than being indicative of mental illness (Roxburgh, 2010). Roxburgh (2010) suggests that the social role of being a medium with a counselling role might itself act as a supportive 'buffer' against stress.

Summary

Social explanations of mediumship have focused on cultural differences (and similarities) in the role of mediumship in a given culture. Modern mediumship practice is undertaken in religious, healing, and secular contexts (where it holds an entertainment role). The language employed within mediumistic exchanges has been explored by a number of researchers in recent years, in particular by Wooffitt and colleagues. This has taken a neutral stance on the ostensible reality of information received by mediums and instead has focused on *how* language is employed in the interaction between the medium and the sitter to provide evidence for the afterlife, which seems to take the form of a series of three 'turns' between the medium and the sitter/members of the audience. Further, mediumship may provide a social (explanatory) framework for anomalous experiences.

👁 Psi explanations

Traditional parapsychological approaches to mediumship have explored the hypothesis that the medium is actually obtaining information from a discarnate source (i.e. a person who is no longer living). This research has sought to evaluate both the accuracy of the information provided by the medium, and whether the alleged spirit controls and spirit entities actually relate to deceased people (Alvarado, 2003). Early researchers attempted to find evidence that the claimed discarnate had actually existed. A third hypothesis is that the medium may be acquiring information by psi, via telepathy, clairvoyance, or precognition on the part of the medium. This is known as the *superpsi* hypothesis (Braude, 2003). The idea that living minds (including that of the medium) might influence mediumistic impressions dates back to thinkers in the Victorian era (Alvarado, 2003).

Exploring the accuracy of information obtained during mediumship

Since the 1880s researchers have been interested in the accuracy of information that is provided by mental mediums in a séance. Early research gauged the accuracy of information given to sitters at a séance, but it was soon realised that information might be picked up from the sitter (telepathically or via sensory cueing). To attempt to control for this, research employed 'proxy' sitters to sit with the medium on behalf of a third person who was not present. Sir William Barrett later devised the 'book test' which asked mediums to obtain information from a deceased personality about the contents and location of a book which could then be looked up by investigators. Several such book tests took place, which often seemed very convincing, that is, information contained in the book passage corresponded to information provided by the medium. Interestingly, some early work attempted to take chance coincidence into account (Roll, 2006).

'Drop in communicators' are discarnate spirits who spontaneously appear in séances and who are unknown to the medium or any of the sitters present. If it could be demonstrated that there were no normal means by which mediums knew of the personality of the drop in communicator, and evidence for that person's existence could be found based on information that the medium gave, then, it could be argued that the medium was displaying genuine psi ability. However, some of these cases could have been due to the medium reading obituaries in newspapers, although other cases cannot be so easily explained.

The cross correspondences have been employed as evidence in support of a survival hypothesis. Between 1901 and 1932 a series of mediumistic communications were received by several mediums which included classical (ancient Greek and Latin) references which made no sense when the scripts were considered in isolation. However, a 'key' appeared in one of the scripts which enabled the scripts to be considered together. Together, they appeared to be providing a message from deceased members of the SPR, including F. W. H. Myers, who was a classical scholar. The idea that this may be due to coincidence was explored by Verrall (one of the mediums involved in the cross correspondences). More recently, Moreman (2003) found that impressive coincidences between randomly selected literary passages are possible (as we have already discussed). However, Roll (2006) notes that one of the more intriguing features of the cross correspondences was that the scripts often contained the sudden introduction of content that seemed unconnected with other contents of the script.

Thinking scientifically → **How to design a mediumship study**

O'Keeffe and Wiseman (2005) note that there are several issues to consider when designing a study to evaluate the accuracy of mediumistic information given to a sitter. In such studies sitters rate the accuracy of statements that mediums have given them.

Firstly, a well-designed study should control for the possibility of sensory leakage. This includes removing the possibility of verbal and unconscious cueing from sitters which may be used by mediums to ascertain whether the information they are providing is correct or not.

Secondly, researchers should accurately assess the generality of statements in the mediums' scripts, given that people are prone to apply Barnum statements to themselves. This may be approached by asking sitters to rate the accuracy of a series of statements, which include their own amid those for other sitters (decoy readings). However, it should be remembered that some statements are not independent from other statements. For example, the statement that someone has recently lost someone *who is male* and a second statement that the deceased *had a beard* are actually related to one another. This should be taken into account with the statistical evaluation of statement endorsement. O'Keeffe and Wiseman note that some prior research has evaluated statements as if they are independent, which could inflate the findings in favour of the psi hypothesis.

Finally, there is need for blind judging of the scripts by sitters (sitters should be blind to which of the scripts was intended for them). This includes the random presentation of the transcript and decoy transcripts making sure that subtle cues (e.g. regarding the time of day and day of the week) are removed from the transcripts.

Another intriguing phenomenon is that of xenoglossy, the apparent fluency in a language other than the native language of the medium during the mediumistic trance. Where this has occurred researchers have sought normal explanations, which include cryptomnesia, obtaining the information from a normal source at an unconscious level, such as being exposed to the language in a book or on the radio or television. Some individuals classified as 'savants' are able to read very rapidly and have incredible memory for information. The savant Daniel Tammet is able to learn a new language from scratch within a very short time period (Tammet, 2006). Hughes (2010) suggests that all individuals may hold the potential for such skills under certain circumstances.

Other early research applied statistical methods to the accuracy of information provided by mediums for specific sitters (O'Keeffe & Wiseman, 2005). In recent years there has been something of a resurrection of research into this area. The resurgence in mediumship research began with research by Schwartz (2002) and Roy and Robertson (2004), with several other studies emerging since that time (Beischel, 2007; Jensen & Cardeña, 2009; Kelly & Arcangel, 2011).

O'Keeffe and Wiseman (2005) observe that the research findings on the accuracy of mediumistic communications have been mixed, with some researchers finding evidence for psi and others finding no such evidence, a pattern which continues to this day. Despite some ingenious research methods designed to rule out normal explanations for mediumship, many experiments have still exhibited other methodological problems. However, more recent research has employed tighter methods and has even included **triple blind** designs: the medium is blind to information about the sitter and feedback from them (both before and during the reading); the rater is blind to the origin of the readings during scoring; and the experimenters who interact with the medium during the readings, and with the rater during scoring, are also blind about information about the rater and the discarnate personality associated with the rater

(Kelly & Arcangel, 2011). Current research at the Windbridge Institute uses a quintuple blind method (Beischel, 2007). Unfortunately, the topic remains taboo for many modern researchers who have an interest in parapsychology, and there are few laboratories which have sought to replicate this work.

The source of the information

Researchers have also been interested in ascertaining the source of the information provided by mediums. Some researchers were interested in the idea of survival after bodily death, but realised that if they could demonstrate ESP among living minds, it would be difficult to ascertain the source of any demonstrated psi awareness (Alvarado, 2003).

Some modern researchers have attempted to explore the source of information and have claimed that their work supports the hypothesis that there is communication from the afterlife (e.g. Schwartz, 2011). However, in line with earlier researchers (such as J. B. Rhine), Bem (2005) notes that "it may be more difficult than it first appears to distinguish alleged communication with deceased persons from extended forms of psi among the living. Because claims for medium-mediated communication with the deceased are more extraordinary to me than claims for psi, I will always opt for the latter when both explanations can account for the data" (p. 182).

Other researchers have adopted a more process-oriented approach and have explored differences in the subjective experiences that mediums have when attempting to pick up information from a living versus a discarnate source. For example, Rock and Beischel (2008) explored differences in phenomenological experiences when mediums gave readings for a discarnate source as compared to a living source. They found that mediums experienced greater intensity of negative affect, higher levels of alteration in body image, greater sense of time alteration, a greater sense of spiritual meaningfulness, higher internal absorption, a larger alteration in state of consciousness, less self-awareness, less control, and a lower score on memory in the discarnate condition as compared to the control condition. Although this does not determine the source of psi, a future study is planned which aims to evaluate differences in the subjective experiences of mediums when they are blind to whether they are attempting to acquire information from a discarnate or a living source.

Summary

Psi hypotheses have been explored by assessing the accuracy of information provided by mediums (attempting to prevent knowledge being obtained by normal means). This body of research is mixed in its outcomes, with some studies finding evidence indicative of ESP while others do not. With increasing methodological improvements and more replications in other laboratories it may eventually be possible to undertake a meta-analysis to see what the overall picture is for this type of research. The question of the source of information (e.g. ESP versus discarnate personalities) is harder to test, and thus, recent research has focused more on phenomenological differences between mediums' subjective psychic experiences with the living and deceased beings.

Thinking critically about mediumship research

What is the best explanatory model for mediumship experiences? Mediumship experiences are complicated and many of the approaches evaluated in this chapter seem to be persuasive. We have observed that mediumship should be explored as an interaction between the medium and the sitter and that the psychology of both the medium and the person interpreting the information is important in understanding the psychology of mediumship experiences.

It seems very likely that mediums are entering a dissociative state of consciousness, and that they may be wired to do so in terms of their biology and personality structure. However, research from a biological perspective does not appear to be consistent, despite the existence of a strong theoretical case. Differences in biology may imply that there are differences in the ways in which each medium engages with the 'mediumistic trance'. These states might be as unique as the people experiencing them. The state which is being accessed does appear to be dissociative in nature, although the idea that mediumship is pathological can be challenged as many mediums are healthy and adapted. It may alternatively be that states associated with mediumship (dissociation) enable access to different 'selves' or 'potentials', some of which may have great creative potential (as in the case of Patience Worth). A classic dissociation argument would suggest that the medium does not acknowledge that these selves are part of the self, but only seem to derive from an external (discarnate or other) source.

There is a lot of support for a cognitive perspective, particularly for the sitters. This suggests that information provided by mediums may sometimes be Barnum statements which appear to apply to the self, when they would apply equally well to other people. The discourse between the medium and the sitter may elevate the chances of this application, as the social turns appear to function to firstly demonstrate knowledge, via the generation of statements which are responded to very quickly by the sitters, followed by an attempt to provide evidence of the existence of the spirits who are providing the information to the medium. This language interaction is clearly demonstrated in a number of contexts, and does appear to, at least superficially, dovetail with cognitive arguments of Barnum statements, which are general statements that apply to a large proportion of the population (and as such, should apply to someone in the audience at a psychic event). However, a social interpretation is neutral as to the reality of the interaction with alleged spirits, and researchers are open to the idea that there could be an ostensible spirit providing the information which is instantiated into the series of turns. For example, Roe (1995) has observed that people are aware of the general nature of a lot of information, but still often come away from readings convinced of some aspects of the reading as genuinely applying to them.

The picture becomes more complex when we consider the nature of the other personalities, and that sometimes the medium seems to provide information to which they should not have access. The question is whether the other self/information derives from another part of the medium's personality or psyche, the result of accessing ESP information or the influence of a discarnate spirit. The paranormal approaches towards mediumship are mixed in their findings, and although there appears to be some evidence for the demonstration of psi information under laboratory conditions by some researchers, other researchers have failed to find such evidence.

Further reading

Braude, S. (1995). *First person plural*. Lanham, MD: Rowman & Littlefield.

Hunter, J. & Luke. D. (Eds.). (2012). *Talking with the spirits: Ethnographies from between the worlds*. Brisbane: Daily Grail.

Chapter 10

Concluding comments

Rather than summarise the contents of this book, we will end by making a few speculations and comments about implications and applications: the implications of what we have covered for our understanding of consciousness; and potentially important applications of some of this knowledge, in particular for mental health practitioners.

However, first, now that you have arrived at the end of this book, let us look once again at the case of Agnes Paquet. How might she have benefited from the accumulation of knowledge that has been achieved in the 120 years since her experience was reported? Perhaps two things might have struck her initially. First, she might be surprised at the diversity of opinions and models on the nature and implications of anomalous experiences, and the lack of consensus between these approaches. For example, despite the slow accumulation of research over the intervening century, the question of whether or not Agnes Paquet's crisis apparition might have contained information that was acquired through paranormal means is ultimately undecided and highly contentious. Likewise, the implications for her well-being are unclear and depend upon a matrix of factors that are only just beginning to be understood (such as the degree of social support received; also the role of protective trait and cognitive factors, such as low cognitive disorganisation and a coherent belief system with which to interpret her experience). Second, she might have been surprised by the methodologies currently employed, the accumulation of knowledge about the human brain, and the reliance on statistics to answer profound questions about human experience.

Agnes Paquet might have seen glimpses of herself in Chapter 3 on individual differences of traits that are predictive of being prone to anomalous experiences. She may have recognised herself as sociable and interested in new experiences, prone to daydreaming and having a vivid imagination. She might have had an external locus of control, seeing her fate in the hands of more powerful 'others'. Or perhaps she often relied upon hunches and her intuition, or had a strong interest in the arts. She might have held paranormal beliefs to help her have a sense of control over her experiences, which, upon reflection, might have made her more amenable to label her experience as anomalous and veridical. Neurological models relate such traits and beliefs to 'neural interconnectedness', either between the hemispheres or between cortical and sub-cortical regions. Such processing might predispose people to see meaning in randomness and to confuse reality and imagination, underpinning hallucinations and attributions of paranormality. Poor sleep quality and tiredness might exacerbate such processes, as we saw in Chapter 7 on apparitions. Might she be satisfied with the explanations proffered thus far? Perhaps, due to the vivid and intense nature of her experience and her seeming to know of her brother's demise before she was told of it, she would prefer a paranormal explanation.

In the chapter on pseudoscience (Chapter 5) it was identified that parapsychology has the hallmarks of a science, falling a little short on some of the benchmarks of good science but performing better than mainstream science on others. However, the potential for fraud as a possible, if unlikely, explanation for results was considered. The following chapter on methodologies and controversies in parapsychology (Chapter 6) illustrated the methodological rigour and advancements made in the field since Victorian times. However, despite some statistically significant meta-analyses, the evidence is disputed and the subjectivity that enters the analytical process through decision making was revealed. Ultimately, interpretations of this evidence may depend on one's predisposition to believe in paranormal phenomena in the first place. As such, perhaps the notion that Agnes Paquet's apparition of her brother was a projection resulting from a telepathic influence might be a convincing and comforting alternative explanation for her, serving a meaningful and potentially healthy function. Alternatively, given the prevalence of religious beliefs at her time, she may prefer to think that her brother's consciousness survived death.

The word consciousness has many different meanings (Natsoulas, 1987), and here we refer to it as the 'stream of conscious experience', the content of our awareness (James, 1890). The study of anomalistic psychology contributes to our understanding of conscious experience in a number of ways. First, it illustrates how it is a construction. For example, in Chapter 7, on apparitions, we saw that what we perceive is sensitive to 'top down processing' and expectation (affecting, for example, whether we interpret and perceive something ambiguous as being anomalous, such as a ghostly presence). Second, it shows how diverse conscious experience is and how truly extraordinary it is. From experiential variations along a sleep–wake continuum, we may have interjections of dreams into waking experience (as in sleep paralysis, hypnagogic and hypnapompic hallucinations and pseudo-hallucinations and apparitions brought about through poor sleep quality), as well as interjections of waking experience into dreams (as in the case of lucid dreaming and, potentially, out-of-body experiences). We may experience radical alterations in our sense of self, our sense of body, time, our thoughts, images and feelings, to the extent that we appear to float above our body, see things that 'are not there', or have a sense of unity with all things – and to do so is relatively common. Third, and more profoundly, rather than simply enabling us to map out experiential territories and types, anomalistic psychology touches upon philosophical questions about the nature of consciousness and the mind–body problem. The French philosopher René Descartes (1596–1650) described the qualitative distinction between our subjective conscious experience, the 'what it feels like' of awareness (today referred to as 'qualia') and the biological system that houses it, our brain and body, neurons, blood, and all. How, he asked, might these coexist and interact? (Of course the phrase 'mind-body problem' separates 'the two' out before we have started.) Some approaches – called monism – argue that mind and brain are the same (one) thing. Either that they are both 'mind' (idealism), or that they are both 'brain' (materialism) (although 'neutral monism' has been proposed, where both are some unidentified third substance). However, Descartes proposed 'dualism', that the mind and body are separate but interacting substances. This position has prevailed in various forms ever since (for an introduction to this area, refer to Susan Blackmore's book *Consciousness*, 2003). In modern psychology dualism is deeply unfashionable. A reductionistic monist stance is typically assumed, where mind is reduced to brain, or 'epiphenomenalism', where the mind arises from the functioning of the brain, but is like a mirage, producing a kind of puppet show that has no causal functioning and is merely an illusory by-product. (This latter position, though, is actually a weak form of dualism.) Nevertheless, if taken seriously, the findings of parapsychology challenge the contemporary materialistic and epiphenomenal views of consciousness. If our consciousness does leave our body in an out-of-body experience, or if we do still have conscious experience when our brain shows no activity (in a near-death experience), if apparitions are left-over bits of consciousness (which bits?) of deceased persons, and if mediums do communicate with said consciousnesses, then we are forced to reconsider dualism as an option (or potentially some form of neutral monism). If our thoughts are causal and can affect the minds and brains of other people, then they are not mere epiphenomena but may reciprocally affect physical systems. Further, if things like telepathy do occur, then how do we know which of our thoughts are 'ours' or whether they originated in the mind/brain of another? How can we be sure that the inkling that we should pop down to see a friend at a particular time was our idea or theirs? Such notions challenge the idea that each of us is a single bounded self that is separate from other single bounded selves. Paranormal phenomena, such as telepathy and crisis apparitions, if taken as 'real', challenge our conceptualisation of consciousness, suggesting that minds are interconnected and affect each other in ways that are not understood scientifically. As neuroscientists do not yet understand how conscious experience is produced by the brain, this has led to alternative perspectives, such as the notion that the brain is a 'receiver' for consciousness, and that consciousness is elsewhere, more widely distributed, like a satellite television picking up radio signals. The philosophical implications of parapsychology alone, let alone the need for a physical theory with which to support its findings, can seem mind-boggling.

Let us now take a practical perspective. Anomalistic psychology has applied implications for conceptualisations of mental health and medical practice.

As noted in several chapters in this book, anomalous and subjective paranormal experiences are often equated with pathology. There is undoubtedly an overlap with pathology, although the relationship might be better conceptualised as a Venn Diagram, with pathology and anomalous experiences overlapping, suggesting that anomalous experiences may occur in a pathological context (the overlapping area) but also in a healthy context; that is, not all anomalous experiences are pathological. In Chapter 3 we discussed the schizotypy construct, and noted that there are two types of 'anomaly-prone' personality – one associated with better health than the other (Goulding, 2005; Holt, Simmonds-Moore & Moore, 2008). As such, anomalous experiences have the potential to be associated with very good mental health, spiritual experiences, and creativity, but they also have the potential for maladjustment and psychopathology (Clarke, 2001). To illustrate this point, a recent survey found that while some subjective paranormal experiences are associated with conflict or personal trauma, others are life enhancing and positively assimilated into the life of the experient (Montinelli & Parra, 2000). Anomalous experiences (and beliefs) per se may therefore *not* be associated with pathology. Rather, 'health' seems to be more associated with how unusual experiences are managed/controlled and assimilated into the overriding cognitive structure and whether the products of anomalous experiences are useful.

In Chapter 7, on mediumship, the overlaps between mediumship, dissociation, and pathology were examined as a special topic. It was noted that mediums often score higher than other people on measures of dissociation. However, in contrast to a pathological interpretation, mediums actually tend to exhibit very good mental health, particularly when they have been working as mediums for a period of time. This might be because experiences which could potentially relate to pathology become controlled, are occurring within a particular (socially acceptable and often religious) context, and are applied beyond the self (Simmonds-Moore, 2011). Likewise, those reporting out-of-body experiences have been found to be significantly more healthy than a psychiatric group, and a control group of college students (Twemlow et al., 1982). Similar patterns are apparent with other anomalous and subjective paranormal experiences.

If a cognitive deficits or dysfunctional view of anomaly-proneness is taken, then reports of anomalous experiences can but be understood in a negative light. If they are associated with distress then they are likely to be seen as symptomatic of some underlying mental disorder. A person who has had a crisis apparition, for example, and who is struggling to understand this experience, who perhaps cannot sleep, is anxious, and is troubled by their experience, may be referred to a psychiatrist for analysis and may be medicated and perhaps given a diagnostic label. It is therefore a challenge for psychologists, given that we have seen in this book that reports of anomalous experiences can be associated with well-being, to better understand the relationship between anomaly proneness and health. More needs to be learnt about when anomalous experiences may and may not be symptomatic, for example, of schizophrenia. This will avoid unnecessary treatment and distress on the part of experients, while also alerting professionals to genuine illnesses that do require treatment. These issues are complex and special counselling may be required for people who have an anomalous experience and are distressed, unsettled or threatened by them. Such an approach needs to avoid stigmatisation, and perhaps, based on the finding that belief systems predict healthy anomalous experiences, needs to help a person fit their anomalous experience into their worldview (Schofield & Claridge, 2007). Such counselling practices are being developed, particularly at the Institut für Grenzgebiete der Psychologie und Psychohygiene (IGPP) in Freiburg, Germany, and the development of a Spirituality Crisis Network in the UK (Simmonds-Moore, 2011). Such problems have been partially considered in a major innovation in DSM-IV, which added a diagnostic category entitled Religious or Spiritual Problem. This new category sought to improve diagnostic assessments when religious and spiritual issues are involved and improve treatment of such problems by stimulating clinical research. For example, how should religious beliefs and anomalous experiences be treated by a counsellor? If one supports the view that they may be veridical, might one be colluding in a delusion? If they are assumed to be delusional, might one be imposing a disease on a person who is not ill, or ill for other reasons? Thus, anomalistic psychology can help to differentiate factors that are associated with health versus illness and also has implications for how clinicians proceed ethically and therapeutically.

In recent years anomalous experiences and beliefs have become acceptable topics for psychologists and health practitioners (in part, due to their inclusion in the DSM IV). Perhaps, in the coming years clinical approaches might move towards developing ways to encourage healthy anomalous and paranormal experiences, rather than making the erroneous assumption that these experiences are, by their very nature, pathological.

On that note, we reach the end of this book. There is much that still needs to be understood about anomalous experiences and beliefs; for example, developing and testing more comprehensive models of anomaly proneness. Perhaps, some questions, such as whether or not ESP occurs, will remain unanswered for a long time, given the ambiguity of the outcomes and the interactions between belief and statistical evidence and the unclear goal posts that are required for 'proof' or disproof. Whatever your opinion on such matters, we hope that this book has given you a valuable taster of this interesting and controversial field that will inspire you to further reading, reflection, and research.

Further reading

Blackmore, S. (2003). *Consciousness: An introduction*. Abingdon: Hodder & Stoughton.

Beloff, J. (1987). Parapsychology and the mind–body problem. *Inquiry: An Interdisciplinary Journal of Philosophy, 30*, 215–225.

Clarke, I. (Ed.) (2001). *Psychosis and spirituality: Exploring the new frontier*. Philadelphia, PA: Whurr Publishers.

Simmonds-Moore, C. (Ed.) (in press). *Essays on exceptional experiences and health*. Jefferson, NC: McFarland.

Glossary

Absorption The tendency to be absorbed in a particular activity to the exclusion of awareness of other events.

Algorithmic approach A logical approach to problem-solving that requires systematic testing of propositions and sub-propositions.

Apophenia The tendency to see meaning and significance in apparently random events.

Arousal system There are several arousal systems in the human body, but, generally, these pertain to alertness and the extent to which one is prepared to react to stimuli, from being relaxed and relatively unreactive to being alert and ready to respond.

Asomatic A sense of being out of touch with one's body.

Autoscopy The experience of seeing one's body as if one was physically removed from it.

Behaviourists Behaviourism was one of the dominant schools of thought within psychology in the 20th century and is based on the principle that all things that humans do can be considered as behaviours which can be shaped through learning.

Boundary thinness A personality trait characterised by 'thin boundaries', between parts of the mind/brain and the person and the environment.

Causal link A relationship whereby one event or variable can logically be said to cause another.

Clairvoyance *See* Extrasensory perception.

Cognitive deficits hypothesis The notion of faulty cognitive processes at work in the appraisal of anomalous experiences.

Confound An extraneous variable in an experimental design that has not been controlled for and that might therefore better explain any effect on the dependent variable than the independent (or treatment) variable.

Correlation A statistical technique that shows how strongly pairs of variables are related. It cannot be assumed that there is a causal link between the variables even if they have a close relationship.

Correlational *See* Correlation.

Counterfactual closeness Speculation about a more extreme outcome which, counter to fact, did not actually occur but which only nearly did.

Cross-modal mapping The combination of information from different sense modalities.

Demand characteristics An experimental artefact whereby participants conform to the perceived demands of the experiment rather than acting naturally as they are expected to.

Depersonalisation A sense that one's self is not 'really there', such that there is awareness of what oneself is doing but no sense of control over the situation.

Double blind An experimental procedure whereby neither the participants nor the experimenter know which condition is which, and so are blind to whoever is receiving the placebo or control treatment until after the study is complete.

Ecological validity The degree to which the research approximates real-life, as opposed to artificial, situations, measures, and methods.

Electroencephalograph Maps the brain's surface electrical activity, recorded from a network of electrodes on the surface of the skull.

Electronic voice phenomenon The presence of anomalous voices on blank tapes, live audio equipment, or digital voice recorders.

Embodied An emphasis on the role that the body has in shaping consciousness.

Entity encounter experience The encounter with a non-physical entity believed to be sentient; for example, religious visions, fairies or little people, demons, black dog apparitions, and ghosts.

Extrasensory perception (ESP) Paranormal cognition (includes telepathy, clairvoyance, and precognition). The acquisition of information about an external object, event or influence without the use of the known sensory channels or logical inference. Information obtained directly from another organism is termed telepathy, or is termed clairvoyance if the information is obtained directly from any non-living source in real-time. If the information comes from the future it is termed precognition.

Falsification The testing of hypotheses in a manner which attempts to disprove them, rather than support them.

Flow A state of total mental absorption in an activity, accompanied by positive affect and a loss of one's sense of self and time.

Frontal lobe Region of the cerebral cortex that is located in front of the parietal lobe and above and in front of the temporal lobe in both cerebral hemispheres of the mammalian brain.

Geomagnetism The Earth's magnetic field, variations in which can be measured.

Heuristic approach An approach to problem-solving that uses approximate 'rule-of-thumb' solutions to problems that are good enough and which eliminate the need for more accurate but more complex solutions.

Hidden causes Potential causes for coincidences that defy ordinary consideration.

Hyperaesthesia Extreme perceptual sensitivity.

Hypnagogic The state of consciousness upon going to sleep in between being awake and being asleep. It is characterised by vivid imagery and auditory phenomena and is when sleep paralysis experiences can occur.

Hypnopompic The state of consciousness upon waking up, in between being asleep and being awake. *See also* Hypnagogic.

Illusion of control A theory, proposed by Langer, that individuals may assume that they can utilise skill in situations determined only by chance and inappropriately perceive the situation to be controllable.

Instrumental activism The guiding cultural principle that action rather than inaction is the more preferable social function.

Introspection The act of looking inward and reporting upon the contents of one's consciousness.

Judgement by availability The evaluation of coincidences based on obviously available probabilities.

Law of truly large numbers Given a big enough sample even very unlikely events are probable.

Magical thinking Thinking characterised by an absence of differentiation between the self and the natural and social worlds, such that coincidences and correlations are thought to have a causal relationship.

Melatonin A hormone produced by the pineal gland that helps to maintain the body's circadian rhythm.

Meta-analysis A statistical procedure for analysing homogeneous series of experiments with mixed results, allowing for the interpretation of the findings as a whole, such as with the ganzfeld series of experiments.

Metachoric experience A hallucinatory experience which seems to be continuous with waking reality.

Mystical experience The individual's direct experience of a relationship to an apparently fundamental but usually unperceivable reality. A profound, temporary, passive, and indescribable transpersonal experience.

Need for control A concept in psychology whereby an individual's need to control events can be quantified.

Occam's razor The selection of a hypothesis that makes the fewest new assumptions, when competing hypotheses are equal in other respects.

Ontology A metaphysical enquiry into the nature of existence and ultimate reality, such as the existence of God or the nature of mind.

Operant conditioning A type of learning that modifies behaviour through its association with a stimulus. *See also* Behaviourists.

Parasympathetic nervous system Part of the autonomic nervous system that is associated with the body at rest.

Parietal lobe Region of the cerebral cortex that is located behind the frontal lobe and above the temporal and occipital lobes in both cerebral hemispheres of the mammalian brain.

Parsimony/parsimonious The simplest or most economical explanation, conforming to Occam's razor.

Peak experience A transient moment of self-actualisation. *See also* Self-actualisation and Flow.

Phenomenology The scientific study of immediate experience. Also, the philosophical doctrine, proposed by Edmund Husserl, that advocates the phenomenological approach as the basis of psychology.

Positive schizotypy A personality trait that is indicative of a tendency to have unusual cognitive-perceptual experiences, such as déjà vu, pseudo-hallucinations, and delusions.

Precognition *See* Extrasensory perception.

Precognitive dreams Dreams incorporating information obtained by precognition.

Prefrontal cortex Part of the frontal lobe in the brain which is involved in planning behaviours.

Principle of equivalent odd matches   Principle by which some 'odd matches' are considered to be less probable than other odd matches that are actually equally improbable. Applies particularly to coincidences that involve oneself as opposed to those occurring to others.

Problem-solving   A branch of research in psychology that explores the logical and cognitive processes required to solve problems.

Prospective experiments   A study whereby participants are selected for the likelihood of experiencing a particular variable and then studied both before and after to see what the effects might be. This is an advanced alternative to ordinary quasi-experimental designs and aims to overcome problems in making a causal link.

Psi   (pronounced like 'sigh') A general term for ESP and PK.

Psychodynamic functions hypothesis   The view that paranormal beliefs are need-serving, such that there is a need to believe.

Psychokinesis (PK)   Literally mind movement. Also known as telekinesis and mind over matter. The direct influence of mental intention on the physical world without the need for motor actions of the body.

Psychosis   Psychopathology associated with a loss of contact with reality, with symptoms such as hallucinations and delusions.

Quasi-experimental   An experimental design which does not randomly allocate participants to groups and so causal links cannot be inferred from the findings. *See also* True experiment.

Rapid eye movement (REM)   One of the two distinct stages of sleep associated with eye movements, a specific pattern of electroencephalograph activity, and paralysis of the body muscles. Dreaming is usually more bizarre during REM sleep.

Reductionism   Considering phenomena in terms of their most simple parts.

Remote staring detection   The anomalous detection of being stared at by an unseen observer, which, if this occurs without the use of the ordinary senses, is a type of extrasensory perception.

Replication   The re-running of a research study to establish if the findings of the original study are repeatable and robust.

Self-actualisation   A term used in humanistic psychology to refer to the full realisation of a person's potential, coined by Abraham Maslow.

Sense of presence   An experience (that may just be 'felt') of a presence of another consciousness in the absence of a real person.

Sensory leakage The unintended transmission of information via ordinary sensory channels in an ESP experiment, such as non-verbal communication or signs of extra handling on the target image.

Sleep paralysis The feeling of being paralysed while the mind is awake.

Social constructionism A sociological theory of knowledge that considers how cognitions and other psychological and social phenomena are shaped by social interactions.

Social marginality hypothesis The sociological approach that considers members of socially marginalised and disadvantaged groups as being the most susceptible to paranormal beliefs, because such beliefs are empowering for the disenfranchised.

Socially transmitted The means by which customs are adopted directly from one's immediate culture, such as family, friends, and the media.

Subliminal The reception of information through the sensory channels below the threshold of conscious awareness.

Suggestibility Being receptive to ideas and suggestions of others, particularly in regard to hypnosis.

Syllogistic reasoning The logical evaluation of whether a conclusion necessarily follows from two given premises.

Sympathetic nervous system Part of the autonomic nervous system that underpins the 'flight or fight' response, mobilising the body for action under stress, making the heart rate faster, for example.

Synaesthesia A sensory experience in one modality that triggers an experience in another modality, such as colours associated with words.

Telepathy *See* Extrasensory perception.

Temporal lobe Region of the cerebral cortex that is located on the lower side portion in both cerebral hemispheres of the mammalian brain.

Transliminality A personality variable indicative of cognitive-perceptual material being more likely to cross the threshold into awareness.

Triple blind Like a double-blind experiment, except that the person doing the analysis does not know which condition is which either. *See also* Double blind.

True experiment An experiment in which participants are randomly allocated to experimental and control conditions so as to eliminate biases in grouping. Only true experiments can establish causal links between variables. *See also* Quasi-experimental.

Vignette A short description of an event, behaviour or person used to control information provided to participants in psychology experiments.

Worldview hypothesis Interprets paranormal belief as the product of a common human approach to 'making sense of the world'.

References

Albas, D. & Albas, C. (1989). Modern magic: The case of examinations. *The Sociological Quarterly, 30*, 603–613.

Alcock, J. (1981). *Parapsychology: Science or magic?* Oxford: Pergamon.

Alcock, J. (2003). Give the null hypothesis a chance: Reasons to remain doubtful about the existence of psi. *Journal of Consciousness Studies, 10*, 29–50.

Alcock, J., Burns, J. & Freeman, A. (Eds.) (2003). Psi Wars: Getting to grips with the paranormal. *Journal of Consciousness Studies, 10*(6–7), 1–246.

Alcock, J. & Otis, L. (1980). Critical thinking and belief in the paranormal. *Psychological Reports, 46*, 479–482.

Alvarado, C. (1982a). Recent OBE detection studies: A review. *Theta, 10*, 35–38.

Alvarado, C. (1982b). ESP during out-of-body experiences: A review of experimental studies. *Journal of Parapsychology, 46*, 209–230.

Alvarado, C. (1989). Trends in the study of out-of-body experiences: An overview of developments since the nineteenth century. *Journal of Scientific Exploration, 3*, 27–42.

Alvarado, C. (2000). Out-of-body experiences. In E. Cardeña, S. Lynn & S. Krippner (Eds.), *Varieties of anomalous experience: Examining the scientific evidence* (pp. 183–218). Washington, DC: American Psychological Association.

Alvarado, C. (2003). The concept of survival of bodily death and the development of parapsychology. *Journal of the Society for Psychical Research, 67*, 65–95.

Alvarado, C. (2005). Historical writings on parapsychology and its contribution to psychology. *PsyPioneer,* December 2005, p. 270. Accessed in March 2010 from: www.woodlandway.org/PDF/20. PSYPIONEERFoundedbyLesliePrice.pdf

Alvarado, C. (2008a). Apparitions of the living seen shortly before their deaths. *Journal of Near-Death Studies, 27,* 77–80.

Alvarado, C. (2008b). Note on online books and articles about the history of dissociation. *Journal of Trauma & Dissociation, 9,* 107–118.

Alvarado, C. & Zingrone, N. (2008). Headaches and out-of-body experiences: A research note. *Journal of the Society for Psychical Research, 72,* 107–110.

American Psychiatric Association. (1994). *The Diagnostic and Statistical Manual of Mental Disorders* (DSM-IV).

Arcangel., D. (2008). Placement of apparitions. *Journal of Near-Death Studies, 26,* 303–306.

Astin, J., Harkness, E. & Ernst, E. (2000). The efficacy of "distant healing": A systematic review of randomized trials. *Annals of Internal Medicine, 132,* 903–910.

Atwater, F. (2004). The hemi-sync process. Accessed in February 2008 from: http://www.monroeinstitute.com/PBWeditor/upload/File/the_hemisync_process_2004.pdf.

Auton, H., Pope, J. & Seeger, G. (2003). Isn't it strange: Paranormal beliefs and personality traits. *Social Behavior and Personality, 31,* 711–720.

Ayeroff, F. & Abelson, R. (1976). ESP and ESB: Belief in personal success at mental telepathy. *Journal of Personality and Social Psychology, 2,* 240–247.

Ayers, L., Beaton, S. & Hunt, H. (1999). The significance of transpersonal experiences, emotional conflict, and cognitive abilities in creativity. *Empirical Studies of the Arts, 17,* 73–82.

Bak, M., Myin-Germeys, I., Delespaul, P., Vollebergh, W., de Graaf, R. & van Os, J. (2003). Do different psychotic experiences differentially predict need for care in the general population? *Comprehensive Psychiatry, 46,* 192–199.

Barker, J. (1967). Premonitions of the Aberfan disaster. *Journal of the Society of Psychical Research, 44,* 169–181.

Barrett, W. (1911). *Psychical research.* London: Williams & Norgate.

Beischel, J. (2007). Contemporary methods used in laboratory-based mediumship research. *Journal of Parapsychology, 71,* 37–68.

Beloff, J. (1993). *Parapsychology: A Concise History*. London: Athlone Press.

Bem, D. (1994). Response to Hyman. *Psychological Bulletin, 115*, 25–27.

Bem, D. (2005). Review of the book "The afterlife experiments: Breakthrough scientific evidence of life after death". *Journal of Parapsychology, 69*, 173–183.

Bem, D. (2011). Feeling the future: Experimental evidence for anomalous retroactive influences on cognition and affect. *Journal of Personality and Social Psychology, 100*, 407–425.

Bem, D. & Honorton, C. (1994). Does psi exist? Replicable evidence for an anomalous process of information transfer. *Psychological Bulletin, 115*, 4–18.

Bem, D., Palmer, J. & Broughton, R. (2001). Updating the ganzfeld database: A victim of its own success? *Journal of Parapsychology, 65*, 207–218.

Bender, H. (1966). The Gotenhafen Case of correspondence between dreams and future events: A study of motivation. *International Journal of Neuropsychiatry, 2*, 398–407.

Bentall, R. (1990). The illusion of reality: A review and integration of psychological research on hallucinations. *Psychological Bulletin, 107*, 82–95.

Bentall, R. (2003). *Madness explained: Psychosis and human nature*. London: Penguin books.

Bentall, R. & Slade, P. (1985). Reality testing and auditory hallucinations: A signal-detection analysis. *British Journal of Clinical Psychology, 24*, 159–169.

Berlitz, C. (1974). *The Bermuda triangle*. New York: Doubleday.

Blackmore, S. (1980). The extent of selective reporting of ESP ganzfeld studies. *European Journal of Parapsychology, 3*, 123–219.

Blackmore, S. (1983). Are out-of-body experiences evidence for survival? *Anabiosis: The Journal of Near-Death Studies, 3*, 137–155.

Blackmore, S. (1984). A postal survey of OBEs and other experiences. *Journal of the Society for Psychical Research, 52*, 225–244.

Blackmore, S. (1987). Where am I? Perspectives in imagery and the out-of-body experience. *Journal of Mental Imagery, 11*, 53–66.

Blackmore, S. (1990). The lure of the paranormal: What makes so many people believe in psychic phenomena? *New Scientist, 1735*, 62–65.

Blackmore, S. (1993). Near-death experiences in India: They have tunnels too. *Journal of Near-Death Studies, 11*, 205–217.

Blackmore, S. (1994). Are women more sheepish?: Gender differences in belief in the paranormal. In L. Coley & R. White (Eds.), *Women and parapsychology* (pp. 68–89). New York: Parapsychology Foundation.

Blackmore, S. (1996a). *In search of the light: The adventures of a parapsychologist.* Amherst, New York: Prometheus Books.

Blackmore, S. (1996b). Near-death experiences. *Journal of the Royal Society of Medicine, 89,* 73–76.

Blackmore, S. (1997). Probability misjudgement and belief in the paranormal: A newspaper survey. *British Journal of Psychology, 88,* 683–689.

Blackmore, S. (1998). Experiences of anoxia: Do reflex anoxic seizures resemble NDEs? *Journal of Near-Death Studies, 17,* 111–120.

Blackmore, S. (2003). *Consciousness: An introduction.* Abingdon: Hodder & Stoughton.

Blackmore, S. & Troscianko, T. (1985). Belief in the paranormal: Probability judgements, illusory control, and the "chance baseline shift". *British Journal of Psychology, 76,* 459–468.

Blackmore, S. & Troscianko, T. (1989). The physiology of the tunnel. *Journal of Near-Death Studies, 8,* 15–28.

Blanke, O. & Arzy, S. (2005). The out-of-body experience: Disturbed self-processing at the temporo-parietal junction. *The Neuroscientist, 11,* 16–24.

Boden, M. & Berenbaum, H. (2004). The potentially adaptive features of peculiar beliefs. *Personality and Individual Differences, 37,* 707–719.

Bösch, H., Steinkamp, F. & Boller, E. (2006). Examining psychokinesis: The interaction of human intention with random number generators—A meta-analysis. *Psychological Bulletin, 132,* 497–523.

Braithwaite, J. (2004). Magnetic variances associated with 'haunt-type' experiences: A comparison using time-synchronised baseline measurements. *European Journal of Parapsychology, 19,* 3–28.

Braithwaite, J. & Dent, K. (2011). New perspectives on perspective-taking mechanisms and the out-of-body experience. *Cortex, 47,* 628–632.

Braithwaite, J. & Townsend, M. (2006). Research note: Sleeping with the entity – a quantitative magnetic investigation of an English castle's reputedly 'haunted' bedroom. *European Journal of Parapsychology, 20,* 65–78.

Braude, S. (1995). *First person plural.* Lanham, MD: Rowman & Littlefield.

Braude, S. (2003). *Immortal remains: The evidence for life after death.* Lanham, MD: Rowman & Littlefield.

Britton, W. & Bootzin, R. (2004). Near-death experiences and the temporal lobe. *Psychological Science, 15,* 254–258.

Broad, C. (1953). *Religion, philosophy and psychical research.* London: Routledge & Kegan Paul.

Broad, W. & Wade, N. (1982). *Betrayers of the truth: Fraud and deceit in science.* Oxford: Oxford University Press.

Brod, J. (1997). Creativity and schizotypy. In G. Claridge (Ed.), *Schizotypy: Implications for illness and health* (pp. 274–298). New York: Oxford University Press.

Broughton, R. (1992). *Parapsychology: The controversial science.* London: Rider.

Brown, D. & Sheldrake, R. (2001). The anticipation of telephone calls: A survey in California. *Journal of Parapsychology, 65,* 145–156.

Brugger, P. (2001). From haunted brain to haunted science: A cognitive neuroscience view of paranormal and pseudoscientific thought. In J. Houran & R. Lange (Eds.), *Hauntings and Poltergeists: Multidisciplinary Perspectives* (pp. 195–213). Jefferson, NC: McFarland.

Brugger, P., Dowdy, M. & Graves, R. (1994). From superstitious behavior to delusional thinking: The role of the hippocampus in misattributions of causality. *Medical Hypotheses, 43,* 397–402.

Brugger, P., Gamma, A., Muri, R., Schäfer, M. & Taylor, K. (1993). Functional hemispheric asymmetry and belief in ESP: Towards a 'neuropsychology of belief'. *Perceptual and Motor Skills, 77,* 1299–1308.

Brugger, P. & Graves, R. (1997). Testing vs. believing: Magical ideation in the judgement of contingencies. *Cognitive Neuropsychiatry, 2,* 251–272.

Brugger, P., Regard, M. & Landis, T. (1991). Belief in extrasensory perception and illusory control: A replication. *Journal of Psychology, 125,* 501–502.

Brugger, P., Regard, M., Landis, T., Cook, N., Krebs, D. & Niederberger, J. (1993). 'Meaningful' patterns in visual noise, effects of lateral stimulation and the observer's belief in ESP. *Psychopathology, 26,* 261–265.

Brugger, P. & Taylor, K. (2003). ESP: Extrasensory perception or effect of subjective probability? *Journal of Consciousness Studies, 10,* 221–246.

Bruner, A. & Revulski, S. (1961). Collateral behavior in humans. *Journal of Experimental Analysis of Behavior, 4*, 349–350.

Bunge, M. (1980). Demarcating science from pseudo-science. *Beyond the fringe of science symposium*, McGill University, 19 February 1980.

Bünning, S. & Blanke, O. (2005). The out-of-body experience: Precipitating factors and neural correlates. *Progress in Brain Research, 150*, 331–350.

Bush, N. (2010). Distressing western near-death experiences: Finding a way through the abyss. In J. Holden, B. Greyson & D. James (Eds.), *The handbook of near-death experiences: Thirty years of investigation* (pp. 63–86). Santa Barbara, CA: Praeger.

Caird, D. (1987). Religiosity and personality: Are mystics introverted, neurotic, or psychotic? *British Journal of Social Psychology, 26*, 345–346.

Cardeña, E., Lynn, S. & Krippner, S. (2000). *Varieties of anomalous experience: Examining the scientific evidence*. Washington, DC: American Psychological Association.

Chalmers, A. (1999). *What is this thing called science?* Maidenhead, Berks: Open University Press.

Chalmers, D. (1999). *First-person methodologies in the science of consciousness*. Accessed in May 2007 from: http//consc.net/papers/firstperson.html.

Chambers, V. (2004). A shell with my name on it: The reliance upon the supernatural during the First World War. *Journal for the Academic Study of Magic, 2*, 79–102.

Chapman, L., Chapman, J., Kwapil, T., Eckblad, M. & Zinser, M. (1994). Putatively psychosis-prone subjects 10 years later. *Journal of Abnormal Psychology, 103*, 171–183.

Charpak, G. & Broch, H. (2004). *Debunked: ESP, telekinesis, and other pseudoscience*. Baltimore, MD: John Hopkins University Press.

Cheyne, J. (2002). Situational factors affecting sleep paralysis and associated hallucinations: Position and timing effects. *Journal of Sleep Research, 11*, 169–177.

Cheyne, J. & Girard, T. (2004). Spatial characteristics of hallucinations associated with sleep paralysis. *Cognitive Neuropsychiatry, 9*, 281–300.

Cheyne, J. & Girard, T. (2009). The body unbound: Vestibular-motor hallucinations and out-of-body experiences. *Cortex, 5*, 201–215.

Claridge, G. (Ed.) (1997). *Schizotypy: Implications for illness and health.* Oxford: Oxford University Press.

Claridge, G. & Beech, T. (1995). Fully and quasi-dimensional constructions of schizotypy. In A. Raine, T. Lencz & S. Mednick (Eds.), *Schizotypal personality* (pp. 192–216). New York: Cambridge University Press.

Claridge, G., Clark, K., Powney, E. & Hassan, E. (2008). Schizotypy and the Barnum effect. *Personality and Individual Differences, 44,* 436–444.

Clarke, D. (1995). Experience and other reasons given for belief and disbelief in the paranormal and religious phenomena. *Journal of the Society for Psychical Research, 60,* 371–384.

Clarke, I. (Ed.) (2001). *Psychosis and spirituality: Exploring the new frontier.* Philadelphia, PA: Whurr Publishers.

Cohen, J. (1960). *Chance, skill and luck: The psychology of guessing and gambling.* London: Pelican.

Cohen, J. (1992). A power primer. *Psychological Bulletin, 112,* 155–159.

Collins, H. & Pinch, T. (1982). *Frames of meaning: The social construction of extraordinary science.* London: Routledge Kegan Paul.

Colman, A. (1987). *Facts, fallacies and frauds in psychology.* London: Hutchinson.

Cook, A. & Irwin, H. (1983). Visuospatial skills and the out-of-body experience. *Journal of Parapsychology, 47,* 23–35.

Cook, C. & Persinger, M. (1997). Experimental induction of the "sensed presence" in normal subjects and an exceptional subject. *Perceptual and Motor Skills, 85,* 683–693.

Cory, C. (1919). Patience Worth. *Psychological Review, 26,* 397–407.

Costa, P. & McCrae, R. (1992). *Professional manual: Revised NEO personality inventory (NEO PI-R) and NEO five-factor inventory (FFI).* Florida: Psychological Assessment Resources.

Council, J., Bromley, K., Zabelina, D. & Waters, C. (2007). Hypnotic enhancement of creative drawing. *International Journal of Clinical Experimental Hypnosis, 55,* 467–485.

Crawley, S., French, C. & Yesson, S. (2002). Evidence for transliminality from a subliminal card guessing task. *Perception, 31,* 887–892.

Crow, T. (2008). Craddock & Owen vs. Kraepelin: 85 years late, mesmerized by 'polygenes'. *Schizophrenia Research, 103,* 156–160.

Csikszentmihalyi, M. (1992). *Flow: The psychology of happiness.* London and Sydney: Ryder.

Dag, I. (1999). The relationships among paranormal beliefs/locus of control and psychopathology in a Turkish college sample. *Personality and Individual Differences, 26*, 723–737.

Dagnall, N., Parker, A. & Munley, G. (2008). News events, false memory and paranormal belief. *European Journal of Parapsychology, 23*, 173–188.

Dalton, K. (1997). *The relationship between creativity and anomalous cognition in the ganzfeld*. Unpublished PhD Thesis, University of Edinburgh.

Dalton, K., Zingrone, N. & Alvarado, C. (1999). Exploring out-of-body experiences, dissociation, absorption, and alterations of consciousness with a creative population in the ganzfeld. *Proceedings of the Parapsychological Association 43rd Annual Convention*, 48–67.

Davies, M. & Kirkby, H. (1985). Multidimensionality of the relationship between perceived control and belief in the paranormal: Spheres of control and types of paranormal phenomena. *Personality and Individual Differences, 6*, 661–663.

de Pablos, F. (1998). Spontaneous precognition during dreams: Analysis of one-year naturalistic study. *Journal of the Society for Psychical Research, 62*, 423–433.

de Pablos, F. (2002). Enhancement of precognitive dreaming by cholinesterase inhibition: A pilot study. *Journal of the Society for Psychical Research, 66*, 88–102.

Dennett, D. (2007). *Breaking the spell: Religion as a natural phenomenon*. London: Penguin.

Diaconis, P. & Mosteller, F. (1989). Methods of studying coincidences. *Journal of the American Statistical Association: Applications & Case Studies, 84*, 853–861.

Dr Seuss. (1973). *Did I ever tell you how lucky you are?* New York: Random House.

Dunne, J. (1927). *An experiment with time*. London: MacMillan.

Easter, A. & Watt, C. (2011). It's good to know: How treatment knowledge and belief affect the outcome of distant healing intentionality for arthritis sufferers. *Journal of Psychosomatic Research, 71*, 86–89.

Easton, S., Blank, O. & Mohr, C. (2009). A putative implication for fronto-parietal connectivity in out-of-body experiences. *Cortex, 45*, 216–227

Edge, H. (1993). The medium as healer and clown: An interpretation of mediumship in Bali. *Journal of the American Society for Psychical Research, 87*, 171–183.

Edge, H., Morris, R., Palmer, J. & Rush, J. (1986). *Foundations of parapsychology: Exploring the boundaries of human capability*. Boston: Routledge & Kegan Paul.

Edwards, E. (2001). A house that tries to be haunted: Ghostly narratives in popular film and television. In J. Houran & R. Lange (Eds.), *Hauntings and poltergeists: Multidisciplinary perspectives* (pp. 82–119). Jefferson, NC: McFarland.

Egner, T. & Gruzelier, J. (2003). Ecological validity of neurofeedback: Modulation of slow wave EEG enhances musical performance. *Neuroreport: For Rapid Communication of Neuroscience Research, 14*, 1221–1224.

Emmons, C. & Sobal, J. (1981). Paranormal beliefs: Testing the social marginality hypothesis. *Sociological Focus, 14*, 49–56.

Esgate, A. & Groome, D. (2001). Probability and coincidence. In R. Roberts & D. Groome (Eds.), *Parapsychology: The science of unusual experience* (pp. 19–34). London: Arnold.

Eudell, E. & Campbell, J. (2007). Openness to experience and belief in the paranormal – a modified replication of Zingrone, Alvarado, and Dalton (1998–1999). *European Journal of Psychology, 22*, 166–174.

Evans, H. (2001). The ghost experience in a wider context. In J. Houran & R. Lange (Eds.), *Hauntings and poltergeists: Multidisciplinary perspectives* (pp. 41–61). Jefferson, NC: McFarland.

Evans, J. (1997). Semantic activation and preconscious processing in schizophrenia and schizotypy. In G. Claridge (Ed.), *Schizotypy: Implications for illness and health* (pp. 80–97). New York: Oxford University Press.

Eysenck, H. (1967). Personality and extra-sensory perception. *Journal of the Society for Psychical Research, 44*, 55–71.

Falk, R. (1989). Judgement of coincidences: Mine versus yours. *American Journal of Psychology, 102*, 477–493.

Farias, M., Claridge, G. & Lalljee, M. (2005). Personality and cognitive predictors of New Age practices and beliefs. *Personality and Individual Differences, 39*, 979–989.

Feather, S. & Schmicker, M. (2002). *The gift: The extraordinary experiences of ordinary people*. New York: St. Martin's Paperbacks.

Feist, G. (1999). The influence of personality in artistic and scientific creativity. In R. Sternberg (Ed.), *Handbook of creativity* (pp. 273–596). Cambridge: Cambridge University Press.

Fenwick, P. (2001). The neurophysiology of religious experience. In I. Clarke (Ed.), *Psychosis and spirituality: Exploring the new frontier* (pp. 15–26). London: Whurr Publishers.

Fingelkurts, A. & Fingelkurts, A. (2009). Is our brain hardwired to produce God, or is our brain hardwired to perceive God? A systematic review on the role of the brain in mediating religious experience. *Cognitive Process, 10*, 293–326. Accessed in February 2010 at: http://www.bm-science.com/team/art56.pdf.

Foulkes, D. & Fleisher, S. (1975). Mental activity in relaxed wakefulness. *Journal of Abnormal Psychology, 4*, 66–75.

Francis, L. & Thomas, T. (1996). Mystical orientation and personality among Anglican clergy. *Pastoral Psychology, 45*, 99–105.

Frazer, J. (1922/1957). *The golden bough*. London: MacMillan.

French, C. (2003). Fantastic memories: The relevance of research into eyewitness testimony and false memories for reports of anomalous experiences. *Journal of Consciousness Studies, 10*, 153–174.

French, C. (2010). Reflections of a (relatively) moderate skeptic. In S. Krippner & H. Friedman (Eds.), *Debating psychic experience: Human potential or human illusion* (pp. 53–64). Oxford: Praeger.

French, C., Haque, U., Bunton-Stasyshyn, R. & Davis, R. (2009). The 'Haunt' project: An attempt to build a 'haunted' room by manipulating complex electromagnetic fields and infrasound. *Cortex, 45*, 619–629.

French, C. & Santomauro, J. (2007). Something wicked this way comes: Causes and interpretations of sleep paralysis. In S. Della Sala (Ed.), *Tall tales about the mind and brain: Separating fact from fiction* (pp. 390–398). Oxford: Oxford University Press.

French, C., Santomauro, J., Hamilton, V., Fox, R. & Thalbourne, M. (2008). Psychological aspects of the alien contact experience. *Cortex, 44*, 1387–1395.

French, C. & Wilson, K. (2007). Cognitive factors underlying paranormal beliefs and experiences. In S. Della Sala (Ed.), *Tall tales about the mind and brain: Separating fact from fiction* (pp. 3–22). Oxford: Oxford University Press.

Frenkel, E., Kugelmass, S., Nathan, M. & Ingraham, L. (1995). Locus of control and mental health in adolescence and adulthood. *Schizophrenia Bulletin, 21,* 219–226.

Friedland, N. (1992). On luck and chance: Need for control as a mediator of the attribution of events to luck. *Journal of Behavioral Decision Making, 5,* 267–282.

Friedman, H. & Schustack, M. (2006). *Personality: Classic theories and modern research* (3rd ed.). London: Pearson.

Furnham, A. & Varian, C. (1988). Predicting and accepting personality test scores. *Personality and Individual Differences, 9,* 735–748.

Furuya, H., Ikezoe, K., Shigeto, H., Ohyagi, Y., Arahata, H., Araki, E. & Fujii, N. (2009). Sleep- and non-sleep-related hallucinations – Relationship to ghost tales and their classifications. *Dreaming, 19,* 232–238.

Gabbard, G. & Twemlow, A. (1984). *With the eyes of the mind: An empirical analysis of out-of-body states.* New York: Praeger Scientific.

Gallagher, C., Kumar, V. & Pekala, R. (1994). The anomalous experiences inventory: Reliability and validity. *Journal of Parapsychology, 58,* 402–428.

Gallagher, T. & Lewis, J. (2001). Rationalists, fatalists, and the modern superstitious: Test-taking in introductory sociology. *Sociological Inquiry, 71,* 1–12.

Garrett, E. (2002). *Adventures in the supernormal.* New York: Helix Press.

Genovese, J. (2005). Paranormal beliefs, schizotypy, and thinking styles among teachers and future teachers. *Personality and Individual Differences, 39,* 93–102.

Gianotti, L., Faber, P. & Lehmann, D. (2002). EEG source locations after guessed random events in believers and skeptics of paranormal phenomena. *International Congress Series, 1232,* 439–441.

Gianotti, L., Mohr, C., Pizzagalli, D., Lehmann, D. & Brugger, P. (2001). Associative processing and paranormal belief. *Psychiatry and Cognitive Neurosciences, 55,* 595–603.

Gmelch, G. (2001). *Inside pitch: Life in professional baseball.* Washington, DC: Smithsonian Institution Press.

Gould, R. (1921). Superstitions among Scottish college girls. *The Pedagogical Seminary, 28,* 203–248.

Goulding, A. (2005). Healthy schizotypy in a population of paranormal believers and experients. *Personality and Individual Differences, 38*, 1069–1083.

Goulding, A. & Parker, A. (2001). Finding psi in the paranormal: Psychometric measures used in research in paranormal beliefs/experiences and in research on psi-ability. *European Journal of Parapsychology, 16*, 73–101.

Gow, K., Lang, T. & Chant, D. (2004). Fantasy-proneness, paranormal beliefs and personality features in out-of-body experiences. *Contemporary Hypnosis, 21*, 107–125.

Granqvist, P., Fredrikson, M., Unge, P., Hagenfeldt, A., Valind, S., Larhammar, D., et al. (2005). Sensed presence and mystical experiences are predicted by suggestibility, not by the application of transcranial weak complex magnetic fields. *Neuroscience Letters, 375*, 69–74.

Gray, T. & Mill, D. (1990). Critical abilities, graduate education (Biology vs. English), and belief in unsubstantiated phenomena. *Canadian Journal of Behavioural Science, 22*, 162–172.

Gray, W. (1991). *Thinking critically about New Age ideas*. Belmont, CA: Wadsworth.

Greeley, A. (1975). *The sociology of the paranormal: A reconnaissance*. Beverly Hills, CA: Sage.

Green, C. & McCreery, C. (1975). *Apparitions*. London: Hamish Hamilton.

Greene, J. (1987). *Memory, thinking, and language*. London: Methuen.

Greyson, B. (1983). The near-death experience scale: Construction, reliability, and validity. *Journal of Nervous and Mental Disease, 171*, 369–375.

Greyson, B. (1991). Near-death experiences precipitated by suicide attempt: Lack of influence of psychopathology, religion, and expectations. *Journal of Near-Death Studies, 9*, 183–188.

Greyson, B. (2000a). Near-death experiences. In E. Cardeña, S. Lynn & S. Krippner (Eds.), *Varieties of anomalous experiences* (pp. 315–352). Washington, DC: American Psychological Association.

Greyson, B. (2000b). Dissociation in people who have near-death experiences: Out of their bodies or out of their minds? *Lancet, 355*, 460–463.

Greyson, B. (2003). Incidence and correlates of near-death experiences in a cardiac care unit. *General Hospital Psychiatry, 25*, 269–276.

Greyson, B. (2010). Implications of near-death experiences for a postmaterialist psychology. *Psychology of Religion and Spirituality, 2*, 37–45.

Greyson, B., Williams Kelly, E. & Kelly, E. (2010). Explanatory models for near-death experiences. In M. Holden, B. Greyson & D. James (Eds.), *The handbook of near-death experiences: Thirty years of investigation* (pp. 213–234). Santa Barbara, CA: Praeger.

Grimshaw, G., Bryson, F., Atchley, R. & Humphrey, M. (2010). Semantic ambiguity resolution in positive schizotypy: A right hemisphere interpretation. *Neuropsychology, 24*, 130–138.

Grof, S. (ND). *Psychology of the future: Lessons from modern consciousness research.* Accessed in January 2011 from: www.stanislavgrof.com/pdf/Psychology%20of%20the%20Future.Stan%20Gro_long.pdf.

Grof, S. & Grof, C. (1989). *Spiritual emergency.* New York: St. Martin's Press.

Groth-Marnat, G. & Pegden, J. (1998). Personality correlates of paranormal belief: Locus of control and sensation seeking. *Social Behavior and Personality, 26*, 291–296.

Gruzelier, J. (in press). The mind-body connection, healing and exceptional experiences. In C. Simmonds-Moore (Ed.), *Exceptional experiences and health: Essays on the mind, body and human potential.* Jefferson, NC: McFarland.

Guilford, J. (1967). *The nature of human intelligence.* New York: McGraw-Hill.

Gurney, E., Myers, F. & Podmore, F. (1886). *Phantasms of the living.* London: Society for Psychical Research & Truber.

Hacking, I. (1988). Telepathy: Origins of randomization in experimental design. *Isis, 70*, 427–451.

Hageman, J., Peres, J., Moreira-Almeida, A., Caixeta, L., Wickramasekera, I. & Krippner, S. (2010). The neurobiology of trance and mediumship in Brazil. In S. Krippner & H. Friedman (Eds.), *Mysterious minds: The neurobiology of psychics, mediums and other extraordinary people* (pp. 85–111). Santa Barbara, CA: Praeger.

Haraldsson, E. (1985). Representative national surveys of psychic phenomena: Iceland, Great Britain, Sweden, USA and Gallup's multinational survey. *Journal of the Society for Psychical Research, 53*, 145–158.

Haraldsson, E. & Houtkooper, J. (1991). Psychic experiences in the multinational human values study: Who reports them? *Journal of the American Society for Psychical Research, 85*, 145–165.

Hartmann, E. (1991). *Boundaries in the mind: A new psychology of personality*. New York: Basic Books.

Hartmann, E., Harrison, R. & Zborowski, M. (2001). Boundaries in the mind: Past research and future directions. *North American Journal of Psychology, 3*, 347–368.

Hastings, A., Hutton, M., Braud, W., Bennett, C., Berk, I., Boynton, T., Dawn, C., Ferguson, E., Goldman, A., Greene, E., Hewett, M., Lind, V., McLellan, K. & Steinbach-Humphrey, S. (2002). Psychomanteum research: Experiences and effects on bereavement. *Omega: Journal of Death and Dying, 45*, 211–228.

Hayano, D. (1978). Strategies for the management of luck and action in an urban poker parlour. *Urban Life, 6*, 475–488.

Herodotus (2009). *The histories*. Accessed in February 2011 from: www. digireads.com.

Hill, D. (1968). *Magic and superstition*. London: Hamlyn Publishing.

Hill, D. & Persinger, M. (2003). Application of transcerebral, weak (1 microT) complex magnetic fields and mystical experiences: Are they generated by field-induced dimethyltryptamine release from the pineal organ? *Perceptual and Motor Skills, 97*, 1049–1050.

Hines, T. (2003). *Pseudoscience and the paranormal*. New York: Prometheus Books.

Hobson, J. A. & McCarly, R. W. (1977). The brain as a dream-state generator: An activation-synthesis hypothesis of the dream process. *American Journal of Psychiatry, 134*, 1335–1348.

Holden, J. (2010). Veridical perception in near-death experiences. In M. Holden, B. Greyson & D. James (Eds.), *The handbook of near-death experiences: Thirty years of investigation* (pp 185–212). Santa Barbara, California: Praeger.

Holden, J., Long, J. & MacLurg, B. (2010). Characteristics of Western near-death experiencers. In J. Holden, B. Greyson & D. James (Eds.), *The handbook of near-death experiences: Thirty years of investigation* (pp. 109–133). Santa Barbara, CA: Praeger.

Holt, N. (2007). *Creativity, states of consciousness and anomalous cognition: The role of epistemological flexibility in the creative process*. Unpublished Doctoral thesis, University of Northampton.

Holt, N. (in press). The muse in the machine: Creativity, anomalous experiences and mental health. In C. Simmonds-Moore (Ed.), *Essays on exceptional experiences and health*. Jefferson, NC: McFarland.

Holt, N., Delanoy, D. & Roe, C. (2004). Creativity, subjective paranormal experiences and altered states of consciousness. *Proceedings of the Parapsychological Association 47th Annual Convention*, 433–436.

Holt, N. & Lewis, R. (2009). *A2 psychology 2008 AQA a specification: The student's textbook*. Bancyfeli, Carmarthen: Crown House Publishing.

Holt, N., Simmonds-Moore, C. & Moore, S. (2008). Benign schizotypy: Investigating differences between clusters of schizotypy on paranormal belief, creativity, intelligence and mental health. *Proceedings of Presented Papers: The Parapsychological Association 51st Annual Convention*, 82–96.

Honorton, C. (1977). Psi and internal attention states. In B. Wolman (Ed.), *Handbook of parapsychology* (pp. 435–472). New York: Van Nostrand Reinhold.

Honorton, C. (1985). Meta-analysis of psi ganzfeld research: A response to Hyman. *Journal of Parapsychology, 49*, 51–91.

Honorton, C. (1995). Impact of the sender in ganzfeld communication: Meta-analysis and power estimates. *Proceedings of Presented Papers: The Parapsychological Association 38th Annual Convention*, 132–140.

Honorton, C. & Ferrari, D. (1989). "Future telling": A meta-analysis of forced-choice precognition experiments, 1935–1987. *Journal of Parapsychology, 53*, 281–308.

Honorton, C., Ferrari, D. & Bem, D. (1992). Extroversion and ESP performance: A meta-analysis and a new confirmation. In L. Henkel & G. Schmeidler (Eds.), *Research in parapsychology 1990* (pp. 35–38). Metuchen, NJ: Scarecrow Press.

Honorton, C. & Harper, S. (1974). Psi-mediated imagery and ideation in an experimental procedure for regulating perceptual input. *Journal of the American Society for Psychical Research, 68*, 156–168.

Hood, B. (2009). *Supersense: From superstition to religion – the brain science of belief*. London: Constable.

Honegger, B. (1979). Correspondence. *Parapsychology Review, 10*, 24–26.

Horsfall, S. (2000). The experience of Marian apparitions and the Mary cult. *The Social Science Journal, 37*, 375–384.

Houran, J., Ashe, D. & Thalbourne, M. (2003). Encounter experiences in the context of mental boundaries and bilaterality. *Journal of the Society for Psychical Research, 67*, 260–280.

Houran, J. & Thalbourne, M. (2001). Further study and speculation on the psychology of 'entity encounter experiences'. *Journal of the Society for Psychical Research, 65*, 26–37.

Houran, J., Wiseman, R. & Thalbourne, M. (2002). Perceptual-personality characteristics associated with naturalistic haunt experiences. *European Journal of Parapsychology, 17*, 17–44.

Hufford, D. (2001). An experience centered approach to hauntings. In J. Houran & R. Lange (Eds.), *Hauntings and poltergeists: Multidisciplinary perspectives* (pp. 18–40). Jefferson NC: McFarland.

Hughes, J. (2010). A review of Savant Syndrome and its possible relationship to epilepsy. *Epilepsy and Behavior, 17*, 147–152.

Hunt, H., Dougan, S., Grant, K. & House, M. (2002). Growth enhancing versus dissociative states of consciousness: A questionnaire study. *Journal of Humanstic Psychology, 42*, 90–106.

Hyman, R. (1985a). A critical historical overview of parapsychology. In P. Kurtz (Ed.), *A skeptic's handbook of parapsychology* (pp. 3–96). Buffalo, NY: Prometheus.

Hyman, R. (1985b). The ganzfeld: A critical appraisal. *Journal of Parapsychology, 49*, 3–49.

Hyman, R. (1994). Anomaly or artifact? Comments on Bem and Honorton. *Psychological Bulletin, 115*, 19–24.

Hyman, R. (2010). Parapsychology's Achilles heel: Persistent inconsistency. In S. Krippner & H. Friedman (Eds.), *Debating psychic experience: Human potential or human illusion* (pp. 43–52). Oxford: Praeger.

Hyman, R. & Honorton, C. (1986). A joint communiqué: The psi ganzfeld controversy. *Journal of Parapsychology, 50*, 351–364.

Inglis, D. & Holmes, M. (2003). Highland and other haunts: ghosts in Scottish tourism. *Annals of Tourism Research, 30*, 50–63.

Ipsos MORI. (2007). Survey on beliefs. Accessed in February 2011 from: http://www.ipsos-mori.com/researchpublications/ researcharchive/246/Survey-on-Beliefs.aspx.

Irwin, H. (1985). *Flight of mind: A psychological study of the out-of-body experience*. Metchuchen, NJ: The Scarecrow Press.

Irwin, H. (1990). Fantasy-proneness and paranormal beliefs. *Psychological Reports, 66*, 655–658.

Irwin, H. (1993). Belief in the paranormal: A review of the empirical literature. *Journal of the American Society for Psychical Research, 87,* 1–39.

Irwin, H. (1999). *An introduction to parapsychology* (3rd ed.). Jefferson, NC: McFarland.

Irwin, H. (2000). The disembodied self: An empirical study of dissociation and the out-of-body experience. *Journal of Parapsychology, 64,* 261–276.

Irwin, H. (2003). *An introduction to parapsychology* (4th ed.). Jefferson, NC: McFarland.

Irwin, H. (2009). *The psychology of paranormal belief: A researcher's handbook.* Hatfield: University of Hertfordshire Press.

Irwin, H. & Watt, C. (2007). *An introduction to parapsychology* (5th ed.). Jefferson, NC: McFarland.

Jahoda, G. (1969). *The psychology of superstition.* Middlesex: Penguin Books.

James, W. (1890/1986). *The principles of psychology.* New York: Penguin Books.

James, W. (1895). Review of "report on the census of hallucinations". *Psychological Review, 2,* 69–75.

Janoff-Bulman, R. (1992). *Shattered assumptions: Towards a new psychology of trauma.* New York: Free Press.

Jansen, K. (1997). The ketamine model of the near-death experience: A central role for the N-Methyl-D-Aspartate receptor. *Journal of Near-Death Studies, 16,* 5–26.

Jawer, M. (2006). Environmental sensitivity: Inquiry into a possible link with apparitional experience. *Journal of the Society for Psychical Research, 70,* 25–47.

Jensen, C. & Cardeña, E. (2009). A controlled long-distance test of a professional medium. *European Journal of Parapsychology, 24,* 53–67.

Johns, L. (2005). Hallucinations in the general population. *Current Psychiatry Reports, 7,* 162–167.

Kaptchuk, T. (1998). Intentional ignorance: A history of blind assessment and placebo controls in medicine. *Bulletin of the History of Medicine, 72,* 389–433.

Kaptchuk, T., Friedlander, E., Kelley, J., Sanchez, M., Kokkotou, E., Singer, J., Kowalczykowski, M., Miller, F., Kirsch, I. & Lembo, A. (2010). Placebos without deception: A randomized controlled trial in irritable bowel syndrome. *PLoS ONE, 5,* 1–7.

Keinan, G. (1994). Effects of stress and tolerance of ambiguity on magical thinking. *Journal of Personality and Social Psychology, 67*, 48–55.

Keinan, G. (2002). The effects of stress and desire for control on superstitious behavior. *Personality and Social Psychology Bulletin, 28*, 102–108.

Kelly, E. & Arcangel, D. (2011). An Investigation of mediums who claim to give information about deceased persons. *Journal of Nervous and Mental Disease, 199*, 11–17.

Kennedy, J., Kanthamani, H. & Palmer, J. (1994). Psychic and spiritual experiences, health and well-being, and meaning in life. *Journal of Parapsychology, 58*, 353–383.

Keren, G. & Wagenaar, W. (1985). On the psychology of playing blackjack: Normative and descriptive considerations with implications for decision theory. *Journal of Experimental Psychology: General, 114*, 133–158.

Koffel, E. & Watson, D. (2009). Unusual sleep experiences, dissociation, and schizotypy: Evidence for a common domain. *Clinical Psychology Review, 29*, 548–559.

Kohls, N. & Walach, H. (2007). Psychological distress, experiences of ego loss and spirituality: Exploring the effects of spiritual practice. *Social Behavior and Personality, 35*, 1301–1316.

Kolb, B. & Whishaw, I. (1996). *Fundamentals of human neuropsychology* (4th ed.). New York: W. H. Freeman.

Krippner, S. (2011). Candomblé, Umbanda, and Kardecismo mediums in Recife, Brazil. *Paranthropology, 2*, 9–13.

Krippner, S. & Achterberg, J. (2000). Anomalous healing experiences. In E. Cardeña, S. Lynn & S. Krippner (Eds.), *Varieties of anomalous experience: Examining the evidence* (pp. 353–395). Washington, DC: American Psychological Association.

Krippner, S. & Friedman, H. (Eds.) (2010). *Debating psychic experience: Human potential or human illusion*. Oxford: Praeger.

Kuhn, T. (1962). *The structure of scientific revolutions*. Chicago, IL: University of Chicago Press.

Kumar, V. & Pekala, R. (2001). Relation of hypnosis-specific attitudes and behaviors to paranormal beliefs and experiences: A technical review. In J. Houran & R. Lange (Eds.), *Haunting and poltergeists: Multidisciplinary perspectives* (pp. 260–279). Jefferson, NC: McFarland.

Kumar, V., Pekala, R. & Cummings, J. (1993). Sensation seeking, drug use and reported paranormal beliefs and experiences. *Personality and Individual Differences, 14*, 685–91.

LaBerge, S. & Gackenbach, S. (2000). Lucid dreaming. In E. Cardeña, S. Lynn & S. Krippner (Eds.), *The varieties of anomalous experience* (pp. 151–182). Washington, DC: American Psychological Association.

Lange R. & Houran J. (1997). Context-induced paranormal experiences: Support for Houran and Lange's model of haunting phenomena. *Perceptual and Motor Skills, 84*, 1455–1458.

Lange R. & Houran, J. (2002). Ambiguous stimuli brought to life: The psychological dynamics of hauntings and poltergeists. In J. Houran & R. Lange (Eds.), *Hauntings and poltergeists: Multidisciplinary perspectives* (pp. 280–306). Jefferson, NC: McFarland.

Langer, E. (1975). The illusion of control. *Journal of Personality and Social Psychology, 32*, 311–328.

Langer, E. & Roth, J. (1975). Heads I win, tails it's chance: The illusion of control as a function of the sequence of outcomes in a purely chance task. *Journal of Personality and Social Psychology, 32*, 951–955.

Laski, M. (1961). *Ecstasy*. Bloomington: Indiana University Press.

Lawrence, T. (1993). Gathering in the sheep and goats: A meta-analysis of forced-choice sheep-goat ESAP studies, 1947–1993. *Proceedings of the Parapsychological Association 36th Annual Convention*, 75–86.

Lawrence, T. (1995). How many factors of paranormal belief are there? A critique of the Paranormal Belief Scale. *Journal of Parapsychology, 59*, 3–25.

Lawrence, T., Edwards, C., Barraclough, N., Church, S. & Hetherington, F. (1995). Modelling childhood causes of paranormal belief and experience: Childhood trauma and childhood fantasy. *Personality and Individual Differences, 19*, 209–215.

Leahey, T. & Leahey, G. (1983). *Psychology's occult doubles: Psychology and the problem of pseudoscience*. Chicago, IL: Nelson-Hall.

Leder, D. (2005). 'Spooky actions at a distance': Physics, psi and distant healing. *The Journal of Alternative and Complementary Medicine, 11*, 923–930.

Levin, J. & Mead, L. (2008). Bioenergy healing: A theoretical model and case series. *Explore: The Journal of Science and Healing, 4*, 201–209.

Levin, R., Gilmartin, L. & Lamontanaro, L. (1998). Cognitive style and perception: The relationship of boundary thinness to visual-spatial processing in dreaming and waking thought. *Imagination, Cognition and Personality, 18*, 25–41.

Lilienfeld, S. (2005). The 10 commandments of helping students distinguish science from pseudoscience in psychology. *Observer, 18*, 39–40, 49–51.

Lilienfeld, S., Lynn, S. & Lohr, J. (2003). Science and pseudoscience in clinical psychology: Initial thoughts, reflections, and considerations. In S. Lilienfeld, S. Lynn & J. Lohr (Eds.), *Science and pseudoscience in clinical psychology* (pp. 1–14). New York: Guilford Press.

Littlewood, J. (1953). *A mathematician's miscellany*. London: Methuen.

Lobach, E. & Bierman, D. (2004). Who's calling at this hour? Local sidereal time and telephone telepathy. In S. Schmidt (Ed.), *Proceedings of the Parapsychological Association 47th Annual Convention*, 91–97.

Loftus, E. & Hoffman, H. (1989). Misinformation and memory, the creation of new memories. *Journal of Experimental Psychology: General, 118*, 100–104.

Long, J. & Holden, J. (2007). Does the arousal system contribute to near-death and out-of-body experiences? A summary and response. *Journal of Near-Death Studies, 25*, 135–169.

Loughland, C. & Williams, L. (1997). A cluster analytic study of schizotypal trait dimensions. *Personality and Individual Differences, 23*, 877–883.

Lubart, T. (2000–2001). Models of the creative process: Past, present and future. *Creativity Research Journal, 3 & 4*, 295–308.

Luke, D. (2007). *The psychology and parapsychology of beliefs about luck and their relation to beliefs about psi and psi performance*. Unpublished PhD thesis, The University of Northampton, UK.

Luke, D., Delanoy, D. & Sherwood, S. (2008). Psi may look like luck: Perceived luckiness and beliefs about luck in relation to precognition. *Journal of the Society for Psychical Research, 72*, 193–207.

Luke, D. & Friedman, H. (2009). The neurochemistry of psi reports and associated experiences. In S. Krippner & H. Friedman (Eds.), *Mysterious minds: The neurobiology of psychics, mediums, and other extraordinary people* (pp 163–186). Santa Barbara, CA: Praeger.

Luke, D. & Kittenis, M. (2005). A preliminary survey of parapsychological experiences with psychoactive drugs. *Journal of Parapsychology, 69*, 305–327.

Luke, D., Roe, C. & Davison, J. (2008). Testing for forced-choice precognition using a hidden task: Two replications. *Journal of Parapsychology, 72*, 133–154.

Lukoff, D. (2007). Visionary spiritual experiences. *Southern Medical Journal, 100*, 635–641.

Lukoff, D., Lu, F. & Turner, R. (1992). Toward a more culturally sensitive DSM-IV: Psychoreligious and psychospiritual problems. *Journal of Nervous and Mental Disease, 180*, 673–682.

Lundahl, C. (1999). Parallels between near-death experiences prophetic visions and prophecies from the Bible and Mormon Holy Writ. *Journal of Near-Death Studies, 17*, 193–203.

Lyvers, M., Barling, N. & Harding-Clark, J. (2006). Effect of belief in "psychic healing" on self-reported pain in chronic pain sufferers. *Journal of Psychosomatic Research, 60*, 59–61.

MacDonald, D. (2000). Spirituality: Description, measurement, and relation to the Five Factor Model of Personality. *Journal of Personality, 68*, 153–197.

MacDougall, D. (1907). Hypothesis concerning soul substance together with experimental evidence of the existence of such substance. *Journal of the American Society for Psychical Research, 1*, 237–244

Maher, M. (1999). Riding the waves in search of the particles: A modern study of ghosts and apparitions. *Journal of Parapsychology, 63*, 47–80.

Maher, M. (2000). Quantitative investigation of the General Wayne Inn. *Journal of Parapsychology, 64*, 365–390.

Mahowald, M. & Schenck, C. (2001). Nocturnal dissociation: Awake? Asleep? Both? Or neither? *Sleep and hypnosis, 3*, 131–134.

Malinowski, B. (1948). *Magic, science and religion, and other essays.* Boston: Beacon Press.

Maltby, J. & Day, L. (2001). Spiritual involvement and belief: The relationship between spirituality and Eysenck's personality dimensions. *Personality and Individual Differences, 30*, 187–192.

Maltby, J., Macaskill, A. & Day, L. (2010). *Personality, individual differences and intelligence* (2nd ed.). London: Pearson.

Marks, D. (1981). Sensory cues invalidate remote viewing experiments. *Nature, 292*, 171.

Marks, D. & Kammann, R. (1978). Information transmission in the remote viewing experiments. *Nature, 274*, 680–681.

Marks, D. & Kammann, R. (1980). *The psychology of the psychic.* Buffalo, NY: Prometheus Books.

Martindale, C. (1977–1978). Creativity, consciousness and cortical arousal. *Journal of Altered States of Consciousness, 3*, 69–87.

Martindale, C. (1999). Biological bases of creativity. In R. Sternberg (Ed.), *Handbook of creativity* (pp. 137–152). Cambridge, UK: Cambridge University Press.

Maslow, A. (1971). *The further reaches of human nature.* New York: Viking.

Mason, O. & Budge, K. (2011). Schizotypy, self-referential thinking and the Barnum effect. *Journal of Behavior Therapy and Experimental Psychiatry, 42*, 145–148.

Masters, K., Spielmans, G. & Goodson, J. (2006). Are there demonstrable effects of distant intercessory prayer? A meta-analytic review. *Annals of Behavioral Medicine, 32*, 21–26.

Mathews, R. & Blackmore, S. (1995). Why are coincidences so impressive? *Perceptual and Motor Skills, 80*, 1121–1122.

Mauskopf, S. & McVaugh, M. (1980). *The elusive science: Origins of experimental psychical research.* Baltimore: Johns Hopkins University Press.

Mavromatis, A. (1987). *Hypnagogia: The unique state of consciousness between wakefulness and sleep.* London: Routledge and Kegan Paul.

McCarty, D. & Chesson, A. (2009). A case of sleep paralysis with hypnopompic hallucinations. *Journal of Clinical Sleep Medicine, 15*, 83–84.

McClenon, J. (1990). Chinese and American anomalous experiences: The role of religiosity. *Sociological Analysis, 51*, 53–67.

McClenon, J. (2001). The sociological investigation of haunting cases. In J. Houran & R. Lange (Eds.), *Hauntings and poltergeists: Multidisciplinary perspectives* (pp. 62–81). Jefferson NC: McFarland.

McCrae, R. (1994). Openness to experience: Expanding the boundaries of factor V. *European Journal of Personality, 8*, 251–272.

McCreery, C. (1997). Hallucinations and arousability: Pointers to a theory of psychosis. In G. Claridge (Ed.), *Schizotypy: Implications for illness and health* (pp. 251–273). New York: Oxford University Press.

McCreery, C. (2006). *Dreams and psychosis: A new look at an old hypothesis.* Accessed in October 2011 from: http://www.celiagreen.com/charlesmccreery/dreams-and-psychosis.pdf.

McCreery, C. & Claridge, G. (2002). Healthy Schizotypy: The case of out-of-body experiences. *Personality and Individual Differences, 32*, 141–154.

McCue, P. (2002). Theories of haunting: A critical overview. *Journal of the Society for Psychical Research, 66*, 1–21.

McGarry, J. & Newberry, B. (1981). Beliefs in paranormal phenomena and locus of control: A field study. *Journal of Personality and Social Psychology, 41*, 725–736.

McNally, R. (2003). Is the pseudoscience concept useful for clinical psychology? The demise of pseudoscience. *The Scientific Review of Mental Health Practice, 2*, 97–101.

Mednick, S. (1962). The associative basis of the creative process. *Psychological Review, 69*, 220–232.

Metzinger, T. (2005). Out-of-body experiences as the origin of the concept of a "soul". *Mind & Matter, 3*, 57–84.

Miles, P. & True, G. (2003). Reiki – Review of a biofield therapy: History, theory, practice and research. *Alternative Therapies, 9*, 62–72.

Milgram, S. (1963). Behavioral study of obedience. *Journal of Abnormal and Social Psychology, 67*, 371–378.

Milton, J. (1999). Should ganzfeld research continue to be crucial in the search for a replicable psi effect? Part I. Discussion paper and introduction to an electronic mail discussion. *Journal of Parapsychology, 63*, 309–334.

Milton, J. & Wiseman, R. (1997). *Guidelines for extrasensory perception research*. Hertfordshire: University of Hertfordshire Press.

Milton, J. & Wiseman, R. (1999). Does psi exist? Lack of replication of an anomalous process of information transfer. *Psychological Bulletin, 125*, 387–391.

Montinelli, D. & Parra, A. (2000). Conflictive psi experiences: A survey with implications for clinical parapsychology. *Proceedings of the 43th Annual Convention of the Parapsychological Association*, 178–191.

Moody, R. (1976). *Life after life*. New York: Bantam.

Moody, R. (1994). A latter day psychomanteum. In D. Bierman (Ed.), *Proceedings of the 37th Annual Convention of the Parapsychological Association*, 335–336.

Moore, D. (2005). *Three in four Americans believe in the paranormal*. Accessed in February 2011 from: http://www.gallup.com/poll/16915/Three-Four-Americans-Believe-Paranormal.aspx.

Moreira-Almeida, A., Neto, F. & Cardeña, E. (2008). Comparison of Brazilian Spiritist mediumship and dissociative identity disorder. *Journal of Nervous and Mental Disease, 196*, 420–424.

Moreman, C. (2003). A re-examination of the possibility of chance coincidence as an alternative explanation for mediumistic communication in the Cross Correspondences. *Journal of the Society for Psychical Research, 67*, 225–242.

Morgan, H., Turner, D., Corlette, P., Absalom, A., Adapa, R., Arana, F., Pigott, J., Gardner, J., Everitt, J., Haggard, P. & Fletcher, P. (2011). Exploring the impact of ketamine on the experience of illusory body ownership. *Biological Psychiatry, 69*, 35–41.

Morgan, R. & Morgan, D. (1998). Critical thinking and belief in the paranormal. *College Student Journal, 32*, 135–139.

Morris, R. L. (1991). Comment. *Statistical Science, 6*, 393–395.

Morris, R., Dalton, K., Delanoy, D. & Watt, C. (1995). Comparison of the sender/no sender condition in the ganzfeld. *Proceedings of Presented Papers, The Parapsychological Association 38th Annual Convention*, 244–259.

Moulton, S. & Kosslyn, S. (2008). Using neuroimaging to resolve the psi debate. *Journal of Cognitive Neuroscience, 20*, 182–192.

Mousseau, M-C. (2003). Parapsychology: Science or pseudo-science? *Journal of Scientific Exploration, 17*, 271–282.

Mueller, A. & Roberts, R. (2001). Dreams. In R. Roberts & D. Groome (Eds.), *Parapsychology: The science of unusual experience* (pp. 86–101). London: Arnold.

Muldoon, S. (1936). *The case for astral projection*. Chicago, IL: The Aries Press.

Munro, C. & Persinger, M. (1992). Relative right temporal-lobe theta activity correlates with Vingiano's Hemispheric Quotient and the "sensed presence". *Perceptual and Motor Skills, 75*, 899–903.

Murray, C. & Fox, J. (2005). The out-of-body experience and body image: Differences between experients and nonexperients. *The Journal of Nervous and Mental Disease, 193*, 70–72.

Murray, C. & Wooffitt, R. (Eds.) (2010) Anomalous experiences and qualitative research. Special Issue, *Qualitative Research in Psychology, 7*(1), 1–83.

Murray, C. (2010). Developing a dissociational account of out-of-body experiences. In M. Smith (Ed.), *Anomalous experiences: Essays from parapsychological and psychological perspectives* (pp. 161–176). Jefferson, NC: McFarland.

National Science Foundation. (2000). *Science and Technology: Public Attitudes and Public Understanding: Belief in the Paranormal or*

Pseudoscience. Accessed in March 2011 from: http://www.nsf.gov/statistics/seind00/access/c8/c8s5.htm.

Natsoulas, T. (1987). The six basic concepts of consciousness and William James' stream of thought. *Imagination, Cognition and Personality, 6*, 289–319.

Negro, P., Palladino-Negro, P. & Louzã, M. (2002). Do religious mediumship dissociative experiences conform to the sociocognitive theory of dissociation? *Journal of Trauma and Dissociation, 3*, 51–73.

Nelson, K., Mattingly, M., Lee, S. & Schmitt, F. (2006). Does the arousal system contribute to near-death experience? *Neurology, 66*, 1003–1009.

Nelson, L., Mattingly, M. & Schmitt, F. (2007). Out-of-body experiences and arousal. *Neurology, 68*, 794–795.

Neppe, V. & Palmer, J. (2004). Subjective anomalous events: Perspectives for the future, voices from the past. In M. Thalbourne & L. Storm (Eds.), *Parapsychology in the twenty-first century: Essays on the future of psychical research* (pp. 242–271). Jefferson, NC: McFarland.

Neppe, V. & Palmer, J. (2009). Subjective anomalous events: Perspectives for the future, voices from the past. In M. Thalbourne & L. Storm (Eds.), *Parapsychology in the twenty-first century: Essays on the future of psychical research* (pp. 242–271). Jefferson, NC: McFarland.

Nettle, D. (2006). Schizotypy and mental health amongst poets, visual artists, and mathematicians. *Journal of Research in Personality, 40*, 876–890.

Nicol, J. (1985). Fraudulent children in psychical research. In P. Kurtz (Ed.), *A skeptic's handbook of parapsychology* (pp. 275–286). Buffalo, NY: Prometheus.

Norlander, T. & Gustafson, R. (1998). Effects of alcohol on a divergent thinking figural fluency test during the illumination phase of the creative process. *Creativity Research Journal, 11*, 265–274.

Norlander, T., Kjellgren, A. & Archer, T. (2003). Effects of flotation- versus chamber-restricted environmental stimulation technique (REST) on creativity and realism under stress and non-stress conditions. *Imagination, Cognition and Personality, 22*, 341–357.

Noyes, R. & Kletti, R. (1976). Depersonalization in the face of life-threatening danger: A description. *Psychiatry, 39*, 19–27.

O'Keeffe, C. & Parsons, S. (2010). Haunting experiences: An integrative approach. In M. Smith (Ed.), *Anomalous experiences: Essays from parapsychological and psychological perspectives* (pp. 108–119). Jefferson, NC: McFarland.

O'Keeffe, C. & Wiseman, R. (2005). Testing alleged mediumship: Methods and results. *British Journal of Psychology, 96*, 165–179.

Ono, K. (1987). Superstitious behavior in humans. *Journal of the Experimental Analysis of Behavior, 47*, 261–271.

Osis, K. & McCormick, D. (1980). Kinetic effects at the ostensible location of an out-of-body projection during perceptual testing. *Journal of the American Society for Psychical Research, 74*, 319–329.

Palmer, G. & Braud, W. (2002). Exceptional human experiences, disclosure, and a more inclusive view of physical, psychological, and spiritual well-being. *Journal of Transpersonal Psychology, 34*, 29–61.

Palmer, J. (1978). The out-of-body experience: A psychological theory. *Parapsychology Review, 9*, 19–22.

Palmer, J. (1979). A community mail survey of psychic experiences. *Journal of the American Society for Psychical Research, 73*, 221–251.

Palmer, J. (2003). ESP in the ganzfeld: Analysis of a debate. *Journal of Consciousness Studies, 10*, 51–68.

Palmer, J. (2009). Out-of-body and near-death experiences as evidence for externalization or survival. In C. Murray (Ed.), *Scientific psychological perspectives on out-of-body and near-death experiences* (pp. 159–170). New York: Nova Science Publishers.

Parker, A. (2000). A review of the ganzfeld work at Gothenburg University. *Journal of the Society for Psychical Research, 64*, 1–15.

Parnia, S., Waller, D., Yeates, P. & Fenwick, P. (2001). A qualitative and quantitative study of the incidence, features and aetiology of near-death experiences in cardiac arrest survivors. *Resuscitation, 48*, 149–156.

Parra, A. (2006). 'Seeing and feeling ghosts': Absorption, fantasy-proneness and healthy schizotypy as predictors of crisis apparition experiences. *Journal of Parapsychology, 70*, 357–372.

Parra, A. (2009). Out-of-body experiences and hallucinatory experiences: A psychological approach. *Imagination, Cognition and Personality, 29*, 211–223.

Parra, A. & Espinoza Paul, L. (2009). Exploring the links between nocturnal hallucinatory experiences and personality characteristics. *European Journal of Parapsychology, 24*, 139–154.

Pekala, R. & Cardeña, E. (2000). Methodological issues in the study of altered states of consciousness and anomalous experiences. In

E. Cardeña, S. Lynn & S. Krippner (Eds.), *Varieties of anomalous experiences* (pp. 47–82). Washington, DC: American Psychological Association.

Pekala, R., Kumar, V. & Cummings, J. (1992). Types of high hypnotically susceptible individuals and reported attitudes and experiences of the paranormal and the anomalous. *Journal of the American Society for Psychical Research, 86*, 135–150.

Pekala, R., Kumar, V. & Marcano, G. (1995). Anomalous/paranormal experiences, hypnotic usceptibility, and dissociation. *Journal of the American Society for Psychical Research, 89*, 13–332.

Pérez-Fabello, M. & Compos, A. (2011). Dissociative experiences, creative imagination, and artistic production in students of Fine Arts. *Creativity Research Journal, 23*, 38–41.

Persinger, M. (1989). Psi phenomena and temporal lobe activity: The geomagnetic factor. In L. Henkel & R. Berger (Eds.), *Research in Parapsychology 1988* (pp. 121–156). Metuchen, NJ: Scarecrow Press.

Persinger, M. (1993). Paranormal and religious beliefs may be mediated differentially by subcortical and cortical phenomenological processes of the temporal (limbic) lobes. *Perceptual and Motor Skills, 76*, 247–251.

Persinger, M. (1996a). Hypnosis and the brain: The relationship between subclinical complex partial epileptic-like symptoms, imagination, suggestibility, and changes in self-identity. In R. Kunzendorf, N. Spanos & B. Wallace (Eds.), *Hypnosis and imagination* (pp. 283–305). New York: Baywood.

Persinger, M. (1996b). Hypnosis and the brain: The relationship between subclinical complex partial epileptic-like symptoms, imagination, suggestibility, and changes in self-identity. In R. Kunzendorf, N. Spanos & B. Wallace (Eds.), *Hypnosis and imagination* (pp. 283–305). New York: Baywood Publishing Co., Inc.

Persinger, M. & Derr, J. (1989). Geophysical variables and behavior: LIV. Zeitoun (Egypt) apparitions of the Virgin Mary as tectonic strain-induced luminosities. *Perceptual and Motor Skills, 68*, 123–128.

Persinger, M. & Koren, S. (2001). Predicting the characteristics of haunt phenomena from geomagnetic factors and brain sensitivity: Evidence from field and experimental studies. In J. Houran & R. Lange (Eds.), *Hauntings and poltergeists: Multidisciplinary perspectives* (pp. 179–194). Jefferson, NC: McFarland.

Persinger, M. & Koren, S. (2005). A response to Granqvist et al. "Sensed presence and mystical experiences are predicted by suggestibility, not by the application of transcranial weak magnetic fields". *Neuroscience Letters, 380*, 346–347.

Persinger, M., Koren, S. & O'Connor, R. (2001). Geophysical variables and behavior: CIV. Power-frequency magnetic field transients (5 microtesla) and reports of haunt experiences within an electronically dense house. *Perceptual and Motor Skills, 92*, 673–674.

Persinger, M. & Makarec, K. (1987). Temporal lobe epileptic signs and correlative behaviours displayed by normal populations. *The Journal of General Psychology, 114*, 179–195.

Persinger, M. & Makarec, K. (1992). The feeling of a presence and verbal meaningfulness in context of temporal lobe function: Factor analytic verification of the muses? *Brain and Cognition, 20*, 217–226.

Persinger, M. & Makarec, K. (1993). Complex partial epileptic signs as a continuum from normals to epileptics: Normative data and clinical populations. *Journal of Clinical Psychology, 49*, 33–45.

Persinger, M. & Richards, P. (1991). Tobacyk's paranormal belief scale and temporal lobe signs: Sex differences in the experiences of ego-alien intrusions. *Perceptual and Motor Skills, 73*, 1151–1156.

Persinger, M., Tiller, S. & Koren, S. (2000). Experimental simulation of a haunt experience and elicitation of paroxysmal electrocephalographic activity by transcerebral complex magnetic fields: Induction of a synthetic 'ghost'? *Perceptual and Motor Skills, 90*, 659–674.

Pizzagalli, D., Lehmann, D., Gianotti, L., Koenig, T., Tanaka, H., Wackermann, J. & Brugger, P. (2000). Brain electric correlates of strong belief in paranormal phenomena: Intracerebral EEG source and regional Omega complexity analyses. *Psychiatry Research: Neuroimaging, 100*, 139–154.

Planer, F. (1980). *Superstition*. London: Cassell.

Popper, K. (1963). *Conjectures and refutations: The growth of scientific knowledge*. New York: Basic Books.

Radin, D. (1997). *The conscious universe: The scientific truth of psychic phenomena*. New York: HarperCollins.

Radin, D. (2004). Electrodermal presentiments of future emotions. *Journal of Scientific Exploration, 18*, 253–273.

Radin, D. & Ferrari, D. (1991). Effects of consciousness on the fall of dice: A meta-analysis. *Journal of Scientific Exploration, 5*, 61–83.

Radin, D. & Nelson, R. (1989). Evidence for consciousness-related anomalies in random physical systems. *Foundations of Physics, 19*, 1499–1514.

Radin, D. & Nelson, R. (2003). Research on mind–matter interactions (MMI): Individual intention. In W. Jonas & C. Crawford (Eds.), *Healing, intention and energy medicine: Research and clinical implications* (pp. 39–48). Edinburgh: Churchill Livingstone.

Radin, D. & Rebman, J. (1995). Are phantasms fact or fantasy? A preliminary investigation of apparitions evoked in the laboratory. *Journal of the Society for Psychical Research, 61*, 85–87.

Radner, D. & Radner, M. (1982). *Science and unreason.* Belmont, CA: Wadsworth.

Randi, J. (1983a). The Project Alpha experiment: Part 1. The first two years. *Skeptical Inquirer, 7*, 24–33.

Randi, J. (1983b). The Project Alpha experiment: Part 2. Beyond the laboratory. *Skeptical Inquirer, 8*, 36–45.

Rattet, S. & Bursik, K. (2001). Investigating the personality correlates of paranormal belief and pre-cognitive experience. *Personality and Individual Differences, 31*, 433–444.

Reed, G. (1988). *The psychology of anomalous experience.* New York: Prometheus Books.

Reinsel, R. (2003). Dissociation and mental health in mediums and sensitives: A pilot survey. In S. Wilson (Ed.), *Proceedings of the Parapsychological Association 46th Annual Conference*, 200–221.

Rhine, J. (1934). *Extra-sensory perception.* Boston: Boston Society for Psychical Research.

Rhine, L. (1961). *Hidden channels of the mind.* New York: Morrow.

Rhine, J. (1974). Security versus deception in parapsychology. *Journal of Parapsychology, 38*, 99–121.

Rice, T. (2003). Believe it or not: Religious and other paranormal beliefs in the United States. *Journal for the Scientific Study of Religion, 42*, 95–106.

Richet, C. (1884). La suggestion mentale et le calcul des probabilités. *Revue Philosophique, 18*, 609–674.

Ridolfo, H., Baxter, A. & Lucas, J. (2010). Social influence in paranormal belief: Popular versus scientific support. *Current Research in Social Psychology, 15*, 33–41.

Ring, K. & Cooper, S. (1997). Near-death and out-of-body experiences in the blind: A study of apparent eyeless vision. *Journal of Near-Death Studies, 16*, 101–147.

Roberts, M. & Seager, P. (1999). Predicting belief in paranormal phenomena: A comparison of conditional and probabilistic reasoning. *Applied Cognitive Psychology, 13*, 443–450.

Robertson, T & Roy, A. (2001). A preliminary study of the acceptance by non-recipients of mediums' statements to recipients. *Journal of the Society for Psychical Research, 65*, 91–106.

Rock, A. & Beischel, J. (2008). Quantitative analysis of research mediums' conscious experiences during a discarnate reading versus a control task: A pilot study. *Australian Journal of Parapsychology, 8*, 157–179.

Roe, C. (1991). Cold reading strategies. *Proceedings of Presented Papers from the Parapsychological Association 34th Annual Convention*, 470–480.

Roe, C. (1995). Pseudopsychics & the Barnum effect. *European Journal of Parapsychology, 11*, 76–91.

Roe, C. (1996). Clients' influence in the selection of elements of a psychic reading. *Journal of Parapsychology, 60*, 43–70.

Roe, C. (1998). Belief in the paranormal and attendance at psychic readings. *Journal of the American Society for Psychical Research, 92*, 25–51

Roe, C. (1999). Critical thinking and belief in the paranormal: A re-evaluation. *British Journal of Psychology, 90*, 85–98.

Roe, C. (2010). The role of altered states of consciousness in extrasensory experiences. In M. Smith (Ed.), *Anomalous experiences: Essays from parapsychological and psychological perspectives* (pp. 25–49). New York: Praeger.

Roe, C. , Davey, R. & Stevens, P. (2003). Are ESP and PK aspects of a unitary phenomenon? A preliminary test of the relationship between ESP and PK. *Journal of Parapsychology, 67*, 343–366.

Rogo, D. (1985). J. B. Rhine and the Levy scandal. In P. Kurtz (Ed.), *A skeptic's handbook of parapsychology* (pp. 313–326). Buffalo, NY: Prometheus.

Roll, W. (2006). On apparitions and mediumship: An examination of the evidence that personal consciousness persists after death. In L. Storm & M. Thalbourne (Eds.), *Essays on the possibility of life after death: The survival of human consciousness* (pp. 142–173). Jefferson, NC: McFarland.

Roll, W. & Persinger, M. (1998). Is ESP a form of perception? Contributions from a study of Sean Harribance. *Proceedings of Presented Papers from the Parapsychological Association 41st Annual Conference*, 199–209.

Rosenthal, R. (1966). *Experimenter effects in behavioral research.* New York: Appleton-Century-Crofts.

Rosenthal, R. (1979). The "file-drawer" problem and tolerance for null results. *Psychological Bulletin, 86*, 638–641.

Rosenthal, R. & Rubin, D. (1989). Effect size estimation for one sample multiple-choice type data: Design, analysis, and meta-analysis. *Psychological Bulletin, 106*, 332–337.

Rotter, J. (1990). Internal versus external control of reinforcement: A case history of a variable. *American Psychologist, 45*, 489–493.

Rouw, R. & Scholte, H. (2007). Increased structural connectivity in grapheme-color synesthesia. *Nature Neuroscience, 10*, 792–797.

Roxburgh, E. (2010). *The psychology and phenomenology of spiritualist mental mediumship.* Unpublished doctoral thesis, University of Northampton.

Roy, A. & Robertson, T. (2004). Results of the application of the Robertson-Roy protocol to a series of experiments with mediums and participants. *Journal of the Society for Psychical Research, 68*, 18–34.

Sabom, M. (1983). *Recollections of death: A medical investigation.* New York: Harper & Row.

Sabom, M. (1998). *Light and death: One doctor's fascinating account of near-death experiences.* Michigan: Zondervan.

Sagan, C. (1979). *Broca's brain: Reflections on the romance of science.* New York: Random House.

Schlitz, M. & Radin, D. (2003). Telepathy in the ganzfeld: State of the evidence. In W. Jonas & C. Crawford (Eds.), *Healing, intention and energy medicine* (pp. 75–82). London: Harcourt Health Sciences.

Schlitz, M., Wiseman, R., Watt, C. & Radin, D. (2006). Of two minds: Sceptic-proponent collaboration within parapsychology. *British Journal of Psychology, 97*, 313–322.

Schmeidler, G. (1985). Belief and disbelief in psi. *Parapsychology Review, 16*, 1–4.

Schmeidler, G. & Edge, H. (1999). Should ganzfeld research continue to be crucial in the search for a replicable psi effect? Part II. Edited ganzfeld debate. *Journal of Parapsychology, 63*, 335–388.

Schmidt, S., Erath, D., Ivanova, V. & Walach, H. (2009). Do you know who is calling? Experiments on anomalous cognition in phone call receivers. *The Open Psychology Journal, 2*, 12–18.

Schmidt, S., Schneider, R., Utts, J. & Walach, H. (2004). Distant intentionality and the feeling of being stared at: Two meta-analyses. *British Journal of Psychology, 95*, 235–247.

Schofield, K. & Claridge, G. (2007). Paranormal experiences and mental health: Schizotypy as an underlying factor. *Personality and Individual Differences, 43*, 1908–1916.

Schott, G. & Bellin, W. (2001). An examination of the validity of positive and negative items on a single-scale instrument. *Evaluation and Research in Education, 15*, 84–94.

Schouten, S. (1993). Are we making progress? In L. Coly & J. McMahon (Eds.), *Psi research methodolodgly: A re-examination* (pp. 295–322). New York: Parapsychology Foundation.

Schredl, M. (2009). Frequency of precognitive dreams. Association with dream recall and personality variables. *Journal of the Society for Psychical Research, 73*, 83–91.

Schulter, G. & Papousek, I. (2008). Believing in paranormal phenomena: Relations to asymmetry of body and brain. *Cortex, 44*, 1326–1335.

Schwartz, G. (2002). The afterlife experiments: Breakthrough scientific evidence of life after death. New York: Atria books.

Schwartz, G. (2011). Photonic measurement of apparent presence of spirit using a computer automated system. *Explore: The Journal of Science and Healing, 7*, 100–109.

Schwartz, S. & Dossey, L. (2010). Nonlocality, intention and observer effects in healing studies: Laying a foundation for the future. *Explore: The Journal of Science and Healing, 6*, 295–307.

Seligman, R. (2005a). From affliction to affirmation: Narrative transformation and the therapeutics of Candomblé mediumship. *Transcultural Psychiatry, 42*, 272–294.

Seligman, R. (2005b). Distress, dissociation, and embodied experience: Reconsidering the pathways to mediumship and mental health. *Ethos: Journal of the Society for Psychological Anthropology, 33*, 71–99.

Sessa, B. (2008). Is it time to revisit the role of psychedelic drugs in enhancing human creativity? *Journal of Psychopharmacology, 22*, 821–827.

Sheldrake, R. (2000). Telepathic telephone calls: Two surveys. *Journal of the Society for Psychical Research, 64*, 224–232.

Sheldrake, R. & Smart, P. (2003a). Videotaped experiments on telephone telepathy. *Journal of Parapsychology, 67*, 187–206.

Sheldrake, R. & Smart, P. (2003b). Experimental tests for telephone telepathy. *Journal of the Society for Psychical Research, 67*, 184–199.

Shermer, M. (1997). *Why people believe weird things: Pseudo-science, superstition, and bogus motions of our time.* New York: MJF Books.

Shermer, M. (2010). The sensed-presence effect. *Scientific American, 302*, 34–34.

Sherwood, S. (2002). Relationship between the hypnagogic/hypnopompic states and reports of anomalous experiences. *Journal of Parapsychology, 66*, 127–150.

Sherwood, S. & Roe, C. (2003). A review of dream ESP studies conducted since the Maimonides dream ESP programme. *Journal of Consciousness Studies, 10*, 85–109.

Shrimali, S. & Broota, K. (1987). Effect of surgical stress on belief in God and superstition: An in situ investigation. *Journal of Personality and Clinical Studies, 3*, 135–138.

Sidgwick, E. (1891). On the evidence for clairvoyance. Part 1. *Proceedings of the Society for Psychical Research, 7*, 30–99.

Simmonds, C. (2003). *Investigating schizotypy as an anomaly-prone personality.* Unpublished PhD thesis, University of Northampton.

Simmonds, C. & Roe, C. (2000). Personality correlates of anomalous experiences, perceived ability and beliefs: Schizotypy, temporal lobe signs and gender. *Proceedings of the 43rd Annual Parapsychological Association Convention*, 276–291.

Simmonds-Moore, C. (2009–2010). Sleep patterns, personality and subjective anomalous experiences. *Imagination, Cognition and Personality, 29*, 71–86.

Simmonds-Moore, C. (Ed.) (in press). *Essays on exceptional experiences and health.* Jefferson, NC: McFarland.

Simons, D. & Chabris, C. (1999). Gorillas in our midst: Sustained inattentional blindness for dynamic events. *Perception, 28*, 1059–1074.

Skinner, B. (1948). "Superstition" in the pigeon. *Journal of Experimental Psychology, 38*, 168–172.

Slade, P. & Bentall, R. (1988). *Sensory deception: Towards a scientific analysis of hallucinations.* London: Croom Helm.

Smith, C., Johnson, J. & Hathaway, W. (2009). Personality contributions to belief in paranormal phenomena. *Individual Differences Research, 7*, 85–96.

Smith, D. (2008). *Muses, madmen, and prophets: Hearing voices and the borders of sanity*. New York: Penguin.

Smith, M. (1998). *Perceptions of one's own luck: The formation, maintenance and consequences of perceived luckiness*. Unpublished doctoral thesis, University of Hertfordshire, Hertfordshire, UK.

Smith, M. (2003). The role of the experimenter in parapsychological research. *Journal of Consciousness Studies, 10*, 69–84.

Smith, M., Foster, C. & Stovin, G. (1998). Intelligence and paranormal belief: Examining the role of context. *Journal of Parapsychology, 62*, 65–77.

Smith, M. & West, D. (2002). Investigating an anomalous human image on CCTV. *Journal of the Society for Psychical Research, 66*, 41–46.

Smith, M., Wiseman, R., Harris, P. & Joiner, R. (1996). On being lucky: The psychology and parapsychology of luck. *European Journal of Parapsychology, 12*, 35–43.

Soal, S. & Goldney, K. (1943). Experiments in precognitive telepathy. *Proceedings of the Society for Psychical Research, 47*, 21–150.

Spanos, N., DuBreuil, C. & McNulty, S. (1995). The frequency and correlates of sleep paralysis in a university sample. *Journal of Research in Personality, 29*, 285–305.

Spanos, N. & Moretti, P. (1988). Correlates of mystical experience and diabolical experiences in a sample of female university students. *Journal for the Scientific Study of Religion, 27*, 105–116.

Stanford, R. (1990). An experimentally testable model for spontaneous psi events: A review of related evidence and concepts from parapsychology and other sciences. In S. Krippner (Ed.), *Advances in parapsychological research* (Vol. 6, pp. 54–167). NC: McFarland.

Steinkamp, F. (2002). *Parapsychology, philosophy, and the mind: Essays honoring John Beloff*. Jefferson, NC: McFarland.

Steinkamp, F., Milton, J. & Morris, R. (1998). A meta-analysis of forced-choice experiments comparing clairvoyance and precognition. *Journal of Parapsychology, 62*, 193–218.

Stent, G. (1972). Prematurity and uniqueness in scientific discovery. *Scientific American, 227*, 84–93.

Stevenson, I. (1960). A review and analysis of paranormal experiences connected with the sinking of the *Titanic*. *Journal of the American Society for Psychical Research, 54*, 153–171.

Stokes, D. (1985). Parapsychology and its critics. In P. Kurtz (Ed.), *A skeptic's handbook of parapsychology*. Buffalo, NY: Prometheus Books.

Storm, L. & Ertel, S. (2001). Does psi exist? Comment on Milton and Wiseman's (1999) meta-analysis of ganzfeld research. *Psychological Bulletin, 127*, 424–433.

Storm, L., Tressoldi, P. & Di Risio, L. (2010). Meta-analysis of free-response studies, 1992–2008: Assessing the noise reduction model in parapsychology. *Psychological Bulletin, 136*, 893–893.

Strassman, R. (2001). *DMT: the spirit molecule*. Rochester, VT: Park St. Press.

Stuart-Hamilton, I., Nayak, L. & Priest, L. (2006). Intelligence, belief in the paranormal, knowledge of probability and aging. *Educational Gerontology, 32*, 173–184.

Swami, V., Chamorro-Premuzic, T. & Shafi, M. (2010). Psychology in outerspace: Personality, individual difference, and demographic predictors of beliefs about extraterrestrial life. *European Psychologist, 15*, 220–228.

Taft, R. (1969). Peak experiences and ego permissiveness: An exploratory factor study of their dimensions in normal persons. *Acta Psychologica, 29*, 35–64.

Tammet, D. (2006) *Born on a Blue Day: Inside the extraordinary mind of an autistic savant*. New York: Free Press.

Tandy, V. (2000). Something in the cellar. *Journal of the Society for Psychical Research, 64*, 129–140.

Tandy, V. & Lawrence, T. (1998). The ghost in the machine. *Journal of the Society for Psychical Research, 62*, 360–364.

Targ, E., Schlitz, M. & Irwin, H. (2000). Psi-related experiences. In E. Cardeña, S. Lynn & S. Krippner (Eds.), *Varieties of anomalous experience: Examining the scientific evidence* (pp. 219–252). Washington, DC: American Psychological Association.

Targ, R. & Puthoff, H. (1974). Information transmission under controls of sensory shielding. *Nature, 252*, 602–607.

Tart, C. (1998). Six studies of out-of-body experiences. *Journal of Near-Death Studies, 17*, 73–99.

Tart, C., Puthoff, H. & Targ, R. (1980). Information transmission in remote viewing experiments. *Nature, 284*, 191.

Teigen, K. (1995). How good is good luck – The role of counterfactual thinking in the perception of lucky and unlucky events. *European Journal of Social Psychology, 25*, 218–302.

Teigen, K. (1996). Luck. The art of a near miss. *Scandinavian Journal of Psychology, 37*, 156–171.

Teigen, K. (1998). Hazards mean luck: Counterfactual thinking in reports of dangerous situations and careless behavior. *Scandinavian Journal of Psychology, 39*, 235–248.

Teigen, K., Evensen, P., Samoilow, D. & Vatne, K. (1999). Good luck and bad luck: How to tell the difference. *European Journal of Social Psychology, 29*, 981–1010.

Tellegen, A. & Atkinson, G. (1974). Openness to absorbing and self-altering experiences ("absorption"), a trait related to hypnotic susceptibility. *Journal of Abnormal Psychology, 83*, 268–277.

Terhune, D. (2006). Dissociative alterations in body image among individuals reporting out-of-body experiences: A conceptual replication. *Perceptual and Motor Skills, 103*, 76–80.

Terhune, D. (2009). The incidence and determinants of visual phenomenology during out-of-body experiences, *Cortex, 45*, 236–242.

Terhune, D. & Smith, M. (2006). The induction of anomalous experiences in a mirror-gazing facility: Suggestion, cognitive perceptual personality traits and phenomenological state effects. *Journal of Nervous and Mental Disease, 194*, 415–421.

Thalbourne, M. (1982/2003). *A glossary of terms used in parapsychology*. London: William Heinemann.

Thalbourne, M. (1995). Science versus showmanship: A history of the Randi hoax. *Journal of the American Society for Psychical Research, 89*, 344–366.

Thalbourne, M. A. (1997). Paranormal belief and superstition: How large is the association. *Journal of the American Society for Psychical Research, 91*, 221–226.

Thalbourne, M. (2001). Measures of the sheep-goat variable, transliminality, and their correlates. *Psychological Reports, 88*, 339–350.

Thalbourne, M. (2005). Research Note: Creative personality and belief in the paranormal. *European Journal of Parapsychology, 20*, 79–84.

Thalbourne, M. Crawley, S. & Houran, J. (2003). Temporal lobe lability in the highly transliminal mind. *Personality and Individual Differences, 35*, 1965–1974

Thalbourne, M. & Houran, J. (2000). Transliminality, the mental experience inventory and tolerance of ambiguity. *Personality and Individual Differences, 28*, 853–863.

Thalbourne, M., Houran, J., Alias, A. & Brugger, P. (2001). Transliminality, brain function and synesthesia. *The Journal of Nervous and Mental Disease, 189*, 190–192.

Thalbourne, M. & Maltby, J. (2008). Transliminality, thin boundaries, unusual experiences, and temporal lobe lability. *Personality and Individual Differences, 44*, 1617–1623.

Thalbourne, M. & Nofi, O. (1997). Belief in the paranormal, superstitiousness and intellectual ability. *Journal of the Society for Psychical Research, 61*, 365–371.

Thompson, S., Armstrong, W. & Thomas, C. (1998). Illusions of control, underestimations, and accuracy: A control heuristic explanation. *Psychological Bulletin, 123*, 143–161.

Tobacyk, J., Nagot, E. & Miller, M. (1988). Paranormal beliefs and locus of control: A multidimensional examination. *Journal of Personality Assessment, 52*, 241–246.

Toneatto, T. (1999). Cognitive psychopathology of problem gambling. *Substance Use and Misuse, 34*, 1593–1604.

Truzzi, M. (1976). Editorial. *The Zetetic, 1*, 2–6.

Truzzi, M. (1996). Pseudoscience. In G. Stein (Ed.), *The encyclopedia of the paranormal* (pp. 560–575). Amherst, NY: Prometheus.

Tversky, A. & Kahneman, D. (1974). Judgement under uncertainty: Heuristics and biases. *Science, 185*, 1124–1131.

Twemlow, S., Gabbard, G. & Jones, F. (1982). The out-of-body experience: A phenomenological typology based on questionnaire responses. *American Journal of Psychiatry, 139*, 450–455.

Ullman, M., Krippner, S. & Vaughan, A. (1973/2002). *Dream telepathy: Experiments in extrasensory perception.* Charlottesville, VA: Hampton Roads

Utts, J. (1991). Replication and meta-analysis in parapsychology. *Statistical Science, 6*, 363–403.

Utts, J. (1995). An assessment of the evidence for psychic functioning. *Journal of Parapsychology, 59*, 289–320.

Van de Castle, R. (1977). Sleep and dreams. In B. Wolman (Ed.), *Handbook of parapsychology* (pp. 473–499). New York: Van Nostrand Reinhold.

Van Ginkel, R. (1990). Fishermen, taboos, and ominous animals: A comparative perspective. *Anthrozoos, 4*, 73–81.

Van Lommel, P., van Wees, R., Meyers, V. & Elfferich, I. (2001). Near-death experience in survivors of cardiac arrest: A prospective study in the Netherlands. *Lancet, 358*, 2039–2045.

Von Daniken, E. (1968). *Chariots of the gods? Unsolved mysteries of the past*. London: Souvenir Press.

Vyse, S. (1997). *Believing in magic: The psychology of superstition*. Oxford: Oxford University Press.

Wagenmakers, E., Wetzels, R., Borsboom, D. & van der Maas, H. (2011). Why psychologists must change the way they analyze their data: The case of psi. *Journal of Personality and Social Psychology, 100*, 426–432.

Wagner, G. & Morris, E. (1987). "Superstitious" behavior in children. *The Psychological Record, 37*, 471–488.

Wagner, M. & Monnet, M. (1979). Attitudes of college professors towards ESP. *Zetetic Scholar, 5*, 7–17.

Walach, H., Bösch, H., Lewith, G., Naumann, J., Schwarzer, B., Falk, S. et al. (2008). Effectiveness of distant healing for patients with chronic fatigue syndrome: A randomised controlled partially blinded trial (EUHEALS). *Psychotherapy and Psychosomatics, 77*, 158–166.

Walsh, R. & Vaughan, F. (1993). *Paths beyond ego: The transpersonal vision*. Los Angeles: Tarcher/Perigree.

Walter, T. (2008). Mourners and mediums. *Bereavement Care, 27*, 47–50.

Watt, C. (2005a). Parapsychology's contribution to psychology: A view from the front line. *Journal of Parapsychology, 69*, 215–232.

Watt, C. (2005b). Psychological factors. In J. Henry (Ed.), *Parapsychology: Research on exceptional experiences* (pp. 64–79). London: Routledge.

Watt, C., Watson, S. & Wilson, L. (2007). Cognitive and psychological mediators of anxiety: Evidence from a study of paranormal belief and perceived childhood control. *Personality and Individual Differences, 42*, 335–343.

Weaver, Z. (2009). *History of the society for psychical research*. Accessed in February 2011 from: www.spr.ac.uk.

Weisberg, R. (2006). *Creativity: Understanding innovation in problem solving, science, invention and the arts*. Hoboken, NJ: John Wiley.

West, L. (1962). *Hallucinations*. New York: Grune & Stratton.

Wilde, D. & Murray, C. (2008). The evolving self: Finding meaning in near-death experiences using Interpretative Phenomenological Analysis. *Mental Health, Religion & Culture, 12*, 1–17.

Wilde, D. & Murray, C. (2009). An interpretative phenomenological analysis of out-of-body experiences in two cases of novice meditators. *Australian Journal of Clinical and Experimental Hypnosis, 37*, 90–118.

Wilde, D. & Murray, C. (2010). Interpreting the anomalous: Finding meaning in out-of-body and near-death experiences. *Qualitative Research in Psychology, 7*, 57–72.

Williams, B., Ventola, A. & Wilson, M. (2010). *Apparitional experiences: A primer on parapsychological research and perspectives.* Accessed in March 2011 from: www.publicparapsychology.org/Public %20Parapsych/Apparitional%20Experiences%20Primer%20 Final.pdf.

Williams, C. (1997). *The role of imagination in the construction of anomalous experience.* Unpublished PhD Thesis, Edinburgh University.

Williams, E., Francis, L. & Robbins, R. (2007). Personality and paranormal belief: A study among adolescents. *Pastoral Psychology, 56*, 9–14.

Willin, M. (1996). A ganzfeld experiment using musical targets. *Journal of the Society for Psychical Research, 61*, 1–17.

Wilson, K. & French, C. (2006). The relationship between susceptibility to false memories, dissociativity and paranormal belief and experience. *Personality and Individual Differences, 41*, 1493–1502.

Wilson, S. & Barber, T. (1983). The fantasy-prone personality: Implications for understanding imagery, hypnosis, and parapsychological phenomena. In A. Sheikh (Ed.), *Imagery: Current theory, research, and application* (pp. 340–397). New York: Wiley.

Windholz, G. & Diamant, L. (1974). Some personality traits of believers in extraordinary phenomena. *Bulletin of the Psychonomic Society, 3*, 125–126.

Winkelman, M. (1986). Trance states: A theoretical model and cross-cultural analysis. *Ethos, 14*, 174–203.

Winkelman, M. (1992). *Shamans, priests and witches: A cross-cultural study of magico-religious practitioners.* Tempe: University of Arizona Press.

Winkelman, M. (2000). *Shamanism: The neural ecology of consciousness and healing.* Westport, CT and London: Bergin and Garvey.

Wiseman, R. (2011). *Paranormality: Why we see what isn't there.* London: Macmillan.

Wiseman, R. & Greening, E. (2005). 'It's still bending': Verbal suggestions and alleged psychokinetic ability. *British Journal of Psychology, 96*, 115–127.

Wiseman, R. & Morris, R. (1995). Recalling pseudo-psychic demonstrations. *British Journal of Psychology, 86*, 113–125.

Wiseman, R. & Smith, M. (1994). A further look at the detection of unseen gaze. *Proceedings of Papers Presented at the 37th Annual Parapsychological Association Convention*, 465–478.

Wiseman, R., Smith, M., Freedman, D., Wasserman, T. & Hunt, C. (1995). Examining the remote staring effect: Two further studies. *Proceedings of Papers Presented at the 38th Annual Parapsychological Association Convention*, 480–490.

Wiseman, R., Smith, M. & Kornbrot, D. (1996). Exploring possible sender-to-experimenter acoustic leakage in the PRL autoganzfeld experiment. *Journal of Parapsychology, 60*, 97–128.

Wiseman, R. & Watt, C. (2002). Experimenter differences in cognitive correlates of paranormal belief and in psi. *Journal of Parapsychology, 66*, 371–385.

Wiseman, R. & Watt, C. (2004). Measuring superstitious belief: Why lucky charms matter. *Personality and Individual Differences, 37*, 1533–1541.

Wiseman, R. & Watt, C. (2005). The psychology of luck. *Psychology Review, 11*, 17–19.

Wiseman, R. & Watt, C. (2006). Belief in psychic ability and the misattribution hypothesis: A qualitative review. *British Journal of Psychology, 97*, 323–338.

Wiseman, R., Watt, C., Greening, E., Stevens, P. & O'Keeffe, C. (2002). An investigation into the alleged haunting of Hampton Court Palace: Psychological variables and magnetic fields. *Journal of Parapsychology, 66*, 388–408.

Wolfradt, U. (1997). Dissociative experiences, trait anxiety and paranormal belief. *Personality and Individual Differences, 23*, 15–19.

Wolfradt, U. & Meyer, T. (1998). Interrogative suggestibility, anxiety and dissociation among anxious patients and normal controls. *Personality and Individual Differences, 25*, 425–432.

Wolfradt, U., Oubaid, V., Straube, E., Bischoff, N. & Mischo, J. (1999). Thinking styles, schizotypal traits and anomalous experiences. *Personality and Individual Differences, 27*, 821–830.

Wooffitt, R. (2001). Raising the dead: Reported speech in medium–sitter interaction. *Discourse Studies, 3*, 351.

Wooffitt, R. (2007). Epistemic authority and neutrality in the discourse of psychic practitioners: Toward a naturalistic parapsychology. *Journal of Parapsychology, 71*, 69–101.

Wooffitt, R. & Gilbert, H. (2008). Discourse, rhetoric, and the accomplishment of mediumship in stage demonstrations. *Mortality, 13*, 222–240.

Wooffitt, R. & Holt, N. (2011). *Looking in and speaking out: Introspection, consciousness, communication.* Exeter: Imprint Academic.

Wooffitt, R., Holt, N. & Allistone S. (2010). Introspection as institutional practice: Reflections on the attempt to capture conscious experience in a parapsychology experiment. *Qualitative Research in Psychology, 7*, 5–20.

Wulff, D. (2000). Mystical experience. In E. Cardeña, S. Lynn & S. Krippner (Eds.), *The varieties of anomalous experience* (pp. 397–440). Washington, DC: American Psychological Association.

Wuthnow, R. (1976). Astrology and marginality. *Journal for the Scientific Study of Religion, 15*, 157–168.

Young, H., Bentall, R., Slade, P. & Dewey, M. (1987). The role of brief instructions and suggestibility in the elicitation of auditory and visual hallucinations in normal and psychiatric subjects. *Journal of Nervous and Mental Disease, 175*, 41–48.

Zingrone, N., Alvarado, C. & Cardeña, E. (2010). Out-of-body experiences and physical body activity and posture: Response from a survey conducted in Scotland. *Journal of Nervous and Mental Disease, 198*, 163–165.

Zingrone, N., Alvarado, C. & Dalton, K. (1998–1999). Psi experiences and the "Big Five": Relating the NEO-PI-R to the experience claims of experimental subjects. *European Journal of Parapsychology, 14*, 31–51.

Zuckerman, M., Kolin, E., Price, L. & Zoob, I. (1964). Development of a sensation-seeking scale. *Journal of Consulting Psychology, 28*, 477–482.

Zusne, L. & Jones, W. (1989). *Anomalistic psychology: A study of magical thinking* (2nd ed.). Hillsdale, NJ: Lawrence Erlbaum.

Index

Note: Page numbers in bold refer to Glossary.

Rhine, J. B., 90, 98, 111–12, 189
Richet, Charles, 95, 96
right hemisphere, 50–2, 131–2, 147, 182
see also hemispheric dominance
ritual healing theory, 142–3
rituals, 55–66, 114, 115, 130, 131, 142, 143, 175, 182

scepticism, 6, 30–1, 86, 95, 116, 118
schizotypy, 34, 38, 42–4, 47, 50, 52, 134, 138, 145, 159, 165, 166, 181, 195, **202**
science, definition of, 77–9
séance, 89, 95, 97, 174–5, 179, 186
selective reporting, 95, 108, 110–11, 112, 119
sensation seeking, 34–6, 52
sense of presence, 10, 39, 49, 52, 120, 128, 129, 131, 133–5, 138, 160, **203**
sensitivity, 18, 30, 43, 52, 138–9, 141, 147–8
sensory leakage, 27, 102–3, 108, 187, **204**
sleep, 5, 26–7, 35, 99, 129, 133, 134–6, 140, 155, 157, 159–61, 162–3, 165, 171, 175, 182, 193, 194, 196
sleep paralysis, 10–11, 134–5, 159–60, **204**
social marginality hypothesis, 12, 73, **204**
socio-cultural approaches, 141–3, 166–7, 184–5

Society for Psychical Research, 8, 14, 173, 176
spirits, 1, 10, 40, 89, 115, 130, 142, 143–4, 146, 153, 173–6, 179, 182, 184, 186, 191
Spiritualism, 40, 44, 45, 89, 143, 173–4, 176, 182, 184
spiritual, 8, 120, 167, 170–2, 189, 196–7
subliminal perception, 18, 30, 33, 44, 94, 100, 102, **204**
superstition, 55–72
definition of, 56–8
susceptibility to suggestion, 18, 28, 30, 37, 120, 132, 137, 141, **204**

taboos, 57–8
telepathy, 1, 3, 18, 20, 64–5, 67, 74, 90, 91, 96, 98, 145, 186, 195, **200**
definition of, 97
telephone telepathy, 20, 21
see also extrasensory perception
temporal lobes, 34, 48–50, 131–3, 140, 141, 147, 158, 161, 166, **204**
time reversal effects, 100
transliminality, 43–4, 47, 138–9, 141, **204**
transpersonal psychology, 7–9, 14
trauma, 5, 30, 34, 38, 53–4, 70, 128, 138, 143–4, 145, 147, 165–6, 196
type one error, 49–51, 95, 105, 176

Wegener, Alfred, 79
worldview hypothesis, 13, 73, 205

Reading guide

This table identifies where in the book you'll find relevant information for those of you studying or teaching A-level. You should also, of course, refer to the Index and the Glossary, but navigating a book for a particular set of items can be awkward and we found this table a useful tool when editing the book and so include it here for your own convenience.

TOPIC	AQA(A)	PAGE
Anomalistic experience: Pseudoscience	x	77
Anomalistic experience: Parapsychology	x	77, 94
Explanations: Coincidence	x	19
Explanations: Probability judgements	x	19
Explanations: Superstitious behaviour	x	55, 58, 61
Explanations: Magical thinking	x	55, 61
Explanations: Personality factors	x	33
Research: Psychic healing	x	87, 97, 111, 114
Research: Near death and out of body experience	x	149
Research: Psychic mediumship	x	173